Saints under Siege

THE NEW AND ALTERNATIVE RELIGIONS SERIES
General Editors: Timothy Miller and Susan J. Palmer

Saints under Siege

The Texas State Raid on
the Fundamentalist
Latter Day Saints

EDITED BY

Stuart A. Wright and James T. Richardson

NEW YORK UNIVERSITY PRESS

New York and London

NEW YORK UNIVERSITY PRESS
New York and London
www.nyupress.org

References to Internet websites (URLs) were accurate at the time of writing.
Neither the author nor New York University Press is responsible for URLs
that may have expired or changed since the manuscript was prepared.

Library of Congress Cataloging-in-Publication Data

Saints under siege : the Texas State raid on the Fundamentalist Latter
Day Saints / edited by Stuart A. Wright and James T. Richardson.
p. cm. — (The new and alternative religions series)
Includes bibliographical references and index.
ISBN 978-0-8147-9528-6 (cl : alk. paper) — ISBN 978-0-8147-9529-3
(pb : alk. paper) — ISBN 978-0-8147-9530-9 (ebook)
1. Fundamentalist Church of Jesus Christ of Latter Day Saints—History—
21st century. 2. Church and state—Texas—Eldorado Region—History—
21st century. 3. Eldorado Region (Texas)—Church history—21st century.
I. Wright, Stuart A. II. Richardson, James T., 1941–
BX8680.M534E43   2011
261.7'208828933—dc22   2011015727

New York University Press books are printed on acid-free paper,
and their binding materials are chosen for strength and durability.
We strive to use environmentally responsible suppliers and materials
to the greatest extent possible in publishing our books.

Manufactured in the United States of America

c 10 9 8 7 6 5 4 3 2 1
p 10 9 8 7 6 5 4 3 2 1

Contents

Abbreviations

ACLU	American Civil Liberties Union
ACM	anticult movement
AFF	American Family Foundation
AIL	Apostles of Infinite Love
ATF	U.S. Bureau of Alcohol, Tobacco, Firearms and Explosives
BCTF	British Columbia Teachers' Federation
CAN	Cult Awareness Network
CCT	crime control theater
CEST	Cognitive-Experiential Self-Theory
CEV	Combat Engineering Vehicle
CFF	Citizens' Freedom Foundation
CIAOSN	Le Centre d'information et d'avis sur les organisations sectaires nuisibles (Center for Information and Advice on Harmful Sectarian Organizations (Belgium))
COG	Children of God
CPS	Child Protective Services
DCS	Department of Community Services
DFPS	Department of Family and Protective Services
DOCS	Department of Community Services
DPS	Department of Public Safety
FLDS	The Fundamentalist Church of Jesus Christ of Latter Day Saints
GIGN	Groupe d'Intervention de la Gendarmerie Nationale (National Gendarmerie Intervention Group)
HB	House Bill
HRT	Hostage Rescue Team
ICSA	International Cultic Studies Association
ISOT	In Search of Truth
LDS	The Church of Jesus Christ of Latter-day Saints
LSJ	[Leroy S. Johnson] Meeting House
MHMR	Mental Health and Mental Retardation

NRM	New Religious Movement
NSW	New South Wales
OKC	Ogyen Kunzang Choling
RCMP	Royal Canadian Mounted Police
SB	Senate Bill
SRT	Special Response Team
SSSR	Society for the Scientific Study of Religion
UEP	United Effort Plan
UPS	United Parcel Service
YFZ	Yearning for Zion

Preface and Acknowledgments

Texas now has the distinction of being home to two of the most dramatic government raids on religious sects in recent U.S. history. The deadly federal raid on the Branch Davidians outside Waco in 1993 stands as the most memorable law enforcement debacle in modern times, resulting in the deaths of 86 people and the destruction of an entire religious community. Fifteen years later the Texas state raid on the Fundamentalist Church of Jesus Christ of Latter Day Saints (FLDS) in Eldorado led to the unprecedented mass custodial detention of 439 sect children by child protection officials. Fortunately the latter raid produced no shootings or deaths. But the state's massive roundup of FLDS children carved out its own unique place in the annals of American history. It is a peculiar distinction for a state that promotes an image of rugged independence and less government. It appears that the fear and loathing of unconventional religious communities trumps other core cultural values in the Lone Star State. But to be fair, Texas is not alone. As the contributors to this volume make clear, government raids on minority religious communities have become more commonplace in North America and Europe over the last twenty-five years.

We thought it critical to document and analyze this latest state-sect conflict for a number of reasons. First, the FLDS has been the target of state raids in the past, most prominently in 1953 in Arizona. The sect has a raid history that invites a comparative analysis, not simply with other embattled groups but with previous raids on its own community. Second, the 2008 state raid was launched on a fraudulent complaint by a mentally disturbed woman who claimed she was abused by her FLDS spiritual husband. The extent to which state investigators failed to corroborate the veracity of the caller's claims before mobilizing a massive raid to lay siege to the Yearning for Zion Ranch begs explanation. Third, the state's decision to take into custody more than four hundred sect children was an extreme measure by any legal standard; the ill-advised action was later overruled by the Texas Court of Appeals and the Texas Supreme Court.

The explanations by child protection officials for this overreach were later found to be based on egregious exaggerations of threatened children. And, finally, in reconstructing the events and circumstances leading up to the FLDS raid, we were troubled by decisions and actions of the state that targeted a minority religion for differential treatment. Not surprisingly, we found there was much more to the Texas state raid than one could determine from simply reading the press releases by the Department of Family and Protective Services or listening to the nightly news coverage. We felt strongly that this incident deserved closer scrutiny and systematic scholarly examination.

We are grateful to FLDS representatives who agreed to speak to us and allowed us access to other members in the community. In the wake of the raid, we were concerned that besieged sect members might be unwilling to talk to outsiders. Certainly they would have been justified in expressing some reticence and doubting our motives. The FLDS faced a barrage of unfavorable media, public criticism, and official condemnation in the days and weeks following the raid. We were fortunate, however, to find courteous and congenial people genuinely perplexed by the government's actions and eager to tell their own story. We especially thank Dowayne Barlow for his assistance in helping us to make contacts with key FLDS leaders, gather information and documents, and obtain an invitation to attend an event marking the first anniversary of the raid, among other things. Without his help, this project would have been much more difficult.

We also want to acknowledge the contribution of other parties who were drawn to this unpleasant incident for different reasons. Brooke Adams, who covered the raid and its aftermath for the *Salt Lake Tribune*, kindly supplied dozens of copies of the newspaper covering raid-related stories. The coverage by Adams and other *Tribune* staff was simply the best we encountered. Adams's reporting was outstanding, and her blogging on the case also proved to be very insightful.

Mary Batchelor, the executive director of Principle Voices, an education and advocacy organization supporting polygamous families, helped us better understand Mormon polygamy history and culture. Ms. Batchelor's nonprofit organization works with legislators, media, and the Utah State Attorney General's Office to counter stereotyping and push for decriminalization. Principle Voices hosts women's support groups to explore issues of self-esteem, identity, roles, and the unique challenges of being a woman in the Fundamentalist culture. She attended the first anniversary of the FLDS raid event in San Angelo where we made our initial contact.

Linda Werlein, the chief executive officer of the Hill Country Community Mental Health and Mental Retardation Center in Kerrville, was instrumental in explaining how Texas child protection officials adopted an anticult framing of the FLDS that inflated or exaggerated the child abuse claims. Ms. Werlein and her staff were asked by the Department of Family and Protective Services (DFPS) to assist in counseling the FLDS children taken into state custody after the raid. They found, however, that the claims of child abuse were unfounded and began questioning the state's sources of evidence. Ms. Werlein said that the child abuse claims were linked to "cult experts" consulting with the DFPS, and their efforts to challenge the "experts" were rebuffed. Ms. Werlein's observations about the FLDS children and the nature of the evidence during the temporary period of state custody were discerning and perceptive. We are grateful that she was willing to share her experience and insights with us.

Stuart Wright acknowledges support from the Jack Shand Travel Grant, an award made by the Society for the Scientific Study of Religion. The Shand grant helped to support travel to San Angelo and Eldorado, where he conducted field work and interviews in 2009. This support proved to be invaluable to the initial networking that was necessary to launch the project and to the collaboration that eventually became this book.

Finally, we thank New York University Press and our editor, Jennifer Hammer, for recognizing the potential of this work from the outset and carrying it forward. Jennifer has provided incisive comments and advice throughout the editing process and has been delightful to work with. Her assistant, Gabrielle Begue, deserves special mention; she was terrifically efficient and splendidly thorough. We also want to acknowledge the managing editor, Despina Papazoglou Gimbel, and Rita Bernhardt for her excellent copyediting work. As the editing of book manuscripts go, this was a relatively painless endeavor.

Introduction

STUART A. WRIGHT AND JAMES T. RICHARDSON

On April 3, 2008, Texas state police and the Department of Family and Protective Services (DFPS) raided the Yearning for Zion Ranch near Eldorado, Texas, a community of eight hundred members of the Fundamentalist Church of Jesus Christ of Latter Day Saints (FLDS), a Mormon sect that continues to practice polygamy. State officials claimed they had evidence of a "widespread pattern and practice" of child sexual abuse and underage marriage. The massive state raid was triggered by phone calls to the Newbridge Family Shelter hotline in San Angelo, Texas, from March 29 to April 3, from an alleged sixteen-year-old girl inside the FLDS community who said she was raped and beaten by her forty-nine-year-old spiritual husband.[1]

The young girl identified herself as Sarah Jessop and claimed to be the seventh wife of a man she identified as Dale Barlow. According to court documents, she told authorities that her husband choked her, hit her in the chest, and forced himself on her sexually. One of the beatings was so severe that it left her with broken ribs, and she claimed that she had to be taken to the hospital. Sarah said she was forced to marry at fifteen years of age, had an eight-month-old infant child, and was several weeks pregnant at the time of the phone calls. The desperate young mother said that she was not allowed to leave the Yearning for Zion (YFZ) Ranch by herself. She requested help from the domestic violence shelter and child protection officials to escape the ranch and flee the abusive relationship.

Four days after the initial call was made to the domestic violence shelter, the Texas state raid was launched to rescue Sarah, arrest Dale Barlow, and garner evidence of child sexual abuse against FLDS leaders. Following an extensive two-day search of the Yearning for Zion Ranch, however, DFPS and state police were unable to find the young girl anywhere on the property. Despite not finding the purported victim or the alleged perpetrator, Dale Barlow, child protection authorities took 439 children into state custody and a grand jury indicted 12 FLDS men on charges of sexual assault of a minor.[2] It was the largest state custodial detention of children in U.S. history. Officials

Figure I.1. Cavalcade of raid team vehicles streaming toward the Yearning for Zion Ranch on the morning of April 3. Courtesy of Willie Jessop / FLDS.

defended the action, asserting that all the FLDS children were at risk of child abuse (*Original Petition for Protection of Children* 2008).

Texas state officials later learned that the caller was not Sarah Jessop, as she had claimed, but a mentally disturbed thirty-three-year-old woman from Colorado Springs, Rozita Swinton. Ms. Swinton had been arrested previously for making false charges of abuse to the police. In February 2008 Ms. Swinton called Colorado Springs police and claimed she was a young girl being held in a basement. She was later arrested on making false charges and released on $20,000 bail from the El Paso Colorado County jail. Documents related to Swinton's arrest link her to other phone calls to police by a "Dana Anderson" in October 2007. The caller claimed to be a young woman abused by her pastor at Colorado Springs' New Life Church. In another call Swinton claimed to be a thirteen-year-old student at Liberty High School who said she was being drugged and sexually abused by her father ("Phone Number Could Tie Colorado Woman to Calls" 2008). Two years earlier Swinton had called authorities in Castle Rock, Colorado, saying that she was a sixteen-year-old girl named Jessica who had just given birth to a boy named Jacob. She told police she had been molested by a family member and feared going

Figure I.2. Joint state police raid units on the ground at the YFZ Ranch, second day of the raid, April 4. Courtesy of Willie Jessop / FLDS.

home. Castle Rock police say Swinton led them on a three-day wild-goose chase looking for the girl, who claimed she wanted to give up the baby and kill herself (Rizzo and Manson 2008). In fact, Ms. Swinton has been linked to ten incidents of false claims to child protection and law enforcement agencies across the country since 2006.

The raid on the FLDS by Texas state police and child protection officials was predicated both on Swinton's calls to the Family Shelter hotline as well as thirty to forty hours of calls that Swinton placed to FLDS apostate and anticult movement (ACM) activist Flora Jessop, beginning on March 29. Jessop is the founder of Help the Child Brides, an organization designed to provide assistance to underage FLDS women who are allegedly forced to marry into polygamous relationships. Jessop, who recorded the calls, provided a sympathetic ear and encouraged Swinton to contact Texas officials. Jessop then contacted the Texas Rangers directly and forwarded the recorded calls to them (Garrett 2008). But Swinton was not a member of the FLDS, much less an abused spiritual wife at the YFZ Ranch. Moreover, Dale Barlow, the man accused of abusing her, had never been on the Yearning for Zion Ranch in Texas. Not only did state authorities fail to corroborate the authenticity of Swinton's calls, but the manner in which they arrived at identifying Dale Barlow as the abusive husband was equally questionable. Initially Ms. Swinton did not give Barlow's first name in the calls to the domestic violence hotline. Jessica Carroll, a volunteer at the Newbridge Family Shelter, coaxed Ms. Swinton into providing the full name of her alleged husband by googling the name "Barlow" and "FLDS," and then providing Swinton with a list of names from which to choose. Ms. Carroll located a news article on the Internet about Dale Evans Barlow, who had been convicted on sexual abuse charges in Arizona in 2007. In Ms. Carroll's affidavit of April 2, 2008, she states:

> I told Sarah [Swinton] that I knew she could get in trouble if she told me her husband's name, so I asked her if I had a list of names, could she state yes or no? Sarah said yes. I began with a few random names and when I said the name DALE, she said yes, how did you know? (cited in Richter 2009)

According to pleadings filed by attorneys for the FLDS men charged in Schleicher County criminal court on July 12, 2009, an investigation by Texas Ranger Leslie Brooks Long led to phone calls to Mohave County Sheriff Alan Pashano in an attempt to track down Dale Evans Barlow in the days before the raid (Floyd and Sinclair 2009). Shortly afterward, the Mohave County Sheriff's office notified Schleicher County sheriff David Doran that Barlow had not left Mohave County since 2007 and had never been to the YFZ Ranch. Sheriff Doran conveyed this information to Ranger Long. Officer Long also instructed Schleicher County deputy George Arispe to contact the local medical center to verify the claim by the sixteen-year-old pregnant caller that she had been treated for broken ribs and physical abuse. But the medical center had no such record of treating a person fitting this description (Floyd and Sinclair 2009). Moreover, anti-FLDS activist Flora Jessop, who first received the calls from Swinton and sent the recorded calls to Texas authorities, told news sources that Swinton alternately claimed to be Sarah, Sarah's twin sister, Laura, living in Colorado City, and Laura's friend (Mitchell 2008; Rizzo 2008). Texas officials were aware of the multiple inconsistencies in the recorded calls. Despite these bewildering discrepancies, Ranger Long filed an affidavit in support of an arrest and search warrant in connection with an alleged sexual assault of a minor named "Sarah Jessop" by "Dale Barlow" (*Affidavit for Search and Arrest Warrant* 2008). Curiously Ranger Long failed to inform Judge Barbara Walther, who signed the warrant, that (1) the Mohave County Sheriff's Office had confirmed that Barlow had never left Arizona, (2) the local medical center had no record of treating a pregnant sixteen-year-old girl for physical abuse, and (3) numerous other holes and contradictions were evident in Sarah Jessop's account.

The state's uncorroborated and conflicting information in this case should have raised serious questions among law enforcement investigators. There were clearly insufficient grounds for rushing forward into a high-risk, paramilitary raid. Why were officials in such a hurry? When it became apparent that there was no Sarah Jessop on the ranch in the days following the raid, embarrassed Texas officials belatedly pursued more intensive investigations into the hoax calls. They readily found that the calls could be traced to Swinton's phone in Colorado Springs, not to Eldorado. Since Swinton had an extensive police record, officials were able to obtain a search warrant to search her home. The search yielded several items linking Swinton to the calls (Garrett 2008). In a further embarrassing revelation, the *Denver Post* reported that only a few days after the raid, "an anti-polygamy activist told Texas Rangers that Ms. Swinton was impersonating a child sexual abuse victim at (other) polygamist compounds and could be the same person who triggered the Texas raid" (Garrett 2008).

Other key pieces of evidence were missed because Texas authorities failed to adequately investigate the caller's claims. According to the *Arizona Republic*, officials in Arizona received "a call similar to the one in Texas" within the same week from "a 16-year old girl alleging sexual abuse in the polygamist stronghold in Colorado City" (Crawford 2008; see also Wiseman, this volume). But Arizona officials were suspicious of the calls because they could not be verified. Arizona's attorney general, Terry Goddard, told the newspaper, "I don't have the authority, and local officials don't have the authority, to go in and, based on an unverified phone call, sweep up 400 children. If we found that girl (who made the allegations), we could take her into custody and perhaps her siblings" (Crawford 2008). The sharp contrast between the responses of law enforcement officials in Arizona and Texas to nearly identical "unverified" calls is striking. Arizona's attorney general further informed news sources that his staff "worked with officials in Colorado City and interviewed families" but that they were "unable to find the girl or verify that she exists." "We found nothing to substantiate those allegations," Goddard said (Crawford 2008).

Ms. Swinton also made thirty-five calls to a battered women's shelter in Snohomish, Washington, between March 22 and April 4. The calls were recorded and amounted to 17.6 hours of conversation with a volunteer (Kemp 2008). The story Ms. Swinton conveyed to Snohomish County officials was similar to the one she told Texas authorities, but with significant differences that would have raised questions with investigators had they compared notes. Swinton claimed that her husband, Dale Barlow, had moved her from Texas to Washington three months before. In later calls she claimed that Barlow had moved her to the YFZ Ranch, and she was assigned a new husband, "Uncle Merrill" (Kemp 2008). She also claimed that Dale Barlow was living in Everett, Washington. Ms. Swinton did not block her number, and when the incident was reported to Child Protection Services in Washington, a social worker investigating the allegations used the Internet to conduct a reverse search on the number and traced it to Colorado. The Snohomish County Sheriff's Office also investigated the calls. A detective phoned the number in Colorado and asked to speak with Sarah Jessop. The woman who answered the phone told the detective that he had the wrong number ("Follow Up Report" 2008). A worker at the battered women's shelter, Sandra Woodward, said that she was reluctant to report the calls from Sarah to the Sheriff's Office because the incident seemed "very bizarre." Washington state authorities could not verify the calls and took no further actions.

After determining that the phone calls triggering the YFZ raid were fraudulent, Texas authorities scrambled to avoid a public relations disaster, telling media sources that the calls were "not central" to the state's case. Pressed to respond to this mortifying discovery, Stephanie Goodman, chief spokesperson for Texas's social services agencies, told news reporters, "It doesn't matter"; although the calls "got us to the gates, it's not what caused us to remove the children" (Garrett 2008). But this statement was made before the Texas Court of Appeals found that the state's mass detention of the FLDS children was unlawful and ordered the children returned to their parents. The DFPS appealed to the Texas Supreme Court but to no avail, providing another awkward situation for Texas officials. In an attempt to further defend the agency's actions, Ms. Goodman revised the DFPS framing of the incident, telling reporters, "I cannot help but believe that we changed the culture there" (Langford 2009a). Another spokesman, Patrick Crimmins, offered this statement in defense of the beleaguered DFPS: "We wanted to find out if those children had been abused and neglected and do whatever we needed to do to protect them from being harmed in the future" (Winslow 2009). Crimmins's convoluted logic to "do whatever we needed to do" to protect the children as a rationale for the raid, however, could not be squared with the illegality of the forcible separation of FLDS children from their parents and the apparent misfeasance of officials.

Another disturbing feature of the FLDS raid, and one that is probably the least known by the general public, is the hawkish, military-like style of the raid force. The photos taken by FLDS members and reproduced herein will surprise many readers, since this particular facet of the raid went virtually unreported. The heavily armed raid force included SWAT teams with automatic weapons and agents festooned in camouflage, Kevlar helmets, and vests, and flanked by helicopters, dozens of law enforcement vehicles, and an armored personnel carrier.

Tela Mange, spokesperson for the Texas Department of Public Safety (DPS), refused to disclose the number of personnel deployed in the raid, but various sources suggest that the raid team included the Texas Rangers, officers from four different county sheriff agencies, the San Angelo Police Department, and the Texas Game Wardens (Perkins and O'Donoghue 2008). The *Dallas Morning News* reported that, "in the first week, more than 1,000 personnel were deployed" (Hoppe 2008), although this figure includes post-raid DFPS staff and others. Nonetheless, the raw show of force by the state leads one to believe that officials expected to find a group more akin to a terrorist organization or drug traffickers than a peaceful religious community. Why? The YFZ had not shown any signs of violence, but FLDS members were treated to a Third World–style paramilitary foray. According to FLDS members, snipers were positioned around the perimeter behind limestone rocks carved out of a quarry on the ranch. At least one FLDS member reported having a sniper fire a shot over his head even though sect members were unarmed and offered no resistance. Comparisons to the disastrous 1993 federal raid on the Branch Davidians outside Waco, Texas, were not lost on some observers (see Wright and Fagen, this volume).

The Texas state raid on the FLDS raises a number of sobering questions. How and why did this ill-advised and misconceived raid on a polygamist Mormon sect materialize? Why were authorities in Texas so remiss in sufficiently investigating the questionable and inconsistent claims of the caller or, in the case of Ranger Long, in ignoring contravening evidence and failing to convey such evidence to the judge who signed the warrant? Why did Texas officials elect to use a paramilitary style raid rather than other means of police investigation? Given that many of the state's preconceptions of the FLDS were wrong (including that it could turn violent or become "another Waco," that it constructed underground tunnels and stockpiled weapons, and that it engaged in forced servitude), who were the sources of information? Did officials consider that their sources might have been less than objective?

Figure I.3. Combat Engineering Vehicle manned by paramilitary raid team preparing to enter the YFZ Ranch, April 3. Courtesy of Willie Jessop / FLDS.

Figure I.4. Raid team conducting enforcement operations inside the YFZ Ranch on the morning of the raid, April 3. Courtesy of Willie Jessop / FLDS.

Figure I.5. Enforcement agents with full paramilitary gear and automatic weapons on the ground inside the YFZ Ranch, April 3. Courtesy of Willie Jessop / FLDS.

The contributors to this volume make a rigorous effort to answer these and other questions arising from the FLDS raid. We do not assume that the Texas state raid occurred in a social vacuum. Rather, we explore the historical, social, cultural, and political forces that shaped this incident and help explain how and why it developed. Our approach is a critical one, questioning the simplistic assumption that authorities were merely responding to alleged criminal activity. The situation in this instance is far more complex. Compelling evidence suggests that local authorities and elected officials targeted the FLDS from the outset, harassing them with fines, conducting aerial surveillance, deploying confidential informants, making intimidating remarks and threats, and introducing legislation that was specifically aimed at them (Neil 2008; Richardson and Schreinert, this volume). In the words of one elected official, Harvey Hilderbran, they wanted to make the residents at YFZ feel "unwelcome."

There is also convincing evidence that Texas authorities obtained much of their information about the group from anti-FLDS activists and apostates who constructed an exaggerated threat posed by the fundamentalist Mormons. As such, Texas officials garnered a distorted image of the group, one that portrayed the FLDS as far more menacing and dangerous than it actually was. The combination of antipathies among Texas authorities and inflated threats conveyed by anti-FLDS dissidents greatly increased the likelihood that a raid would occur. Indeed, the most vocal and aggressive anti-FLDS activist, Flora Jessop, was the critical link between the bogus caller, Swinton, and the official rationale for the state raid. As several contributors make clear in this volume, anti-FLDS activists and apostates played to the fears of Texas officials and media, and were significant in the development of conditions that led to the state's overreaction to the fraudulent complaint.

A number of contributors offer comparative analyses to other government raids both historically and across cultures. Indeed, no fewer than seven other state raids on new or minority religions are offered as comparative cases in this volume.[3] These comparisons convey a critically important insight, namely, that the Texas state raid on the FLDS conforms to the same patterns seen in other government raids. Readers will find consistent themes among the chapters as to the key elements and factors that animated the FLDS raid. A principal reason for this thematic consistency is that, increasingly, comparative analysis of government raids on new or minority religions reveals notable parallels. In showing how the Texas raid reveals such striking similarities to other raids, we contend that the raid must be viewed in a broader sociological context. To use the vernacular of sociology, we must see the *general* in the *particular*. Government raids on new or minority religions have increased in recent decades. Preliminary research by religious studies scholars Stuart Wright and Susan Palmer indicate that the number of government raids in the last twenty years has climbed dramatically.[4] States now appear to be more willing to employ this kind of extreme enforcement action against unpopular religions generally, and they appear to be more inclined to use such action as a crude form of investigation. As we might expect, the use of this high-risk, social control mechanism has resulted in numerous instances of abuse of state power and egregious restrictions of the rights of the targeted religious communities (Bradney 1999; Homer 1999; Palmer 1999, 2011; Richardson 1998, 1999, 2004; Swantko 2004, 2009; Wiseman, this volume; Wright 1995, 1999, 2002, 2003, 2009). Thus it should not be surprising to find the same kinds of official miscalculations, overreach, and misfeasance in the Texas raid that we have seen in previous cases. Nor should we be surprised to find organized opponents of new or minority religions forming alliances with state actors prior to government raids.

The volume is organized into three sections. The chapters grouped together in part 1 provide a historical context from which to better understand both the FLDS raid and the record of social control measures taken to restrict the sect by both the state as well as the Church of Jesus Christ of Latter-day Saints (LDS) from which the FLDS had split. Part 2 focuses on how social and cultural constructions of the stigmatized religious community by detractors, the media, child protection authorities, law enforcement, and other state officials shaped the trajectory of the FLDS conflict, and how this conflict follows the patterns of other conflicts involving new or minority religions that led to government raids. Part 3 includes chapters that examine the legal and political aspects of the FLDS case, such as an analysis of Appellate Court decisions, legislative actions targeting the FLDS, comparative cases of custodial detention, and consideration of broader constitutional issues.

In chapter 1 historian Martha Bradley Evans provides a fascinating framework from which to both better understand the embattled Mormon splinter sect and view the recurrent experiences of state raids on the FLDS. Evans reminds us that the Texas raid on the FLDS was not the first.[5] The state of Arizona launched a similar raid on the FLDS community in Short Creek in 1953. The reader will find the similarities between these raids striking. Arizona officials conducted a predawn raid, taking into state custody 263 sect children. As in the Texas case, the FLDS was accused of forcing young girls into the bondage of polygamy and "white slavery." The Arizona National Guard set up tents for the women and children, and the men were jailed awaiting their hearings. After a few days the women and children were bussed to state facilities with the intent to place them in foster homes. The FLDS men endured protracted hearings during which public reaction turned against state officials and the mass detention of the children. In the end, all but one of the underage married women returned with their children to Short Creek, a conclusion that was repeated in Texas. The Arizona governor who engineered the 1953 raid, Howard Pyle, lost his bid for reelection and, overall, the incident was considered a public relations fiasco. Evans carefully describes how this series of events parallels the Texas state raid fifty-five years later and asks: What did we learn?

In chapter 2 Susan Palmer offers brief case histories of government raids on four relatively obscure alternative religious communities in three different countries: the Doukhobors (Canada), the Apostles of Infinite Love (Canada), the Children of God/Family International (Australia), and Ogyen Kunzang Choling (France). Like the FLDS raid of 2008, the purpose of these raids was to investigate child abuse and to "rescue" children. Palmer finds that two factors influenced the local authorities and made them take complaints about the groups seriously. First, the groups' alternative patterns of sexuality, parenting, and child-rearing challenged conventional family norms and values.

Second, the communal and sectarian nature of the groups made it difficult to investigate or verify complaints about the treatment of children through unintrusive methods (i.e., interviewing neighbors, schoolteachers, or local doctors). In summarizing her findings, Palmer identifies four common patterns in the raids on these religious communities across place and time. These include (1) influence of a network of cultural opponents, (2) complicity of the media, (3) interlocking allegations (the tactic of using a barrage of linked allegations to impede the ability of the group to defend itself), and (4) cultural tension and intolerance.

In chapter 3 Ryan Cragun, Michael Nielsen, and Heather Clingenpeel examine the tensions between the LDS and the FLDS, and how these tensions influenced the official reaction to the Texas state raid. They show how the LDS has expended considerable effort to distance itself from polygamy and those who continued the practice after it stopped performing plural marriages in the early 1900s. Following the Texas state raid on the YFZ Ranch, they identify intensified efforts, measures, and strategies by the LDS to marginalize the fundamentalist Mormons. The dynamics of LDS marginalization efforts surrounding the latest government raid on the FLDS are explained as a part of the church's perpetual "quest for respectability." In order to achieve and maintain cultural legitimacy, the church must side with conventional society in condemning the polygamous Mormons even though it could be argued that the FLDS holds more to the doctrinal purity envisioned by founder Joseph Smith.

In chapter 4 Michael Hamilton explores reader responses to the Texas raid on the websites of Utah's two leading newspapers, the *Salt Lake Tribune* and *Deseret News,* in order to gauge attitudes toward the FLDS and the central issue of polygamy. He argues that there is long-standing and deep-seated ambivalence among Utahans about the issue of polygamy and the fundamentalist Mormons who continue to practice "the Principle." Hamilton finds that readers responding to the problem of polygamy tend to employ three linguistic motifs or frames. These include (1) using the language of *sacred experience* to explain or rationalize it, (2) using the language of American patriotism to distance themselves from it, and (3) invoking the language of *libertarianism* to question state and federal power. The three motifs identified by Hamilton form a "regional narrative" that has precedence in LDS history and provide important cultural meanings that are employed to make sense of polygamy for those who persist in the practice of plural marriage.

In chapter 5 Stuart Wright asks why authorities in Texas were so inclined to believe the hoax calls made to a domestic violence hotline, rapidly mobilizing a massive state raid on the slimmest of evidence. The answer appears to be that child welfare officials, local law enforcement, and other moral gatekeepers already concerned about the presence of the FLDS in this West Texas community were predisposed to believe sensational tropes about the sect. Wright finds that DFPS officials and social workers were in contact with "cult experts," ACM actors, and FLDS apostates, and had adopted an anti-cult framing of the problem. Officials accepted allegations uncritically that played to the worst cult stereotypes and atrocity tales. This, in turn, contributed to the perception of an inflated threat by authorities, culminating in an ill-advised government raid. Wright examines and carefully documents the activities of organized opponents to explain the formulation of, and rationale behind, the state's misguided raid.

Stuart Wright and Jennifer Lara Fagen offer a focused and in-depth comparative analysis of the FLDS and Branch Davidian raids in chapter 6. They argue that there are striking parallels in terms of process and structure that have not been acknowledged or fully understood. Wright and Fagen contend that the two raids share important commonalities, including the claims made by detractors and opponents who play to similar motifs or "intrinsic narratives" about the targeted group (child abuse, child rape, slavery/servitude, "brainwashing," the stockpiling of weapons, mass suicide, and terrorism). They find the same social and organizational dynamics operating in the planning and execution of the two raids, and even some of the same anticult activists involved. Though news media and critics have offered superficial comparisons, they find that the similarities are robust and reveal disturbing patterns of state and countermovement actions against these unpopular minority religions which also have broader implications about sect-state conflicts.

In chapter 7 Camille B. Lalasz and Carlene Gonzales analyze the raids on the FLDS as a form of "crime control theater." As they explain, "crime control theater" (CCT) is a construct used to describe very public responses to reported crimes that demonstrate an illusion of crime control but are inefficient and often ineffective in actually controlling the targeted crimes. For instance, after being convicted on conspiracy to commit polygamy charges and given probation after the 1953 raid on Short Creek, the FLDS of Short Creek were allowed to return home and resume their polygamous lifestyles. The same conclusion will likely be made about the residents at the YFZ Ranch. Brown and Gonzales argue that CCT responses may be dangerous, as they are often perceived to be legitimate, even noble, but have the unintended consequences of intensifying the problem or leading to additional negative outcomes. For example, not only have the raids on the FLDS failed to curtail illegal activity from occurring, but these raids also created the unintended negative consequence of causing emotional and psychological harm to FLDS members. The raids themselves caused members to feel that the security and sanctity of their homes had been violated. The forced removal of young children from their families and culture for extended periods of time (e.g., up to two years in the case of the Short Creek raid) likely had detrimental effects on the children's attachment bonds and psychological well-being.

Chapter 8, by Jean Swantko Wiseman, provides a comparative analysis of government raids on the Twelve Tribes in Vermont in 1984 and the FLDS in 2008. Wiseman shows how a prominent ACM organization hired a deprogrammer, Galen Kelly, to formulate a plan to weaken and discredit the Twelve Tribes community at Island Pond, Vermont, in the early 1980s. The strategic plan makes explicit the goal of coalescing organized opponents and apostates, fomenting exaggerated media accounts, gathering damaging evidence, and building a case for child abuse with the intent to impel state action. Moreover, the experiment to disrupt and dissolve the community at Island Pond was offered as a model applicable to other nontraditional religious groups in the future, such as the FLDS. The importance of the model is made pointedly by Kelly in noting that it would propel the ACM past the "quagmire of the movement's increasingly problematic reliance on deprogramming." Wiseman argues that the Kelly plan was institutionalized in the ACM culture and became a template from which to attack new or minority religions, including the FLDS.

In chapter 9, James Richardson and Tamatha Schreinert analyze the political and legislative context of the Texas raid on the FLDS. They document that the state raid was not simply a spontaneous response to hoax phone calls but rather a preconceived, predetermined attack on this disfavored religious community. The presence of the FLDS in Eldorado had been flagged by government officials years before the raid, and evidence suggests that they had been preparing for a confrontation for an extended period. The Texas legislature passed a law in 2005 designed to bolster the state's Child Protective Services (CPS) agency and included provisions directly aimed at the FLDS. Two major provisions amended in the bill were proposed by State Representative Harvey Hilderbran, whose district includes Schleicher County where the raid took place. One provision raised the state's age of consent for marriage from fourteen to sixteen, and the other elevated bigamy from a misdemeanor to a felony. Both these statutes were used in the legal actions taken against the FLDS and its leaders. Local officials also conducted surveillance of the FLDS community, orchestrated frequent visits to the ranch, deployed informants, gathered damaging (though often unverified) information, and essentially conducted a range of preparatory activities in anticipation of the raid. The Associated Press reported shortly after the raid that "State troopers put into action the *plan they had on the shelf* to enter the 1,700-acre compound" ("Texas Authorities Defend Sect Raid" 2008; emphasis added). Other statements by government officials indicated that they were only waiting for a "complaint" or "spark" to mobilize the state control machinery against the YFZ residents (Johnson 2008; Neil 2008). Richardson and Schreinert turn to a sociology of law approach, drawing on the work of Donald Black (1976), to explain how and why unconventional religious groups like the FLDS are targeted by the state and receive differential treatment. A comparison of state responses to widespread sexual abuse charges in the Catholic Church is made to illustrate the differences in the form and function of social control.

In the final chapter Tamatha Schreinert and James Richardson offer a legal analysis of the Appeal Court Opinions with regard to the state's custodial detention of the FLDS children. As a backdrop, they provide an overview of the evolution of child abuse allegations levied against the new religions that emerged in the 1960s. They note that ACM attacks on new religions were successful initially by making charges of "brainwashing." But this strategy ran into legal obstacles in the 1990s. As new religions aged and large numbers of children were born to members, the demographic profiles of the groups changed and so did the ACM strategy of attacks. Coinciding with broader social changes and the growing concern for children, ACM organizations engineered a shift in the social control paradigm by focusing on child abuse allegations as the principal rhetorical weapon to combat "cults." Because child protection laws generally invert the presumption of innocence and place the burden of proof on the accused, families in new religions were forced to defend themselves against perpetual child abuse claims by opponents (Richardson 1999). ACM organizations successfully strategized to make child abuse synonymous with "cults" in the popular media. In this context, Schreinert and Richardson show how government raids have become more common by using the legal tool of child abuse claims. Yet even as state raids have increased, the courts have frequently found such state actions to be illegal and a misuse of the child protection laws as they were intended. Schreinert and Richardson analyze the Texas Appeals Court rulings in the FLDS case to illustrate how state actions distort and misapply laws regarding child protection in order to attack minority faiths.

Collectively the contributions to this volume provide compelling evidence of social intolerance and state repression of unpopular minority faiths in general, and the FLDS in particular. Research shows that over time government raids have become the weapon of choice by state agents, collaborating with organized opponents of the targeted groups and recruiting sympathetic or sensationalist media, or both, to leverage unfavorable public opinion in their campaigns of social control. The legal anomalies posed by social efforts to protect children have been exploited by partisan interests to vilify and attack marginalized religious groups using the complicit force of the state. At the same time the expansion of state enforcement and use-of-force operations has produced a kind of "mission creep" (Kraska and Cubellis 1997) in which law enforcement has shown a disturbing propensity to use raids as a new tool to conduct crude forms of investigation. Paramilitary, high-risk operations such as raids, dynamic entries, rapid-response insertions, strike force operations, or close-quarters combat blur the historical and legal distinction between "investigation" and "enforcement" (Kraska 2001; Kraska and Kappeler 1996). It is well established in criminal justice research and protocols that raids are violent, destructive, potentially injurious, and sometimes deadly (McMains and Mullins 2006). As such, the tactic of the raid should be used judiciously and only in the most extreme cases where clear evidence of armed resistance or imminent danger to law enforcement is present. The FLDS community at Eldorado presented no such danger. The massive paramilitary response of state control agents in Texas to the fraudulent charge of abuse in an isolated, individual case was grossly disproportionate to any real threat. Here the analysis of the raid by Brown and Gonzales in chapter 7 as a form of "crime control theater" has added meaning. There was little practical or logistical need for a massive show of force in Eldorado. So what was the real intent of this elaborate paramilitary operation?

The scholars who contributed to this work have asked the harder questions and looked beyond the superficial answers. For example, claims by the state that the raid and custodial detention of FLDS children were "necessary," especially at a cost of more than $14 million to taxpayers (Moritz 2008), have proved to be indefensible given the poor job by the Department of Family and Protective Services in otherwise routine supervision. Roughly a year after the FLDS raid, the *Houston Chronicle* reported that "nearly half of all Texas children killed by abuse belonged to families previously investigated by Texas Child Protective Services—a statistic that has shown no improvement since 2004 despite efforts to save more children"

(Langford 2009b). Between 2004 and 2009 at least 1,227 children died of abuse in Texas, and 516 of those children came from families with CPS histories. Another *Houston Chronicle* report found hundreds of violations of neglect, mistreatment, and abuse of children at state residential treatment centers from mid-2008 through April 2010 (Langford and Ramshaw 2010). According to the report, children were choked, stripped, and beaten by staffers at the facilities. In a few cases staffers encouraged "staged fights" between children by rewarding the winners with prizes such as after-school snacks. More disturbing, no criminal indictments were sought against the perpetrators, and their names were kept secret by DFPS. Most of the residential treatment centers have remained open for business despite multiple violations of abuse and mistreatment (Langford and Ramshaw 2010). This pitiable record suggests that the state could have better spent taxpayer dollars in the ordinary supervision of children under the care of DFPS. There was no history of child deaths at the YFZ Ranch, and yet the underfunded DFPS spent precious dollars and disproportionate resources to address an exaggerated threat. Several contributors to this volume (Brown and Gonzales; Wright and Fagen) offer an explanation of the state's rabid overreaction as a fitting example of "moral panic."

Much has been made of the practice of plural marriage and the alleged coercion of young brides among the FLDS by a small group of former members, organized opponents, and some news reporters in order to manufacture justification for the raid. But state child protection officials apparently never considered the partisan source of their information. They garnered selective narratives and tropes from antagonistic opponents while evidently failing to consult neutral sources such as religion scholars, historians, or social scientists who have actually studied the FLDS. Had they made such an effort they would have gained a better and more balanced perspective and avoided the highly inflated image of threat perpetuated by ACM activists. But as sociologist David Bromley (1998) has pointed out, disputes or conflicts involving groups labeled "cults" tend to be controlled by oppositional coalitions. The minority religion in question is painted as a "subversive" organization and regarded as dangerous, requiring special control agencies with extraordinary authority. The expectation is that the putative violations alleged by opponents will be frequent and serious, and therefore the religious organization is accorded little deference. As such, "the organization is likely to be confronted with unilateral, pre-emptive, coercive control measures. . . . Command over the dispute settlement apparatus means that the oppositional coalition controls the definition of alleged violations and can widely disseminate information collected during investigation and prosecution processes. The result is a *dispute broadening* process that incorporates a range of organizational attributes and practices as external control organizations define their missions in terms of repressing such groups, operate with numerous allies, and face few restraints" (Bromley 1998, 24).

According to Bromley, once groups are successfully cast as a subversive organization ("cult"), they become embodiments of quintessential evil and are considered an imminent threat to the social order. Thus a countersubversion ideology can be constructed more readily to legitimate expanded social control efforts over the targeted group. New or unconventional religions face great difficulty in defending themselves against allegations, because they typically are in a high social tension relationship with the status quo (e.g., FLDS separatist posture), are easy marks for stereotyping and scapegoating, and have few institutional allies. They are thus vulnerable to well-organized countersubversion campaigns to mobilize state control agencies and generate adverse media and public opinion.

It is our hope that the kind of overreaction by state actors in the raid on Eldorado will dissipate in the future as officials look more closely at the wisdom and potential repercussions of such actions. To this end, we offer here new evidence to the growing body of research challenging the all too common tactic of government raids on minority faiths. We suggest that the investigation of abuse claims at the YFZ Ranch could have been conducted just as effectively and at much less of an emotional cost to the religious community, not to mention the inordinate expense to the state, through routine investigative procedures. It seems clear that new or unconventional religious groups are unjustly singled out and treated differently from established religious organizations when criminal complaints are alleged. After all, the claims of thousands of sexual abuse cases among priests in the Catholic Church in the United States did not lead to government raids and paramilitary forays into parish churches to confiscate evidence. Catholic Churches where suspect priests were concealed or moved around to avoid detection were not the target of SWAT teams, armored tanks, automatic weapons, snipers, and helicopters.[6] The targeting of minority religions for specifically violent and intimidating force reveals a practice of state intolerance and discrimination that is unacceptable in a democratic society guided by the rule of law. It is the uneven and unequal *application* of the law in the cases of new or nontraditional religions that is discriminatory and should be denounced by responsible government and religious leaders, civil liberties organizations, the courts, and conscientious citizens.

From this incident, and other government raids examined in comparative analyses throughout this volume, we can see how state-sanctioned practices of religious intolerance and discrimination play out in society. To put the matter in broad social context, organizations that have a low coincidence of interests with the dominant society and challenge the status quo (such as new or minority religions) are more likely to find themselves labeled illegitimate and face heightened measures of harassment, control, and coercion by institutional authorities. These kinds of social dynamics illustrate how discrimination and inequality continue to function in contemporary society. Minority religions face differential treatment despite established legal and constitutional guarantees designed to protect religious expression and ensure equality. Why? Because relationships of power often trump the law, as Donald Black (1976) has so forcefully demonstrated in his work. If and when marginalized religious organizations such as the FLDS are involved in disputes, they have few institutional allies, confront a broad coalition of opponents, and are more readily assailed. These circumstances make them vulnerable to false charges and claims, and hence to more intense social control actions.

NOTES

1. In some news reports the age of the husband is fifty. The discrepancies appear to be the result of different ages described by the caller who claimed to be Sarah Jessop.

2. The DFPS originally reported taking 468 children into custody but later determined that 29 of the "children" were legal adults. The grand jury indicted twelve men, but one of those indicted was Warren Jeffs who was already serving a sentence in Utah stemming from his arrangement of extralegal marriages between his adult male followers and underage girls. As of this writing, four of the remaining eleven FLDS men have been convicted of sexual assault of a minor, charges stemming from plural marriage to underage women in the group.

3. These include the Apostles of Infinite Love, the Branch Davidians, the Doukhobors, Ogyen Kunzang Choling, The Family International, Twelve Tribes, and the 1953 raid on FLDS at Short Creek, Arizona. Actually we had to delete one group from Susan Palmer's chapter during editing, because the chapter was too long. Had we been able to leave her analysis of the Nuwabians in the chapter, the number of comparative groups would have been eight.

4. Stuart Wright and Susan Palmer have documented fifty-eight government raids on new or minority religions over the last fifty years in nine different countries. Approximately 70 percent have occurred since 1990. Their research is part of another forthcoming book, *Storming Zion*, that will be published by Oxford University Press.

5. Indeed, in her seminal work, *Kidnapped from That Land*, Evans documents three government raids on the FLDS: the first in 1935, the second in 1944, and the third in 1953. The 1953 raid stands out because it was much larger in scale.

6. The first modern raid on the Catholic Church regarding sexual abuse charges took place in Europe as this manuscript was in its final stages. The raid was conducted by thirty Belgian police searching for evidence of abuse by clergy on June 24, 2010. The raid targeted the headquarters of the Roman Catholic Church and the recently retired Cardinal of Belgium. Photos released of the raid, however, do not indicate a paramilitary-style incursion as has been typical of other raids on minority faiths in Europe and other Western countries.

REFERENCES

Black, Donald. 1976. *The Behavior of Law*. New York: Academic Press.
Bradney, Anthony. 1999. "Children of a Newer God: The English Courts, Custody Disputes, and NRMs," pp. 153–71 in Susan J. Palmer and Charlotte E. Hardman (eds.), *Children in New Religions*. New Brunswick, NJ: Rutgers University Press.
Bromley, David G. 1998. "The Social Construction of Contested Exit Roles: Defectors, Whistleblowers, and Apostates," pp. 19–48 in David G. Bromley (ed.), *The Politics of Religious Apostasy*. Westport, CT: Praeger.
Crawford, Amanda J. 2008. "Colorado City CPS Phone Call Resembles One Made in Texas, *Arizona Republic*, April 11. Accessed online at http://www.azcentral.com/.
Floyd, John, and Billy Sinclair. 2009. "The Unrelenting March against the FLDS." July 27. Accessed online at http://texascriminaldefense.com/comments/July09/27a.html.
Garrett, Robert T. 2008. "Colorado Woman May Be Caller Who Sparked CPS Sweep, Officials Say," *Dallas Morning News*, April 19. Accessed online at http://www.dallasnews.com.
"Hilderbran Takes Aim at YFZ Ranch." 2005. *Eldorado Success*, March 24.
Homer, Michael 1999. "The Precarious Balance between Freedom of Religion and the Best Interests of the Child," pp. 187–209 in Susan J. Palmer and Charlotte E. Hardman (eds.), *Children in New Religions*. New Brunswick, NJ: Rutgers University Press.
Hoppe, Christy. 2008. "Texas Had Secret Plan to Separate Polygamist Mothers, Children," *Dallas Morning News*, June 4. Accessed online at http://www.dallasnews.com.
Johnson, Kirk. 2008. "Texas Polygamy Raid May Pose Risk," *New York Times*, April 12.
Kemp, Philip. 2008. "Report of Investigation," Texas Department of Public Safety, Texas Ranger Division, April 19.
Kraska, Peter B. 2001. *Militarizing the American Criminal Justice System*. Boston: Northeastern University Press.
Kraska, Peter B., and Louis J. Cubellis. 1997. "Militarizing Mayberry and Beyond: Making Sense of American Paramilitary Policing." *Justice Quarterly* 14 (December): 607–29.
Kraska, Peter B., and Victor E. Kappeler. 1996. "Militarizing American Police: The Rise and Normalization of Paramilitary Policing." *Social Problems* 44 (1): 1–18.
Langford, Terri. 2009a. "FLDS Case Had as Many Complications as Wives," *Houston Chronicle*, March 29. Accessed online at http://chron.com.
———. 2009b. "Hundreds of Children Die Despite CPS Involvement." *Houston Chronicle*, October 22, p. A6.
Langford, Terri, and Emily Ramshaw. 2010. "Kids at Facilities in Texas Choked, Stripped, Beaten," *Houston Chronicle*, June 6, p. A1.

McMains, Michael J., and Wayne Mullins. 2006. *Crisis Negotiations: Managing Critical Incidents and Hostage Situations in Law Enforcement and Corrections.* 3rd ed. Cincinnati, Ohio: Anderson.

Mitchell, Kirk. 2008. "Details Emerging on Calls That May Have Sparked Raid," *Salt Lake City Tribune*, April 20, p. A17.

Moritz, John. 2008. "Texans' Tab for YFZ Roundup Tops $14 Million." *Fort Worth Star-Telegram*, June 14, p. A1.

Neil, Martha. 2008. "Texas Changed Marriage Age to Restrict Rights of Polygamy Ranch Residents." *ABA Journal*, May 2.

Palmer, Susan J. 1998. "Apostates and Their Role in the Construction of Grievance Claims against the Northeast Kingdom/Messianic Communities," pp. 191–208 in David G. Bromley (ed.), *The Politics of Religious Apostasy.* Westport, CT: Praeger.

———. 1999. "Frontiers and Families: The Children of Island Pond," pp. 153–71 in Susan J. Palmer and Charlotte E. Hardman (eds.), *Children in New Religions.* New Brunswick, NJ: Rutgers University Press.

———. 2011. *The New Heretics of France.* New York: Oxford University Press.

Perkins, Nancy, and Amy Joi O'Donoghue. 2008. "FLDS at Ranch Detail Raid by Texas Officials," *Deseret News*, April 15. Accessed online at http://www.deseretnews.com.

Richardson, James T. 1998. "Apostates, Whistleblowers, Law and Social Control," pp. 171–90 in David G. Bromley (ed.), *The Politics of Religious Apostasy.* Westport, CT: Praeger.

———. 1999. "Social Control of New Religions: From 'Brainwashing' Claims to Child Sex Abuse Allegations," pp. 172–86 in Susan J. Palmer and Charlotte Hardman (eds.), *Children in the New Religions.* New Brunswick, NJ: Rutgers University Press.

———. 2004. *Regulating Religion.* New York: Plenum.

Richter, Donald. 2009. "Law Enforcement Misled the Court to Obtain Search Warrants for the YFZ Ranch." Posted June 4; accessed online at http://www.truthwillprevail.org/index.php?parentid=&index=170.

Rizzo, Russ. 2008. "Seeking Sarah: Colorado Caller Is 'Person of Interest,'" *Salt Lake City Tribune*, April 19, p. A4.

Rizzo, Russ, and Pamela Manson. 2008. "Texas FLDS Case: Was Massive Raid Based on Bogus Call from Colorado Woman?" *Salt Lake Tribune*, April 4. Accessed online at http://sltrib.com.

Swantko, Jean A. 2004. "The Twelve Tribes Communities, the Anti-Cult Movement and Government's Response," pp. 179–200 in James T. Richardson (ed.), *Regulating Religion.* New York: Plenum.

———. 2009. "State-Sanctioned Raids and Government Violations of Religious Freedom: Revealing Similarities of Constitutional Errors in Both the 1984 Island Pond Raid and the 2008 FLDS Raid." Paper presented at the Annual Meeting of CESNUR (Centro Studi sulle Nuove Religioni [Center for Studies on New Religions]), Salt Lake City, June. Available online at http://www.cesnur.org.

Winslow, Ben. 2009. "Raid Again? Texas CPS Defends '08 Actions," *Deseret News*, March 28. Accessed online at http://www.deseretnews.com.

Wright, Stuart A. 1995. *Armageddon in Waco: Critical Perspectives on the Branch Davidian Conflict.* Chicago: University of Chicago Press.

———. 1999. "Anatomy of a Government Massacre: Abuses of Hostage-Barricade Protocols during the Waco Standoff." *Terrorism and Political Violence* 11 (2): 39–68.

———. 2002. "A Critical Analysis of Evidentiary and Procedural Rulings in the Branch Davidian Civil Trial," pp. 101–13 in Derek Davis (ed.), *New Religious Movements and Religious Liberty in America*. Waco, TX: Baylor University Press.

———. 2003. "A Decade after Waco: Reassessing Crisis Negotiations at Mt. Carmel in Light of New Government Disclosures." *Nova Religio* 7 (2): 101–110.

———. 2009. "Revisiting the Branch Davidian Mass Suicide Debate." *Novo Religio* 13 (2): 4–24.

I

Historical Context

1

The Past as Prologue

A Comparison of the Short Creek and
Eldorado Polygamy Raids

MARTHA BRADLEY EVANS

When the story of the raid on the community of the Fundamentalist Church of Jesus Christ of Latter Day Saints (FLDS) at the Eldorado, Texas, Yearning for Zion (YFZ) Ranch rolled out, the past was prologue. The similarities between the Short Creek raid of 1953 and the Eldorado raid of 2008 are striking, resonating in scope, design, and impact. As historians, we teach our students that we are doomed to repeat the mistakes of the past if we do not learn the lessons history has to teach us. This most recent episode reminds us of the profound importance of this idea. In this chapter we compare the 1953 raid on Short Creek to the 2008 raid on the YFZ Ranch in Eldorado, Texas, focusing on corresponding patterns and dynamics. We also analyze the ways in which FLDS members sought to interpret the meaning of the raids through their religious beliefs and experiences. Next, we explore how we might understand the most recent endeavors of the FLDS to build a sacred landscape in Texas and determine the influence of its prophet, Warren Jeffs. Finally, we ask what lessons have been learned from these raids.

Short Creek and Eldorado: A Special Symbiosis

Determined to end the practice of plural marriage once and for all, the mastermind of the raid at mid-century was Governor Howard Pyle of Arizona. His accomplices were the State of Arizona's Attorney General's Office, the Mohave County Supreme Court, and the Juvenile Court, along with more than one hundred officers of the court and other governmental personnel. This massive response to what Pyle conceived as an "insurrection" within state boundaries was partly inspired by the desire to protect the interests of underage girls who were the victims of the "foulest conspiracy" to ensnare them in marriages before the legal age of consent.

A career in radio prepared Pyle for his statewide broadcast the morning of July 26, 1953, at 4:00 am, announcing the raid on the Short Creek polygamists.

> Before dawn today the State of Arizona began and now has substantially concluded a momentous police action against insurrection within its own borders. Arizona has mobilized and used its total police power to protect the lives and futures of 263 children. . . . More than 1,500 peace officers moved into Short Creek. . . . They arrested almost the entire population of a community dedicated to the production of white slaves who are without hope of escaping this degrading slavery from the moment of their birth. (Pyle 1953b)

As would be true for the 2008 Eldorado raid more than half a century later, Arizona state officials acted as *parens patrea* to protect the interests of those unable to protect themselves—the underage, perceived victims of polygamy.

> Here is a community—many of the women, sadly right along with the men—unalterably dedicated to the wicked theory that every maturing girl child should be forced into the bondage of multiple wifehood with men of all ages for the sole purpose of producing more children to be reared to become mere chattel of this totally lawless enterprise. (Pyle 1953a)

Pyle anticipated the raid for two years as the state carefully developed a plan, a rationale and support for an unprecedented invasion of a religious community within the confines of the United States. Working in conjunction with the state Attorney General's Office, Pyle developed ingenious strategies for investigating the behavior and persons involved in the polygamous lifestyle. In April 1951 Pyle hired the Burns Detective Agency in Los Angeles with $10,000 appropriated by the state legislature. "Pretending to be a movie company looking for locations and extras, they packed movie equipment into the town and photographed every adult and child in the community. The polygamists, uneasy but courteous, posed for their pictures, meanwhile cautioning their children to stay nearby." Pyle was mostly disgusted at what Burns found. "When they brought the facts back, photographic and otherwise, we realized that the judge was right, we had a problem," Pyle said in 1984. The agency found significant violations of law—tax fraud, misuse of state electrical power, and living conditions that were, in his mind, "unfit for animals let alone human beings." Homes were generally filthy; some families were living in old cars, in unfinished buildings, and in what he considered to be "subhuman conditions" (Pyle 1984).

Fast forward fifty-five years; a phone call from an alleged sixteen-year-old polygamous girl, pregnant and the alleged victim of both physical and sexual abuse, initiated the Eldorado, Texas, raid by the Department of Family and Protective Services (DFPS) and the Texas Rangers. The complexity of the raid suggests that it was carefully planned before the phone call was ever made; the government was poised and ready for a trigger that would justify the intervention (see Richardson and Schreinert, this volume). Before they began, DFPS and state police informed the governor that they were planning to raid Eldorado on April 3, 2008, because of a call they had received from a sixteen-year-old pregnant polygamous girl. The unidentified young woman reported both physical and sexual abuse on the part of her "spiritual husband" (Hoppe 2008). Three days after the raid began several hundred girls and women were taken into custody and removed from the ranch. Supplies were called in from the Red Cross, Goodfellow Air Force Base, and local shelters. DFPS workers' state-issued credit cards were quickly maxed out. According to one news report, "The Governor's Division of Emergency Management had set up a command post, state agencies had pitched in—including even the Forest Service—and hundreds of state workers had been deployed" (Hoppe 2008). The plan was to transport the women and children to a Salvation Army facility in Midlothian, Texas, where they would separate the mothers from their children. Midlothian was a more secure facility, but at the last minute the Salvation Army chose not to allow the transfer to occur on their site.

For Texas, the specter of the government siege on the Branch Davidian community at Mt. Carmel loomed large, recalling the horrors of that tragedy (Wright 1995). Instead of learning the lesson of the 1953 raid on Short Creek or of the 1993 raid at Waco, the government reacted imprudently by launching a paramilitary raid and inviting the possibility of a violent confrontation. The past became prologue to yet another chapter in the history of the clash between religious and civic values. The women and children of Eldorado became symbolic victims in a moral drama, not unlike what occurred at Waco (Ellison and Bartkowski 1995), for which various external institutions (child protection workers, the courts, the media) claimed to be acting in their best interests.

Fundamentalist Origins and Separation of
Plurality from the Mormon Church

Who are the FLDS and what is their relationship to the Church of Jesus Christ of Latter-day Saints (LDS)? Although several splinter groups left Mormonism beginning in the 1830s in the Midwest, Mormon Fundamentalism was always located in the Great Basin Church. The groups still practicing polygamy today have their roots in the nineteenth-century church and in the doctrines taught by the church's early generation of general authorities, and they have lives and a history that run parallel to that of the mainstream LDS Church beginning with the abandonment of plural marriage that began with the Manifesto of 1890, ending official church sanctioned plurality. The term "fundamentalist" applies to those who continue to practice plural marriage and who believe that they follow the more pure doctrines of the Church, before it caved in to the pressure of the federal government to conform to national mores and religious standards.

Most were long-term members of the Church and children of polygamous parents. They chose to remain loyal to this basic long-standing tenet of their Mormon heritage; many were unwavering in their adherence to "the Principle" as the Church position gradually hardened into active prosecution. But as was true in the nineteenth century, opposition separated out the fainthearted, strengthened the strong, and found willing martyrs. The assumption that God required great sacrifices from the faithful provided meaning to their hardships and rendered even the most menial work sacred.

The FLDS call plural marriage "the Principle," believing that it is central to the efforts of faithful men and women to enter the Celestial Kingdom in the life hereafter. Also called "Celestial Marriage," the "New and Everlasting Covenant," and "Priesthood Work," plural marriage centers around a single patriarch and his multiple wives and many children. It is at the heart of a patriarchal ordering of relationships between men and women and their families. Fundamentalist leader Leroy S. Johnson described the range of "fundamentals" that were at the heart of the movement (Johnson 1983–1984, 4:1635). Members believe that their religious practice is mandated by God and that priestly authority was restored to Joseph Smith in the nineteenth century and transferred to John Taylor, who authorized a few men to continue the practice of plural marriage through the priesthood council organized in 1886.

The fundamentalists based their claim to continual priesthood authority on a purported vision that President John Taylor received in September

1886 at the home of John W. Woolley in Centerville, Utah, where he was hiding. Taylor's son, Apostle John W. Taylor, told friends that his father had left among his papers a revelation concerning the future of plural marriage.[1] The fundamentalists never intended to form a new church separate from Mormonism and they continued to identify themselves as members of the Church of Jesus Christ of Latter-day Saints.

Even today, Colorado City/Hildale is the largest single gathering place for Mormon fundamentalism or what would become known as the FLDS. First settled in the late 1920s by Leroy S. Johnson and other polygamist families, Short Creek, as it was then known, was the frequent subject of intense repression and persecution, including ex-communications during the mid-1930s, arrests for conspiracy, Mann Act violations for transporting women over state borders for immoral purposes, Lindberg kidnapping violations for transporting underage women by polygamist men in the Boyden raids of 1944, and, finally, the large-scale raid of the entire community orchestrated by Arizona Governor Howard Pyle on the armistice day of the Korean War in 1953.

In the fifty-five years between 1953 and 2008, Mormon fundamentalism evolved to become a distinctive religious culture that persisted despite considerable efforts by both the federal and state governments to eliminate it. Its members have been penalized and ostracized. In the same years, a significant dissenter community formed outside fundamentalism to fight for those most vulnerable in the FLDS culture and those who chose to leave.

The Short Creek Raid

In the days leading up to July 26, 1953, word had leaked out of the governor's office and Salt Lake City about the plan for a raid on Short Creek. Knowing that it would be soon, two of John Y. Barlow's sons—Joseph and Dan Barlow—climbed to a vantage point overlooking the town on the red butte where they could detect the stream of government vehicles as it moved slowly out of the Kaibab Forest, with car lights announcing their arrival. When certain that the caravan would within hours arrive at Short Creek, the young men threw sticks of dynamite into the air to warn the people of the town.

Short Creek's men and women met at the schoolhouse, prayed together, and sang "We Thank Thee, O God, for a Prophet." Leroy Johnson spoke to them, encouraging them to consider whether they would be willing to die for their faith. When the parade of government officials—policemen and women, social service matrons, attorneys and reporters pulled into town at

4:00 am, they flashed every spotlight, blasted every horn or alarm, creating chaos and fear in the hearts of all who stood in the schoolyard waiting to find out what would happen to them and their families. Many remembered the lunar eclipse that happened minutes after their arrival, the way the moon sucked the light out of the sky and left it pitch black (Barlow n.d.). They brought with them warrants for thirty-six men and eighty-six women, 122 warrants in all. Rather than polygamy itself, a felony, the charges included rape, statutory rape, carnal knowledge, polygamous living, cohabitation, bigamy, adultery, and misappropriation of school funds. Tied to the initial motivation of child abuse, the government accused group members of having "encouraged, advised, counseled and induced their minor, female children under eighteen years of age to actively participate in said unlawful conduct" (Superior Court of Arizona 1953). No violence resulted. Neither the polygamists nor their government invaders fired guns or resorted to violence.

The National Guard set up a tent at the center of town where they prepared meals for the town members throughout the weeklong siege. They arrested the men and jailed them in the schoolhouse lunchroom. In addition, the government set up a place where all the men and women were fingerprinted. The first evening they took the men to Kingman, Arizona, where they were jailed while awaiting their hearings.

On the fourth day, in the morning, police matrons told the women to pack for a three-day trip. The children and their mothers walked from their homes to the schoolyard, where they waited all afternoon for the five greyhound buses that came at 5:00 pm to take them to their foster homes. Finally, the buses arrived and the women and children were loaded on board. Twenty-two teenage boys stayed behind at Short Creek.

When the buses arrived in Phoenix, they pulled up in front of a National Guard Armory at about 7:00 am. The women and children were assigned to foster homes throughout the area. "We didn't know if we would ever see each other again or not! So as each mother and her children were let out of the bus, we said good-bye with tears streaming down our cheeks" (E. Jessop n.d.).

After the women and children were settled in their new homes they began walking the streets looking for other women from their community. Eventually they found one another and met Saturday mornings at the park to talk. At one point the government sponsored a party for the women and children at Phoenix Park. Eventually they gathered for Sunday School at one of their homes.

During the two years following the Short Creek raid, the women and children endured a protracted series of hearings at the Juvenile Court. In the first months the men received sentences but served their time on probation in their homes at Short Creek. When the ordeal was finally over, all but one of the women who had been underage at the time of her marriage returned with their children to Short Creek. The raid failed to end the practice of a plurality of wives, but it created a central defining myth, linking the FLDS with religious martyrs of every generation.

The Eldorado Raid

Within two months after the Eldorado raid, the state of Texas began returning more than 400 children to their families on the ranch. The Third Circuit Court of Appeals ruled that the state did not produce sufficient proof that the children were in imminent danger. In the appeal, thirty-eight women whose children had been seized argued that the District Court lacked proof and was required to return the children to their parents and had abused its discretion by failing to do so (Kinkade 2008). The appeals court agreed and, according to one news report, "The result will likely be the slow and steady crumbling of efforts to prosecute crimes that are a part of the dogma of the Fundamentalist Church of Jesus Christ of Latter Day Saints" ("Slow and Deliberate" 2008). Judge Barbara Walther ruled, on June 3 in San Angelo, that the children should be returned after the Texas Supreme Court found that authorities had "overreached when they rounded up hundreds of women and children during a sex abuse investigation at the sect's ranch. As isolated as they might be," one reporter wrote, "they're still protected under the law" (Smith 2008). The justices voted in a 6–3 majority to uphold the Appellate Court's decision that the District Court erred in placing the 439 FLDS children in state custody (Adams and Lyon 2008). To get their children back, the parents were required to keep their children in the state of Texas and to take parenting classes, among other conditions imposed by the court.

Linda Werlein, the chief executive officer of the Hill Country Community Mental Health and Mental Retardation (MHMR) Center, submitted a sworn affidavit in the case that described the conditions to which the children had been subjected in detention: "We were told, among other things, that we needed to be careful around the FLDS mothers, that the mothers will not look us in the eye when they address us, that they wear very expensive clothing, and that they will refuse to talk to us unless their attorneys are present" (Smith 2008). What they found was quite different. "My staff and I soon learned that each and everything that we were told was either inaccurate or untrue. In fact, the FLDS women and children were very personable, and would speak freely with us, wore clothes that they had made themselves, and were very open with the MHMR staff. Most of all, I was struck by what wonderful mothers they were" (Smith 2008). Werlein and her staff had, on occasion,

> interceded on the part of the mothers and children in order to get many of their basic needs met. Many of the children were getting sick due to the poor quality of food they were given. . . . There were several other concerns about the living conditions that concerned me; including, lack of blankets, the fact that for two weeks children had to play on concrete floors, children were interrogated for several hours at a time (and given little food), mothers had to bathe babies in buckets (only the MHMR could obtain them for the mothers), and the women had no shower facilities for the first few days of their detention. Because the MHMR workers tried to improve these conditions for the mothers and children, CPS [Child Protective Service] workers labeled us as "sympathizers." (Smith 2008)

Werlein concluded, "The living conditions were terrible. At first there was only one bathroom for all of these people. Teenage boys were forced to share the bathroom with women, teenage girls, and all of the infants" (Smith 2008). Curiously, during all the time she was with the FLDS, she said she never saw a woman under the age of seventeen who was pregnant.

FLDS Interpretations of the Raids: Constructing Religious Meaning

For some FLDS members, the raids have been interpreted as ordeals of faith, allowed by God to test their commitment. Similar to religious martyrs of every era, the polygamists of Short Creek were ready to be persecuted in the name of their faith. Vera Black, the woman who became the test case for the state's ability to take custody of the children of polygamist parents, described the 1953 raid as the "most faith promoting experience I had ever had. It is never to be forgotten. Little do we realize what an extra blessed people we are" (Black n.d.). Even the strain of the prosecution in the court case, *Vera Black vs. the State of Utah*, was framed for Black in this way. "I take no credit for the part our family was so privileged to be chosen to see just how we would stand such a test. I give the Lord every bit of the credit for such a wonderful schooling He put us through. I am proud to be numbered among true and outstanding saints" (Black n.d.). Fred Jessop believed that the 1953 raid made them stronger, more dedicated to their religion:

I'm sure the Lord heard our prayers, and prayers of the children, the Saints, and many, many people not affiliated with this work. But as I say, when the stress is on from the outside it tends to drive the people together. But in peace time people are more inclined to be nettled and offended by the little things that each other do, and thereby they draw apart instead of together. And this is the great test that I think we are in today. And of course it was before the lifetime of any of you people, I guess—isn't it" (F. Jessop n.d.).

Another characterized it slightly differently:

These events of 1953 that we were a part of, and that we are a part of today, is the experience of qualifying ourselves to the point where we can be used in the Lord's work. It doesn't make any difference whether we play our major part on this side of the veil, or the other side. We all know people who are close to us that have gone on and been called to do their major work, you might say, on the other side of the veil. But all of these things are a part of the same experience. And as we go through life some of the events that took place during that time had a good deal of humor involved in it. (Timpson n.d.)

Functioning as a sort of crucible, the raid demonstrated strengths that some did not know they had and, more importantly, proved they were committed to following God's directive.

Louis Barlow was a teacher in the local elementary school in 1953, a beloved patriarch and son of John Y. Barlow. For him, however, the raid was a desecration of their sacred community.

This Raid, this abuse that came upon our fair community! After the invasion and the fear that was put into the lives of every mother and child in that community, followed mock trails, Juvenile hearings, and imprisonment! They desecrated the day! The places where we held Sunday School and meetings were made prisons; the men were put in there and held by sheriffs all the way around—not allowed to talk to their families, treated just as if it was a movement of Adolph Hitler or some movement like that out of the law war! (L. Barlow n.d.)

Barlow tried to frame his understanding of the raid in both religious terms and constitutional rights.

We've been accused of committing sin, violating moral laws under the name and guise of religion. I want to remind you of the basic freedom we have. It is the freedom of life, liberty and the pursuit of happiness. And if any community were to do the things that Governor Pyle accused our community of doing and called it religion, yes, of course, it should be wiped out, smashed and done away with. Accusations of white slave factory, accusations of young women being forced into marriage against their will, accusations of misappropriation of funds, accusations of tax evasion, accusations of any kind and every kind—those accusations are FALSE as they can be! And it is our only hope that the American people will see these things and come to our rescue. (L. Barlow n.d.)

On the other hand, Louis's brother, Alvin S. Barlow, felt part of "a very real, a very live, a very wonderful thing" (A. Barlow n.d.). Although he did not fully understand its significance, he knew even as a youth that the raid would define over time who he was. "Sometimes our experiences in our youth don't quite bring it into focus. We see it in the written story; we hear it told from those that were there, and it takes on a certain atmosphere of historical importance, but the very time that we are living, right now, is as critical a day as ever there was" (A. Barlow n.d.). In 2007 they gathered the stories for the anniversary celebration. Barlow said, "Talk about living in a momentous day when spirits are called on to be valiant! Talk about being able to stand during a period of time when a nation is worse off for its moral character than Sodom and Gomorrah! We have a job to do that is certainly outstanding" (A. Barlow n.d.).

Many of the women taken from their homes with their children in April 2008 also interpreted the raid as a test of their faith. Marie Musser wrote about forgiveness and love, and the test of the teachings she had made her religious core.

This heaven-sent love is first a self-discipline in righteous living. But it empowers us to forgive the wrongs of others and leave judgment to God. Keeping sweet is the conquering of oneself, setting oneself aside and taking on a greater power, a more noble nature—the character of God. . . . It is reachable—this becoming like God. The meekness and the humility increase; and then the thoughts, inspired in heaven, awaken in your mind, guiding you how to love others more. You remember the good in them, and you express it in a prayer of gratitude to God, thanking the Lord for each other. You even gain the power through the vision of heaven to look beyond each other's weaknesses, looking upon what they can become because you seek perfection for yourself and also for others. (Musser n.d.)

For the FLDS, the focus during the 2008 raid was principally the impact on the children. One woman, identified only as Sister Barlow, depicted a scene experienced by them all. Anticipating that the children would be taken from their mothers, she tried to prepare them to handle the anxiety it would create. "Today was a long, tense day," she wrote in her journal on April 23, 2008. "Knowing that any minute our children would be snatched from our sides, loaded on a bus, and taken far away. I spent much of the day talking to the children, telling them what I expected of them when I wasn't with them . . . . I told them that we needed to be sweet when we were separated and to not scream. I told them it was okay to cry but to be calm and know that Heavenly Father would be watching" (Sister Barlow n.d.). An unidentified mother "felt as though [her heart] was being torn from its place." Her children screamed as the CPS officers "pried them from their mothers, children whose arms were wrapped tightly around their mother's neck, refusing to let go, being pulled off." Older children also cried, hugging their mothers before being taken away. "I saw fear in the children's eyes," she wrote,

> pain and anguish in every mother's eyes. The sound, of the awful cries that I know ascended into the heavens! Crying and screaming filled the room, a sound so haunting, so full of hurt and pain, was more than my heart could take, and my own tears began to flow down upon my hot cheeks. . . . I am on the bus now, writing, that the freshness of this experience will be caught on paper. (Sister Barlow n.d.)

The tension between religious rights and reasonable state regulation was put to a test in Eldorado. Many questioned the government's actions in what the FLDS considered to be an infringement on their constitutional protection of religious freedom. Heidi Barlow lamented,

> Oh America! What has Texas done to the public servants? We, as Americans, have always put our trust in the police officers. They are there to protect and assist the safety of our homes and our communities. My little 4-year-old granddaughter was witness to an accident with a 4-wheeler ATV. The accident was investigated by a police officer, as is the routine for accidents. My granddaughter was terrified and ran and hid. When the officer was finished taking pictures and interviewing all concerned, her little heart and mind were so relieved that she said, "A police officer came to our house, and he didn't even steal us!" (Barlow n.d.)

Marion Steed's poem, "This Beautiful Day," written days after the raid on April 8, poignantly captures a sense of the violation of sacred space that transpired at the Yearning for Zion Ranch.

> As I sit beneath this oak so grand,
> And look across this once-sacred land,
> I hear the cars and pick-ups roll by,
> And watch the chopper in the sky.
> The teams of men, about twelve per team,
> Walk into the homes with scarcely a knock,
> They leave a man all decked in black,
> Bullet-proof jackets and guns o'er their back.
> One at each corner, two at the doors,
> The rest are inside, taking all that they want,
> Pictures and letters from loved ones so dear
> Mean nothing to them with their devilish sneer.
> They take, and they take: first the children so dear.
> Then nothing is sacred. They joke and make light,
> Having already desecrated the sacred sites.
> They first say, "Don't drive," then, "Don't walk,"
> Then, "Stay home." But how can I do that,
> With twelve men, or more, standing close at my door?
> So I walk off, where it's quiet, right next to this tree,
> A lizard climbs down and walks over to me.
> He looks at me close, and then hustles right off,
> As the chopper goes over on its next flight.
> And then touches down, alongside our sacred site.
> Then thoughts of our Prophet pick us back up.
> He has sweetly endured at least eighteen months.
> We don't know the details but we do know the way.
> To sweetly endure This Beautiful Day. (Steed n.d.)

In this poem we see the way that one FLDS man struggled to find meaning in the raid, measuring it by his own response. Similarly Maggie Jessop found meaning in her own spiritual journey toward forgiveness. She wrote, "I can't yet say that my children harbor no ill feelings against their oppressors, and I cannot say that they would throw their arms around those who have purposely misled them, severely abusing the innocent trusting nature of children in order to accomplish the sinister designs of a dark crusade."

Even still, she was thankful that she was making progress on the road toward forgiveness. "If I were to line graph my experiences, you would see sharp rises and sudden drops, hills and valleys, in striving to overcome the fears and focus on faith. . . . I think there would be a healthy increase, and I feel happy in the effort of rehabilitation following severe anguish and trauma" (M. Jessop n.d.). Jessop's attitude was amazingly positive, believing the raid had been a test of her faith given her by God. "Experience is a very good thing, for it contributes to the growth of character, but I would like to avoid any unnecessary ones with the CPS. I think I might fare better if I faced off a grizzly bear" (M. Jessop n.d.).

Warren Jeffs, Eldorado, and the FLDS

Why did the FLDS move to Eldorado, Texas, and build a new religious community? The isolated, dry and dusty site of the Yearning for Zion Ranch in Schleicher County, Texas, evokes the sect's deep desire to practice its lifestyle privately in the refuge provided by the vast landscape of West Texas. The site itself speaks volumes about the importance of boundary-making religious beliefs, identifying the line between insiders and outsiders, and the profane world beyond and the sacred world within. The walls surrounding the ranch are both literal and figurative, suggesting the profound difference between the lives of the FLDS and those outside the faith. In important ways, as former FLDS member Ross Chatwin said when he visited the site, "that place is intended more to keep people in than to keep anyone out. They have secrets and they don't want anyone leaving to tell those secrets." Although Chatwin's allusion is somewhat sinister, the site itself is complicit in the establishment and maintenance of meaningful boundaries.

When FLDS leaders first visited Eldorado, they posed as businessmen searching for land that would be used as a hunting retreat for corporate clients (Goodwyn 2008). Warren Jeffs planned the construction of the Yearning for Zion ranch largely in secret, letting only his most faithful and loyal followers know about his intentions. Beyond that privileged core, many believed that he would desert the Colorado City group altogether. Simultaneously they felt the impact of his stringent and harsh administration of church and community affairs. FLDS member Benjamin Bistline characterizes Jeffs as increasingly paranoid after 2002, increasingly "in hiding" (Bistline 2004, 410).

The Church's Salt Lake City lawyer, Rodney Parker, said that the FLDS looked for a new "outpost and retreat" for five hundred of the most faithful members but had no interest in becoming part of the town of Eldorado itself. "People can go there to concentrate and focus on their religious mission without the interferences and pressures they've been subjected to" in both Arizona and Utah. "They're a very private people," Parker said, "and right now they're feeling very picked on" (Moreno 2004). Understandably the citizens of Eldorado reacted in confused ways. Among some local townspeople, the images of Waco lingered large. For the most part, however, they believed that the members of the group should be left alone as long as they did not break the law. Although Jeffs himself never publicly announced his intent in establishing the YFZ Ranch, it is possible to understand this move with a sense of the group's history, theology, and behavior.

The persecution narrative became part of the explanation for the early Mormon Church after the exodus first out of Missouri and then Illinois into the Rocky Mountain region. Warren Jeffs wove a familiar narrative for his followers, portraying himself as a "persecuted" prophet who was surrounded in Colorado City, Arizona, and Hildale, Utah, by apostates and troublemakers (Adams 2006). In some ways this added to his strength, according to Rod Parker: "In the view of the faithful people, that makes him stronger in that he bears up to it (Adams 2006). Carolyn Jessop, former FLDS member and author of the book *Escape,* remembered that "Warren Jeffs had been preaching that the entire earth would soon be at war and all the worthy among the chosen would be lifted from the earth and protected, while God destroyed the wicked" (Jessop and Palmer 2008, 307). Warren talked often about moving the most righteous among them to a more remote location, not naming Texas specifically but a place he called the "center place." According to Jessop, "Warren continued to preach about how it was time for God's chosen to have a temple to do the work God had planned for us" (Jessop and Palmer 2008, 334). By the time the Yearning for Zion Ranch had been built, it had been interpreted, framed, and made meaningful by Warren Jeff's sermons, constant discussion, and the selection of the most loyal followers for this special experience.

Jeffs culled an inner elite from the Colorado City/Hildale Church and sent them to the new "center place" so they could live more perfect lives and he could maintain control over the community. Their intent was "to live such pure and holy lives that God would reach down into their modern–day Zion to take them to heaven" (Choate 2008). At the time Texas had a liberal age-of-consent marriage law, an innate friendliness, and respect for private property. Eldorado was remote; land was cheap and readily available. It seemed the perfect plan (Choate 2008). They went because they believed that their prophet, Warren Jeffs, had heard from God and that God had told him what He wanted them to do.

In addition to being a prophetic movement, the FLDS are millennialists who believe that the Second Coming of Christ is imminent, although the date that it will occur shifts according to the faithfulness of the group. Leroy Johnson predicted, in a 1984 board meeting of the United Effort Plan (UEP), that he would not die before Christ returned to the earth so that he could turn the "Keys of Priesthood Back to Him" (UEP Board Meeting 1984). In the same meeting, he said, "We won't be under any trust law then. It will come under the jurisdiction of the Prophet Joseph Smith and his kingdom. . . . It's been tested pretty much in the courts. The lawyers are afraid of it so let's not make any changes. There is only 14 years and that won't be long. We'll be dealing with the Kingdom of God then." Rulon Jeffs added, "It will be a very great pleasure to have you govern us in the millennium under the direction of Jesus Christ and Joseph Smith" (Bistline 2004, 294).

Between the fall of 1998 and the spring of 1999 rumors about the end of the earth again circulated among the fundamentalists. It was believed that the Lord's faithful would be lifted up and the wicked destroyed. Various dates were mentioned as well, but the most significant prediction centered on June 12, 1999, the 111th anniversary of the birth of Leroy Johnson.

> The people gathered in the parking lot of the LSJ [Leroy S. Johnson] Meetinghouse at 6:00 am on that morning. Fred Jessop welcomed every one there on "this beautiful morning," after which they sang "We Thank Thee O God For A Prophet." After the opening prayer and another song, Louis Barlow addressed the people. Then "Uncle Rulon's Sons of Heleman," were marched past the Brethren, presenting an honor guard before them. A circle prayer was then performed, where the people stood in a circle holding hands. A procession of the people then made their way to the Cottonwood Park, a distance of about two blocks away and there engaged in a daylong celebration. During the day, people went to the store to buy a supply of groceries to take with them to Heaven. The Lift Up event was supposed to take place at midnight. Needless to say, it did not happen, when at that time the people were told that the Lord had given them a six-month extension. (Bistline 2004, 391)

Rulon Jeffs said, "We must be lifted up to be protected. Keep sweet is our only protection." Quoting from Leroy S. Johnson's 1984 sermon, he said, "We will have to have the spirit of God upon us enough to be caught up when the judgments of God go over the earth, then we will be let down again. That is the only way the Lord will protect his people. He says he will protect his Saints if He has to send fire from Heaven to do so; and this he will do" (Bistline 2004, 391–92). Jeffs also publicly claimed that he would live to see the second coming of Jesus Christ. Nevertheless, he turned much of the control over the Church to his son, Warren Jeffs.

At the same time that the government altered its approach to dealing with the members of polygamist groups, a change of leadership occurred in the Colorado City/Hildale group. Rulon Jeffs died and the "keys" to perform plural marriages passed to the hands of his son, Warren. The FLDS reaction to this change and to the increased pressure from the government was dramatic, causing new divisions and turmoil that threatened to destroy the Church.

When Rulon Jeffs died in September 2002 it was rumored that he had twenty-two wives, many of whom his son married during the next year. Warren assumed leadership and within six months, among other efforts to centralize finances, he ordered business owners in the community to relinquish ownership. On July 27, 2003, he issued a revelation that established his spiritual power and marginalized the Barlow contingent, thus justifying his leadership.

And behold I say unto you, my elders, beware, for what you do in secret I shall reward you openly. And you must seek my protection through the repentance of your sins, and the building up of my kingdom, my storehouse, my priesthood on the earth. And if you do not, I shall bring a scourge upon my people to purge the ungodly from among you. And those righteous will suffer with the wicked if I will preserve the pure in heart who are repentant. I the Lord have spoken it and my word shall be obeyed if you would receive my blessings. Honor me, through obedience to my celestial laws, and set your family in order, to abide the spirit of oneness, which is the spirit of the celestial kingdom. My holy love burning in your minds and hearts, bonding it together as one in a new and everlasting covenant, the laws of my holy priesthood. Hear the warning voice, oh ye my people, and repent and make restitution unto me that I may own and bless you in the day of trouble and also in Zion, if you will, for my arm of mercy is stretched out still unto those who will repent and come unto me with full purpose of heart, and I will preserve my servants among you to guide you through my revelations and my power, otherwise you will remain unto those who will receive. Abide in my word. Let my people make restitution unto me, through the repentance of their sins and building up my storehouse and all other things, as I shall direct through my servants even so. Amen. (quoted in Bistline 2004, 396–97)

He then said that for the time being there would be no more meetings and no more marriages or baptisms but that the members were obligated to pay their tithing and support the storehouse, the equivalent of $500 per month (ibid.).

Jeffs had quickly made his mark on the group, although he moved to Hildale in 1998 after living in the group's Salt Lake property for most of his life. He had moved with his father to Southern Utah in 1998, because they believed the Apocalypse was imminent. Pushed and threatened with legal action, and the increased pressure under the regime of Utah Attorney General Mark Shurtleff, the leaders of the FLDS, particularly their new president, Warren Jeffs, recoiled with a sense of urgency, disrupting the temporary calm of the 1990s. Jeffs called for a greater centralization of political and economic power in the person of the prophet, giving rise to a new period of division, fear and excommunication, and blatant disregard for the law and its officers.

Warren was the second son of Rulon's fourth and allegedly favorite wife, Marilyn Steed, and had literally dozens of siblings. When he graduated from Jordan High School in 1973 he was one of nine seniors in the top 3 percent of his class. Before becoming the principal of the Church's private school, Alta Academy, Jeffs taught math, science, and computer programming. His motto was that "perfect obedience produces perfect faith, which produces perfect people" (Adams, 2004).

In the policy changes he made, Warren Jeffs sought to solidify power not only in his person and his position but also in a series of public lectures. In a tape-recorded presentation made in 1995, he instructed his audience to be "perfectly obedient and come out of the world" and to follow God's leader (at the time Rulon Jeffs). "That one man is as God over the people and has the right to rule in all areas of life," he said. Jeffs's family includes forty wives, some having been married to his father first, and fifty-six children. For many members these tapes became the equivalent of sacred texts.

Among some fundamentalists, Jeffs is known as an extremist (Watson 2006), with an exacting set of expectations and standards for those around him. According to one account, "his discipline has hardened into law, and his goal is perfection on earth. To err is to risk one's eternal salvation" (Adams 2004). One supporter said of his leadership: "I believe Warren is trying to accomplish something that even God hasn't heretofore. To be able to pull together a captive group of followers who are measured by a mortal man as being perfectly united in mind and body and purpose" (Adams 2004). Other FLDS members speak with great reverence and respect about Warren's influence on their lives (W. Jessop 2009). In his actions, Jeffs is seen as fulfilling prophecy and the predictions of his ancestors, the latest iteration of Mormon millennialism. In anticipation of the Second Coming of Christ and to avoid complete destruction, a special group of the faithful must join together to prepare the earth. Jeffs predicted that the world would end on Wednesday, April 6, 2005, the 175th anniversary of the LDS. When it did not, he accused members of the group of unfaithfulness and sloth (Dethman 2005). "Dooms-day scenarios and rumors of an impending mass suicide by faithful members of the Fundamentalist Church of Jesus Christ of Latter Day Saints" spread on the Web (Perkins 2005). Colorado City Police Chief Sam Roundy discounted the rumors, claiming that they came from outsiders rather than members of the group. "This rumor will go by just like all the other ones we keep hearing about," he said, "None of these predictions or dates that are given about the end of the world is coming from the FLDS church authorities. It's a bunch of nonsense. The scriptures say that no man knows the time or day of the Lord's coming. These rumors are not coming from here" (Perkins 2005).

As a prophet, Warren Jeffs separated his most loyal followers from those who, historically, had disagreed with the more extreme and orthodox inter-pretation of church law, particularly the communal ownership of property in the United Firm. Jeffs excommunicated such long-term community leaders as Dan and Louis Barlow, dividing these men from their wives and children who were seized as a type of "property" of the firm itself, reflecting an attitude not unlike the nineteenth-century concept of *femme covert*. The tightening of Jeffs's control over his followers, and the loyal group of insiders around both his person and his leadership, is evidence of a specific reaction to outside pressures to conform that originated in the Utah Attorney General's office. Partly the result of his father's death and a shift in leadership to his person, as well as a decade-long split between first warders and second warders over the issue of individual property ownership, a huge fissure emerged in the cul-ture of fundamentalism, which never was a monolithic reality that unified or lumped all polygamists into a single whole but rather was distinguished by individual, charismatic leadership, personality, and circumstances.

About twenty years earlier and perhaps partly because of the experience with the split over property rights embedded in the United Effort Plan that engaged the community in eight years of litigation and split the group in two, leaders of the Church, in 1986, attempted to move much of the UEP's assets into another trust—the Majesty Security Trust—in order to put the assets beyond the reach of potential apostates or disgruntled members. This move solidified power in the hands of three men—the president of the Church, Fred Jessop, and Joseph I. Barlow. Although this effort was thwarted by the lawsuit against the UEP, later under the leadership of Warren Jeffs, this same type of transfer was successful, giving Jeffs enormous power over the coffers of the UEP and the Church more generally. His financial power was immense.

The Enoch narrative, described below, is also key to understanding both the early LDS Zion building efforts and those under the leadership of Warren Jeffs. The pattern for city building that came from Latter-day Saint scripture described a righteous people who lived in Zion, "because they were of one heart and of one mind, and dwelt in righteousness; and there was no poor among them," in a place so pure that it "was taken up into heaven" (Smith 1981 [1835], 133). Joseph Smith's own version, Zion of the New Jerusalem, dealt with people on the earth rather than in heaven. "Then shalt thou and all thy city meet them there, and we will receive them into our bosom, and they shall see us, and we will fall upon their necks, and they shall fall upon our necks, and we will kiss each other." There Enoch and Zion would meet, spanning generations but bringing the most righteous together in the sight of God. "And it shall be Zion which shall come forth out of all the creations which I have made; and for the space of a thousand years the earth shall rest." Both the Latter-day Saints and the FLDS anticipated this happy union of Enoch, of Zion, and of this most recent version at the beginning of the millennium. Harold Bloom describes this kind of coming together as a "transumption," but it is also a blending of historical narrative. A powerful method for making the story of the FLDS the same as that of Joseph Smith's Zion building efforts, it moves the biblical narrative into their own time (Bloom 1992). For the Latter-day Saints this was the express purpose of gathering in Zion, an axis mundi where heaven and earth met. The vision describes this sacralization process.

> Righteousness and truth will I [God] cause to sweep the earth as with a flood to gather out mine elect from the four quarters of the earth, unto a place which I shall prepare, an Holy City, that my people may gird up their loins, and be looking forth for the time of my coming; for there shall be my tabernacle, and it shall be called Zion, a new Jerusalem. The Lord said unto Enoch: Then shalt thou and all thy city meet them there, and we will receive them unto our bosom, and they shall see us; and we will fall upon their necks, and they shall fall upon our necks, and we shall kiss each other. And there shall be mine abode, and it shall be called Zion, which shall come forth out of all the creations which I have made; and for the space of a thousand years the earth shall rest. (Smith 1978; Moses 7, 62–64)

Moreover, Enoch's vision placed the concept of Zion in a particular space, "an eschatology based on geographical contingencies" (Olsen 1985, 74). As William Mulder says so eloquently, "while other millenarians set a time [for the Second Coming] the Mormons appointed a place" (Mulder 1958, 21).

According to historian Steven Olsen, "the vision of Enoch portrays paradise as the product of a strong prophet and his devoted followers living together in divine harmony. It also suggests that when earthly Zion eventually perfected itself, heavenly Zion would descend with Christ at the Second Coming to restore paradise to earth (Olsen 1985, 74–75). Enoch's city became the divine model for "Zion" wherever it was built. Permeated by religion, a concern for the general welfare, "the Lord called his people Zion, because they were of one heart and one mind, and dwelt in righteousness; and there were no poor among them. . . . And it came to pass, in his days, that [Enoch] built a city that was called the City of Holiness, even Zion. . . . and lo, Zion, in process of time, was taken up into heaven. And the Lord said unto Enoch: Behold mine abode forever" (Moses, 7:18–21). In much the same way he had with Enoch, God described for Joseph Smith the covenant he would form with his people.

As noted earlier, the wall surrounding the YFZ Ranch intentionally separated the FLDS from the outside world and its evil influences. Like Enoch, Warren Jeffs asked his followers to live righteous lives and to build a city so perfect that they could be lifted up to heaven. Independent scholar John Walsh characterized the YFZ Ranch as a "gated community," where members were "supposed to be holy and keep God's commandments" (Choate 2008). Referencing the Enoch story from the Bible, Walsh suggested, "if they live their lives in a holy enough manner, they as a whole community would be taken up to heaven to meet Christ and basically be rescued from the wicked Earth" (Choate 2008). Warren built a case for this bold enterprise by saying that Colorado City had been rejected by the Lord because "it was no longer a place for his people where the spirit of God could dwell." Ultimately the Church poured a total of $21 million into the YFZ Ranch for the land, the improvements, and the temple.

If one accepts the argument that Warren identified fully with Enoch, believed the end of the world was imminent, and wanted to build Zion to be lifted up unto heaven, it is safe to assume that he reserved the right for the most faithful to live at the YFZ Ranch. It is clear that despite his physical appearance and the shuffling, quiet way he had addressed the court in Arizona, Jeffs had a more powerful persona in the context of the FLDS world. Even his detractors claimed that he had a compelling presence and could persuade his followers to accept his sometimes outrageous claims or instructions as the word of a man who speaks with God. It is also clear, however, that Jeffs stirred up the FLDS community like no other Church leader before him—dividing the Church between those who were willing to follow his leadership and those who questioned his authority in absolute ways. The YFZ was a sanctuary for only the most faithful; those who had the potential of being lifted up, ready to begin the millennium.

Still another way to understand the ranch at Eldorado is in the context of the general evolution of the sect. The FLDS first organized informally around charismatic leadership and the claim to the priesthood authority critical to the continued practice of plurality. But in the 1990s the group organized more formally when it incorporated as a Church, institutionalizing Church leadership, policy, and procedure in a centralization of power in the person of Church president Rulon Jeffs. Building a second major colony after an eighty-year history on the Colorado Strip, Eldorado perpetuated the expansion of Zion and the maturation of the sect. Historically the temple had always been associated with Zion in the mind of Joseph Smith and his successors, and the ordinances performed within were deemed essential for salvation. In some ways it is surprising that the group did not build a temple sooner. Regardless, the temple at Eldorado symbolized the maturation of the sect, the anticipation it held that heaven and earth would meet

The temple also represented a departure for the FLDS. For decades between 1960 and 1986, the polygamists used the school building for religious meetings in Colorado City/Hildale, but in the 1980s, when the school board discovered the practice, the board put an end to it. Fred Jessop, a UEP trustee proposed the idea of constructing a church building to Leroy Johnson, then prophet of the group. Traditionally the group had rejected the idea of erecting church buildings, suggesting that such buildings would become religious icons or edifices focusing on "things" rather than on faith. Johnson told Jessop that he could construct a "modest" building. When done, the meetinghouse measured 200 feet in width and 270 feet in length. The first meeting held in the building commemorated the date that the Prophet Joseph Smith allegedly appeared in a vision to John Taylor while the latter was in hiding in Centerville, Utah—September 27, 1886—telling him to continue with plural marriage. What became known as the Leroy S. Johnson Meetinghouse reflected the general form of a Latter-day Saint Stake Center, but it was far larger and included a central chamber that was as big as two basketball courts. The most intriguing feature of this chamber was the stage area that ran across the eastern elevation and included a row of large carved, wooden chairs that ran across the stage. Three special chairs at the center and a veil that ran the distance behind the chairs oriented the room and established the priesthood hierarchy in spatial terms. The building was funded, in part, through donations from the members themselves who were promised that, for a $1,000 donation, they would be guaranteed a ticket to Jackson County, Missouri, on the day that the Second Coming was to occur (Bistline 2004, 278).

In Eldorado the group built the very first temple standing eighty feet tall out of limestone blocks and a steel frame. With arched windows, turrets at the corners, and crenellations running across the edge of the roof, the façade is adorned with a short domed steeple, a faint reference to the Nauvoo Temple. An "all-seeing eye" and the inscription, "Holiness to the Lord in the House of the Lord," place this building in the context of the nineteenth-century LDS (Winslow 2006). "The temple, it's magnificent from the outside," said J. D. Doyle, a Texas pilot who has taken an aerial photograph of the ranch (Winslow 2006). "They're pretty close-mouthed about the whole thing. You certainly sense that it's special to them, but they won't talk about it" (Winslow 2006). Indeed, many of the objections to the raid centered on the defilement of this temple. "They kicked in the door. They tore it up," the sect's attorney, Rod Parker, told the *Deseret News.* "More importantly, it was defiled. It's not usable as a temple" (Winslow 2008).

Conclusion

The most striking parallel between the Short Creek and Eldorado raids is the justification that the state made to raid these communities. Both raids were stimulated largely by allegations of child abuse. But these allegations, in both cases, proved to be tenuous, at least as a rationale to conduct massive raids. It would appear that the principal motive for these state raids had more to do with attacking plural marriage and discrediting the groups on a larger public stage than in ferreting out child abuse. The choreography of the grand foray into the lair of the "cult" and the "degradation ceremony" (Garfinkel 1956) that followed in the mass media, depicting FLDS members as perverts, pedophiles, and fanatics, was moral theater. It was the state acting to uphold conventional morality and reinforcing the cultural legitimacy of traditional marriage. Contrary to the guarantee of individual civil rights provided by the Constitution, the families of the FLDS received different, extra-legal treatment seemingly justified by their unique religious beliefs and practices.

In the Short Creek case, Governor Pyle gathered information about alleged marriages through a detective agency and the filming that they conducted under the guise of collecting images for future Hollywood films. A story that was not entirely outrageous in the area of Southern Utah that was often the backdrop to Hollywood westerns, it was, nevertheless, a deception designed to trap and expose the polygamists' deviant lifestyle. The Eldorado raid centered on narratives brought to government officials by apostates who had left the group for a wide range of personal reasons and who had motives to destroy the Church. Empowered by the successful series of child abuse cases that escalated public surveillance of the group in the previous five years, particularly the infamous case of the group's prophet Warren Jeffs, dissenters created a pipeline for stories of the group's secretive culture.[2]

The lesson we might learn from the raids on Short Creek in 1953 and Eldorado in 2008 is that crisis events like these feed into a central defining myth and create religious martyrs but do little to break up beliefs and practices of plural marriage. The polygamists actually practice a form of marriage that does not technically violate the law. Only first wives are in legal marriages and the additional wives are "spiritual wives." Given that the government does not regulate "spiritual" marriage or other forms of intimate private relationships, the elaborate state raids can hardly be justified on legal grounds. Rather, it seems that the state may have substituted the claims of child abuse for the morally offensive practice of plural marriage, taking advantage of both aggressive laws on child protection and the vulnerability of the FLDS, as a separatist community, to this charge.

In both cases, when the court hearings and litigation finally ended, it became glaringly evident that the state had overreached. Following two years of hearings at the Juvenile Court in Arizona after the Short Creek raid, a single underage woman was detained. The most serious charges initially brought by the State of Arizona against the men in the Short Creek community (e.g., rape, statutory rape, and misappropriation of school funds) dissipated after a few years. At Eldorado, all but one of the women taken into custody in the raid was "non-suited," released back to parents and/or allowed to return to the community. Twelve FLDS men have been indicted on charges related to underage marriage. The outcome of these cases remains to be seen. For the most part, FLDS leaders and members experiencing the raids in Arizona and Texas interpreted the incidents as forms of persecution and a testing of their faith. They were able to draw inspiration from many biblical examples of saints, prophets, and martyrs who withstood much greater affliction and torment. It is unlikely that the most recent raid will dampen the resolve of the FLDS community and, indeed, may eventually solidify the group and make it stronger in the face of external opposition. The Eldorado raid, as did the Short Creek raid fifty-five years earlier, appears to have confirmed and invigorated the central defining myth linking the FLDS with religious martyrs of every generation.

NOTES

1. The more the Church insisted on polygamy's nonauthorized status, the more important this link to divine authority became. Accounts of Taylor's vision circulated orally for many years, although a few individuals wrote it down; these included George Q. Cannon, L. John Nuttall, John W. Woolley, Samuel Bateman, Daniel R. Bateman, Charles H. Wilkins, Charles Birrell, George Earl, and Lorin C. Woolley, as well as two women, Julia E. Woolley, and Amy Woolley. The Musser account also states that Taylor gave five of them—Cannon, Wilkins, Samuel Bateman, John W. Woolley, and Lorin C. Woolley—authority to perform plural marriages and to ordain others to do the same. Lorin Woolley was the natural leader of the fundamentalist movement, as other fundamentalists felt that he had been set apart for the work by Church President John Taylor. The Mormon Church excommunicated Woolley in 1924 for "pernicious falsehood" a decade after his father, John Woolley, was dropped from the records of the Church. When Lorin C. Woolley died in September 1934, John Y. Barlow succeeded him as senior member of the council. Before Barlow died in 1949, he had called Leroy S. Johnson and J. Marion Hammon, setting them apart as "Apostles of the Lord Jesus Christ." He also had called Guy H. Musser, Rulon Jeffs, Richard Jessop, Carl Holm, and Alma Timpson to positions of authority. The history of plural marriage in the next half-century would become, in large measure, the history of these men and their posterity, a group who by their union selected for themselves a peculiar destiny.

2. During the late 1990s significant and public cases of child abuse came before the court, stimulating the end of the laissez-faire policy of the Utah Attorney General's office and the development of a new concerted and focused attempt to prosecute violations of law among the polygamist sects.

REFERENCES

Adams, Brooke. 2004. "Warren Jeffs Profile: Thou Shalt Obey." *Salt Lake Tribune,* March 14.
———.2006. "Warren Jeffs: A Wanted Man." *Salt Lake Tribune,* May 10.
Adams, Brooke and Julia Lyon.2008. "Texas Supreme Court Says the State Crossed the Line by Keeping FDS Kids in Custody." *Salt Lake Tribune,* May 30.
Adams, Brooke, Lisa Rosetta, and Pamela Manson. 2006. "Remote S. Dakota Is New Home for FLDS." *Salt Lake Tribune,* May 30.
Barlow, Alvin S. n.d. "1953 Raid on Short Creek." Accessed online at http://www.fldstruth. org (October 30, 2008).
Barlow, Heidi, "Where Is the Trust?" N.d. Accessed online at http://www.truthwillprevail. org (July 12, 2009).

Barlow, Louis. N.d. KSUB Radio Report. "1953 Raid on Short Creek." Accessed online at http://www.fldstruth.org (October 30, 2008).

Barlow, Sister, quoted by Donald Richter. n.d. "What Really Happened at the Coliseum." Accessed online at http://www.truthwillprevail.org (July 12, 2009).

Bistline, Benjamin. 2004. *The Polygamists: A History of Colorado City, Arizona.* 2004. Agreka, LLC.

Black, Vera J. n.d. "1953 Raid on Short Creek." Accessed online at http://www.fldstruth.org (October 30, 2008).

Bloom, Harold. 1992. *The American Religion.* New York: Simon and Schuster.

Choate, Trish. 2008. "Yearning for Zion." *Standard Times Washington Bureau,* May 25.

Dethman, Leigh. 2005. "End of the World Prophecy Fails to Come True." *Deseret News,* April 7.

Dillon, Lucinda. 2000. "Majority in Utah Want Polygamists to Be Prosecuted." *Deseret News,* May 18.

Ellison, Christopher G., and John D. Bartkowski. 1995. "Babies Were Being Beaten: Exploring Child Abuse Allegations at Ranch Apocalypse," pp. 95–110 in Stuart A. Wright (ed.), *Armageddon in Waco.* Chicago: University of Chicago Press.

"FLDS Church Issues Statement on Marriage." 2008. *Deseret News,* June 3.

Garfinkel, Harold. 1956. "Conditions of Successful Degradation Ceremonies." *American Journal of Sociology* 61:420–24.

Goodwyn, Wade. 2008. "Texas Town Wary of Polygamist Sect's Arrival." National Public Radio, September 27. Accessed online at http://www.npr.org/templates/story/story. php?storyID+4629743 (December 2, 2008).

Hoppe, Christy. 2008. "Texas Had Secret Plan to Separate Polygamist Mothers, Children." *Dallas Morning News,* June 4.

Jessop, Carol, with Laura Palmer. 2008. *Escape.* New York: Broadway Books.

Jessop, Evelyn F. n.d. "1953 Raid on Short Creek." Accessed online at http://www.fldstruth. org (October 30, 2008).

Jessop, Fred. n.d. "1953 Raid on Short Creek." Accessed online at http://www.fldstruth.org (October 30, 2008).

Jessop, Maggie. n.d. "Oh, Experience, There's Nothing Like Experience." Accessed online at http://www.truthwillprevail.org (July 12, 2009).

Jessop, Willie. 2009. Presentation at Annual Meeting of CESNUR (Centro Studi sulle Nuove Religioni [Center for Studies on New Religions]), Salt Lake City, Utah, June 13.

Johnson, Leroy S. 1983–1984. *Sermons of Leroy S. Johnson.* 7 vols. Hildale, UT: Twin Cities Courier.

King, Deborah. 2008. "'Keeping Sweet' in San Angelo, Texas." *Huffington Post,* May 28.

Kinkade, Lee Ann. 2008. "We Are (All) Family—Growing Up in an 'Intentional Community' Isn't as Foreign as It Sounds." *Slate,* June 4.

Moreno, Sylvia. 2004. "Polygamous Sect Moves In, and Texas Town Asks 'Why?'" Washingtonpost.com. September 7. Accessed online at http://www.washingtonpost.com/ wp-dyn/articles/All52-2004Sep6.html (December 2, 2008).

Mulder, William. 1958. *Homeward to Zion: The Mormon Migration from Scandinavia.* Minneapolis: University of Minnesota Press.

Musser, Marie, quoted by Donald Richter, "Lest We Forget—Fort Concho." Accessed online at http://www.truthwillprevail.org (July 12, 2009).

Olsen, Steven L. 1985. "The Mormon Ideology of Place: Cosmic Symbolism of the City of Zion, 1830–1846." Ph.D. dissertation, University of Chicago.

Perkins, Nancy. 2005. "FLDS-Doomsday Rumors Infest Web." *Deseret News,* April 5.

Pyle, Howard. 1953a. Quoted in the *Arizona Republic,* July 27.

———. 1953b. Radio Address, July 26. KTAR Radio, Phoenix, Arizona.

———. 1984. Oral interview with Martha S. Bradley, March 14, Phoenix, Arizona.

Richter, Donald. N.d. "What Really Happened at the Coliseum." Accessed online at http://www.truthwillprevail.org (July 12, 2009).

"Slow and Deliberate." 2008. *Arizona Republic,* May 28.

Smith, John L. 2008. "Affidavits Paint a Disturbing Picture of Texas Child Protective Services." *Las Vegas Review-Journal,* June 3.

Smith, Joseph, Jr. 1981 [1835]. *Doctrine and Covenants of the Church of Jesus Christ of Latter Day Saints.* 1981 edition. Salt Lake City, UT: The Church of Jesus Christ of Latter Day Saints.

———. 1978. *The Pearl of Great Price: A Selection from the Revelations, Translations, and Narrations of Joseph Smith.* Salt Lake City, UT: The Church of Jesus Christ of Latter-day Saints.

Steed, Marion, n.d. "This Beautiful Day." Accessed online at http://www.truthwillprevail.org (July 12, 2009).

Superior Court of Arizona, Mohave County. 1953. Arrest Warrants, July 26. Kingman County Courthouse. Photocopy in the possession of the author.

Timpson, Ada B. n.d. "1953 Raid on Short Creek." Accessed online at http://www.fldstruth.org (October 30, 2008).

United Effort Plan (UEP) Board Meeting. 1994. Rulon Jeff's home. September 1, Salt Lake City, Utah.

Watson, Marianne. 2006. Conversation with Martha Bradley, May 27, Casper, Wyoming.

Winslow, Ben. 2006. "FLDS Temple Appears Complete." *Deseret News,* May 10.

———. 2008. "Lawyers for FLDS May Sue." *Deseret News,* June 13.

Wright, Stuart A. 1995. *Armageddon in Waco: Critical Perspectives on the Branch Davidian Conflict.* Chicago: University of Chicago Press.

2

Rescuing Children?

Government Raids and Child Abuse Allegations
in Historical and Cross-Cultural Perspective

SUSAN J. PALMER

The Texas raid on the Yearning for Zion (YFZ) community, now generally considered an egregious and expensive miscalculation, was not the first time that secular authorities have attempted to rescue children from an unconventional communitarian society. In the four cases described below, the authorities were quick to assume that an alternative religious social environment was unwholesome for children.

These four other cases include the Doukhobors, the Apostles of Infinite Love, the Children of God/Family International, and Ogyen Kunzang Choling. Two factors appear to have influenced the local authorities and made them take complaints about the group seriously. First, the groups' alternative, religiously validated patterns of sexuality, parenting, and child rearing challenged conventional family norms and values. Second, the communal and sectarian nature of the groups made it difficult, indeed almost impossible, to investigate or verify complaints about the treatment of children through less intrusive methods (i.e., interviewing neighbors, schoolteachers, or local doctors).

Brief case histories of government raids on four relatively obscure alternative religious communities are presented in this chapter. Like the 2008 raid on the Fundamentalist Church of Jesus Christ Latter Day Saints (FLDS), the purpose of these raids was to investigate child abuse and to "rescue" children. In a manner similar to the YFZ case, these other raids involved a dramatic show of force—guns, helicopters, automatic weapons, and armored vehicles. The communities targeted were hardly paramilitary fortresses or "compounds." Unlike militia or armed survivalist encampments such as the recently raided Hutaree based in Michigan, the members of these communities were not trained as soldiers, and their populations included many, if not mostly, pregnant or nursing mothers, children, teenagers, and elderly people.

In order to explore the causes and consequences of these raids, my accounts of each of these groups are structured as follows:

1. Data are provided concerning the raids on each community, with a brief description of the origins of each community and the beliefs or practices that evoked concern or conflict.
2. Descriptions are given of the circumstances that led up to the raids and the actions of the cultural opponents of these groups, as well as the rationale(s) expressed by secular authorities for the launching of these raids.
3. The short- and long-term impact of these raids—on the children, on their parents, and on the targeted religious communities—is addressed.
4. A comparison of the four raids is drawn to find common features and patterns as well as an explanatory framework offered by placing these histories within the social context of family dynamics, changing concepts of the "child," and nineteenth-century tensions between parents and the state over the ownership of children.

The Doukhobors ("Spirit Wrestlers") of British Columbia

In 1953 the Royal Canadian Mounted Police (RCMP) launched the first in a series of raids on the Doukhobors of British Columbia. This was a surprise raid at dawn, in which approximately 200 children between the ages of seven and fifteen were seized, separated from their parents, and loaded on buses accompanied by social workers. Of these children, 104 were forcibly placed in a dormitory school at New Denver, a remote village on Lake Slocan in the north of British Columbia for up to six years.[1] The Doukhobors complained that during the six-year term parents were not permitted to visit their children and could only speak to them through a wire fence (Woodcock and Avakumovic 1977; Holt 1964).

Again, on the morning of January 18, 1955, the family homes of the Doukhobor settlement in Krestova, British Columbia, were raided simultaneously. The raid was authorized by the provincial government of British Columbia and carried out by the RCMP.

The government's rationale for both these raids was to protect the children's right, as Canadian citizens, to receive an education and acquire literacy. The Doukhobors spoke only Russian inside their community in British Columbia. Since their origins in the 1700s in Russia and the Ukraine, the written Bible and all books were associated with the Fall from Eden, the

Devil, and sin. It was their policy, therefore, to reject the written Bible in favor of an oral tradition of teaching, learning from the "Living Book" (the community), and prompting the Holy Spirit within each person. Their history and beliefs had never been written down but were enshrined within an oral history tradition, notably in their hymns and polyphonic choral works (Janzen 1990).

The B.C. government responded to this situation by deciding that every Doukhobor child must be placed in public school and that all parents who refused to cooperate would have their children taken away from them. A raid was deemed necessary because the RCMP had discovered, in previous investigations into the Kootinoff homes, that the Doukhobor couples did not register their births, weddings, or deaths, and there was no public record of the number of children born into each home (Janzen 1990).

Origins

The Doukhobors, or "Spirit Wrestlers," originated in Russia and the Ukraine around the 1700s, as noted.[2] They were Orthodox Christian anarchists who refused to pledge allegiance to a secular government. Strictly communitarian, they refused to sign contracts or serve in the military. Because of their radical pacifism, they came into conflict with the tsars (Alexander I and Nicholas I). In 1899, after weathering intense persecution owing to their refusal to serve in the Russian army, approximately seventy-five hundred Doukhobors emigrated to Canada and settled in Manitoba and Saskatchewan where the Quakers took them in and helped them adjust to their new environment.

The Doukhobors soon proved to be quite uncooperative as Canadian citizens. They would not pledge an oath of allegiance to the Crown or register marriages, births, and deaths or the ownership of land under the names of private individuals. They were awarded Crown land, but in 1907 around three hundred thousand acres reverted to the Crown, the unfortunate result of their insistence on collective ownership.

External social pressure led to a three-way schism in the Doukhobor community in 1907. The "Independents" (edinolichniki) adopted a cooperative stance toward the secular state by renouncing their communitarian ideals and assenting to the signing of contracts. The "Orthodox Community of Doukhobors" remained loyal to their spiritual leader, Peter Verigin, and preserved their religion and cultural patterns. In 1908 and 1912, Verigin purchased large tracts of land in British Columbia, where he and about eight thousand Community Doukhobors moved to cultivate farms and plant fruit trees. The third schism, the "Sons of Freedom," was a group that, in 1903, had reinterpreted the teachings of Peter Verigin and, in 1907, resisted the government's intrusion into their way of life.

Cultural Opposition and Conflict

The Sons of Freedom demonstrated against the Canadian government's seizure of their lands and the pressure to place their children in public schools by staging nudist marches and launching arson attacks on public buildings, police cars, and motorcycles. In 1928, after Peter Verigin was assassinated, his son assumed the mantle of leadership, and attempted to resolve tensions between the Doukhobors and the larger society. The Sons of Freedom considered him "ungodly" and began to direct their arson attacks against the Orthodox Community of Doukhobors, whom they felt had betrayed their cause by agreeing to the government's demands to register marriages and births, and to buy and own private property, which was against their communitarian and anarchist ideals.

In 1953 a rumor spread among the Doukhobors that the RCMP were setting off bombs and fires with the intention of framing the sect, destroying their community, and using the turmoil as a pretext for taking their children. This resulted in a new wave of bombings and arson attacks, mainly targeting government property, the Canadian Pacific Railway, and the West Kootenay Power and Light Company. In 1962 more bombings and burnings occurred; twenty people died during four years of violent demonstrations. In 1964 ninety men belonging to the Sons of Freedom were sentenced and confined to a prison in Agassiz, British Columbia (Janzen 1990).

In 1932 the Canadian Parliament responded to the Sons of Freedom's nudist demonstrations by passing a law that made public nudity a criminal offense. More than three hundred Doukhobors were subsequently arrested for the crime of public nudity, and some of them ended up serving a three-year prison sentence. One of their leaders, an obese farm wife referred to as "Big Fanny," was photographed by journalists as she was escorted to prison by embarrassed RCMP officers (Holt 1964).

The B.C. provincial government, under Sullivan's Royal Commission (1947–1948) had attempted to negotiate with the Sons of Freedom and to plan a gradual process for integrating them into Canadian society. But in 1952 W. A. C. Bennett's Social Credit government came to power and adopted a less tolerant stance toward the "Doukhobor Problem"; a year later, in 1953, the first raid was launched in which, as noted at the start of the chapter, approximately two hundred Doukhobor children were taken into state custody.

A local journalist and politician, Simma Holt, produced news articles calling for the government to exert more control over the deviant Doukhobors.[3] Holt's 1964 book, *Terror in the Name of God,* features photographs of half-clothed Doukhobor women and their naked children attending village meetings, and her prose offers a striking example of intolerance:

> Lovely bodies, like their minds, soon grow gross and ugly—usually starting in the late teens or early twenties as these youngsters find themselves trapped in frustration, boredom and hate of the dark Sons of Freedom world. . . . Without escape [these children] can never look ahead—never hope for anything better than those who stifle in a mass paranoia and masochism. (Holt 1964, 152)

It is important to note that the cultural opponents of the Doukhobors exhibited little or no interest in the religious rationale behind the displays of nudity, which were simply condemned as obscene displays. Journalists and government officials alike understood the nudist marches as parents "brainwashing" their children and subjecting them to cold weather and humiliation. Historians of the Doukhobors have explained that ritual nudity expressed their identification with Adam and Eve before the Fall and was based on the belief that the Holy Spirit resides within every person (Palmieri 1915). Thus public nudity was intended as a magical act of power, intended to ward off enemies. It was a ritual solution to the threat to their culture,[4] much like the ghost dance was to the Lakota Sioux.

Holt reports that over forty years "a total of 1,112 depredations by the Sons of Freedom have cost Canada's taxpayers a minimum of $20,872,950 in destruction, police and court costs." She claims the raids were necessary because children were being trained by their parents to make and throw bombs, and to burn down houses: "Arson was a mother's lesson in love to her child. Hate was his truth. . . . Thus the child grew up" (Holt 1964, 4).

The Aftermath

The B.C. government raids were "successful" insofar as the children taken into state custody, were forced to learn English and did receive a Canadian education. These Russian anarchists were gradually subdued and assimilated, and split into factions representing varying degrees of accommodation to Canadian society.

But the raids were "unsuccessful" in the long term, because the state's custodial detention of the children proved to have a devastating effect on the families. When the children of New Denver came of age, they filed a class-action lawsuit against the B.C. government, alleging that they had suffered physical and sexual abuse at the hands of their teachers in the state's secular boarding school, and that their families, culture, and identity had been "stolen" from them. The B.C. Ombudsman conducted a full investigation and produced a report called; "Righting the Wrong: The Confinement of the Sons of Freedom Doukhobor Children" (1999). According to this report, the Doukhobor children were "wrongfully removed from their families and community, and wrongfully confined to a prison-like school." The report documented many violations of civil liberties, including rights to language, religion, and culture.

The B.C. Ombudsman called for a formal apology by the B.C. government and, in March 2002, produced a progress report (No.43). John McLaren, a law professor at the University of Vancouver, researched the case and described the B.C. governmental policy as "forced assimilation." He argued that many violations of human rights, as defined by the United Nations, had taken place as a direct result of the raids. In 2005 the children of New Denver won their class-action suit and received financial compensation.[5]

The B.C. government has since made an official "Statement of Regret" but Canada's federal government never apologized, claiming that it was not responsible for actions taken by a different government that was in place fifty years ago. The victims, now middle-aged adults, have since formed a group called "The New Denver Survivors Collective" that continues to research the case and lobby for justice. As a consequence of the raids of the 1950s and 1960s, the Sons of Freedom, the radical branch of the Doukhobors, was disbanded. The Orthodox Community of Doukhobors continues on as compliant Canadian citizens and no longer lives communally. Today there are between thirty thousand and forty thousand Doukhobors in Canada. The majority can be found living in farming communities in the Kootenays where they preserve their cultural heritage by participating in Doukhobor organizations and festivals.[6]

In 2005 there was a proposal to "create a picnic area and sculpture in the town of New Denver to pay homage to the scores of Doukhobor children forced into the town's residential schools. The Doukhobors opposed the plan, however, "citing it as an inappropriate symbol or icon which contravened their religious beliefs, and an unwanted attempt to assimilate them into the community." Walter Swetisloff, a Doukhobor Community representative, spoke out against the project, saying, "It was no picnic for us when we were there, so this picnic site as a reminder was very disrespectful" (Keiran, 2008). An eloquent example of official hubris is found in the response of the British Columbia Teachers' Federation (BCTF) to the "Doukhobor problem." The BCTF formally recommended that "real Canadian homes, radiating the best in our Canadian mode of life" should be "placed amidst" the Doukhobor villages, so that these "fanatical Russian anarchists" might establish intimate contacts with "lovable Canadians" (Janzen 1990, 135).

The Apostles of Infinite Love

Canada's other example of a raid to save children occurred in Quebec in the 1960s and targeted a conservative Catholic sectarian commune formed around a mystical pope known to his disciples as "Father John Gregory."[7]

In the early morning of December 28, 1966, the monastic community of the Apostles of Infinite Love (AIL), situated near the village of St. Jovite, Quebec, was raided by the Quebec Provincial Police.[8] Between fifty and sixty police and Social Welfare officers entered the grounds of the monastery by force, breaking the chain barrier and smashing the glass door of the entrance. Their mission was to search for five boys who had been reported as missing by parents who were former members of the AIL. The officials searched the premises and seized documents but did not find the boys.

The following year two more raids were executed, on February 11 and March 13, 1967. Ten monks were arrested, and eight young girls were taken into custody by Social Welfare officers and placed in foster homes (*Father Jean de la Trinité and the Hidden Children of St. Jovite* 1971).

Eleven years later, on May 1, 1978, a third raid was launched. The monastery's grounds (known as "the Domain") were raided at dawn by a team of twenty police officers arriving in twelve police cars and two helicopters, and accompanied by an immigration officer, two dogs, and a paddy wagon. Several former members accompanied the raid team and assisted in the search as guides. After a five-hour search, during which the police fired guns at monks who were trying to escape into the woods, twelve monks and nuns were arrested and jailed in the police station of the nearest town. Three were retained as witnesses, and one nun spent sixteen days in jail. The pretext of the raid was to find the "hidden children" and to retain the witnesses needed in the upcoming trial of the mystical pope Gregory XVII, who was charged with contempt of court and with the "sequestration of children."[9]

On April 14, 1999, twenty-one years later, a fourth raid was executed by 130 police officers accompanied by Youth Protection workers. They took fourteen children into custody, and doctors examined them for signs of abuse. The raid was a response to allegations by several former members who had grown up in the monastery and claimed that they had been sexually abused and beaten by four of their teachers, including the mystical pope. The police searched the monastery to arrest the four accused members, but they could not be found. The element of surprise was lost, because news of the planned police operation had been broadcast on the front page of a Montreal newspaper, *La Presse,* that same morning. When the case finally went to court, the charges were dropped due to a lack of evidence.

Origins

The Apostles of Infinite Love (Les Apôtres de l'amour infini) is a conservative Catholic schismatic movement founded by Jean-Gaston Tremblay, who was born in Rimouski, Quebec, in 1928 and joined a monastic order, the Frères de la Charité. In 1962 Tremblay visited a mystical pope in France, known as Clément XV.[10] Clément XV ordained Tremblay as a priest and later as a bishop (Cuneo 1998).

In the 1970s Tremblay received a revelation that he was the true successor to Saint Peter, Pope Gregory XVII, the mystical pope of the Last Days. After a falling out with Clement XV, Tremblay founded a monastery near St. Jovite where his followers purchased 365 acres in the Laurentides near Mont Tremblant and constructed a monastery. The Apostles have their own hydroelectric plant and printing press, and they make their own clothing, bread, and cheese.[11]

Cultural Opposition and Conflict

In retrospect, it can be seen that the opposition to the AIL originates mainly from the group's practice of admitting families into their lay order in the monastery. Initially the families live together in trailers, but eventually in most cases husband and wife separate and live apart as celibate Brothers or Sisters. Once the father or mother, or both, are ordained as priests (Pope Gregory XVII advocates the ordination of women), their children are then moved into separate quarters and live as miniature monks and nuns, no longer supervised by their own parents.

In the 1960s a network of different parties formed to oppose the AIL. This network included Catholic bishops, social workers in Youth Protection, and former members (Michel San Pietro 1991). In 1962 Msgr. Eugene Limoges, the Bishop of Mont Laurier, warned his parishioners not to attend the "sacrilegious" ceremonies of Father John "on penalty of being refused the Sacraments" (*"Justice" Put on Trial* 1984).

On December 9, 1965, four Provincial Police cars arrived at the monastery to seize the children. A Belgian priest, Father Andre Tailleu, from Detroit, Michigan, came to Quebec to retrieve the children of his sister, whose husband had joined the monastery in 1964. He won his case in court and took the children to Belgium, where they were placed in a state institution (*"Justice" Put on Trial* 1984).

The first two raids, in December 1966 and February 1967, respectively, were instigated by parents whose adult children joined the AIL or by apostate fathers who lobbied to retrieve their children. The 1966 raid was the result of the lobbying efforts of Ralph Sevigny, whose adult children had joined the Apostles. He formed a network of parents who were frustrated in their efforts to communicate with their spouses inside the monastery and who wanted to see their children in the AIL.

The 1978 raid can be traced to the influence of an "arch apostate," Bill Currier, who joined the St. Jovite monastery with his wife and three children in 1969 and defected in 1973. In 1976 he applied for a writ of habeas corpus to seize his children by force, and he won custody of them at the Supreme Court (*"Justice" Put on Trial* 1984). His wife, Carmen Currier, delivered the oldest daughter to him in May 1977 after a visit from Bill Currier, accompanied by the police. But she enlisted the aid of Mother Superior Germaine to keep the two younger children inside the Order by transferring them to sister monasteries. ("It was a question of conscience," she declared). Father John and three of his disciples were charged with the "sequestration" of children, a crime in French law.[12]

On April 25, 1978, the mystical pope was arrested by the Quebec Provincial Police, detained for a preliminary inquiry in Parthenais Prison for four months, and then sentenced to two years in prison (*"Justice" Put on Trial* 1984).

Youth Protection officials were also caught up in the cause. In September 1979 Maureen Champagneur Gilbert, a former Youth Protection commissioner officer, held a press conference and distributed a tract ("Do We Want a Jonestown in Quebec?") which proposed that the government retain a permanent team of deprogrammers. Two years earlier, in September 1977, two

Youth Protection officers interrogated the boys at the monastery and gave a favorable report, but later in a television interview they expressed vague and dire misgivings. The author of *"Justice" Put on Trial* complains that Quebec's Legal Aid colluded with Bill Currier in allowing him the privilege of their services, although as a resident of Ontario he was technically no longer eligible. The author also claimed that the lawyers of Legal Aid tended to discard their clients who were Apostles just before their upcoming trials (e.g., Carmen Currier) but would offer strong support to their opponents.

The 1999 raid was instigated by two second-generation members. Two youths, the Sevigny brothers, ran away from the monastery in 1984. They found their sister at a nearby monastery and persuaded her to leave also. Fourteen years later, in 1998, the brothers suddenly divulged that they had been sexually abused, and they formed a network of thirty second-generation members, all of whom filed complaints of sexual and physical abuse against the mystical pope and three of his leaders, at the Palais de Justice de Saint Jérôme.

The purpose of the 1999 raid, therefore, was to arrest the three monks and one nun accused of sexual crimes, but none of them was at the monastery. Father John Gregory, who was traveling in France at the time, was ordered to appear in court. According to Father Simon, the chief spokesperson at the monastery, Father Gregory miraculously managed to make the court date on April 28, 1999, barely in time because of a favorable backwind that caused his airplane to arrive half an hour early at the airport where the monks were waiting to whisk him off to court.[13] Because the fifty-one charges referred to events alleged to have occurred more than fifteen years earlier (between 1966 and 1985) no evidence was found to support the charges, and after several court hearings (and considerable media coverage) the case was dismissed.

The Aftermath

One result of the raids is that the Apostles have intensified their sectarian stance toward the larger society. Father Simon, who receives visitors at the monastery, has suggested to me on several occasions that Satan was behind the attacks on Gregory XVIII and was also responsible for the arson attack that demolished their first buildings.[14]

A second result is that no children are present in the monastery today, and novices are no longer permitted to bring their children with them. The AIL compensates for the lack of a second generation by intensifying its missionary efforts in Latin America, the Caribbean, and France. Today Pope

Clement XV's monastery in France houses a few aged monks and has gone underground to avoid persecution in the French *lutte antisecte*. The Apostles of Infinite Love, in contrast, are highly visible. Their Sisters wear dramatic blue tunics and veils and Magnificat badges, and travel door to door, distributing calendars and literature. The Apostles at St. Jovite (Tremblant) continue to welcome visitors to their open-air Sunday Mass and offer spiritual retreats at their monastery.

The Children of God/The Family International

In the early 1990s The Family International (formerly known as the Children of God [COG]) experienced a series of raids that took place in Spain, France, Australia, and Argentina. The rationale for the raids was to investigate allegations of child molestation, child abuse, child prostitution, and "incitement of minors to debauchery."

The first raid occurred in Spain, in July 1990, when regional authorities in Barcelona raided a Family home and took twenty-two children into custody. The parents were charged with "illegal association," with operating an illicit school, fraud, and with inflicting psychological harm on the children. The children were held for twelve months during the court procedure.

By July 1992 the Barcelona Provincial Court had discovered no evidence of abuse, acquitted the parents of all charges, and allowed the children to return home. The decision was appealed before the Spanish Constitutional Court, but the lower-court ruling was upheld. Another appeal was also filed before the Supreme Court of Spain in Madrid, but it was rejected on December 1, 1994.

Space does not permit an analysis of all the raids on The Family International in these different countries. I therefore focus on the raids in Australia because ample documentation of those raids exists. Moreover, the raids in Australia reveal a pattern found in other government raids on the Family as well as other new religious movements (Richardson 1999; Palmer 1999; Wright 1995, this volume; Wright and Fagan, this volume).

On May 15, 1992, more than 130 children were seized at dawn in raids on The Family's communal homes in Sydney and Melbourne. Thirty officers from the Department of Community Services (DCS) and the Police Department stormed the communal houses occupied by the communal Christian fundamentalist group in The Hills district of Sydney's northwest and took 65 children into custody. In Victoria simultaneous raids resulted in the seizure of another 72 children and teenagers (Huxley 1992).

The Melbourne police officers also removed documents and religious literature from the Family homes, claiming that they had received information linking the sect with a "number of deceptions" of businesses in the State of Victoria.

The media had been contacted and were present during these predawn raids. The very next day former members from the United Kingdom and the United States appeared on television programs in Australia, describing their traumatic experiences inside The Family.

The lawyers who represented The Family denounced the raid to the press as "legalized kidnapping" and "fascist lunacy." They complained that the police officers had kicked in doors, waved warrants at astonished parents, and dragged sleeping children as young as two years of age from their beds. They bundled seventy-two children, including a five-year-old boy with cerebral palsy, into waiting buses and drove off to three separate detention centers, refusing the parents access for several days while the interviews and examinations took place (Allison 1992a).

A solicitor, Sean McNally, who worked at the legal firm representing most of the parents, warned: "If the department loses its action, as we expect it will since there is no real evidence the children are in any danger, we will sue for $10 million damages for false imprisonment and psychological harm to the children."

The case resulting from the raid was described as "unique in Australian legal history" (Allison 1992a). According to Greg Fleming, the clerk of Cobham Children's Court at Werrington, the trial was expected to last four months and to cost a minimum of $2.5 million. But the children were released from state custody only one week after the raid, the result of a hearing by the Cobham magistrate, Ian Forsyth. A major condition for their release was that the department had to be allowed regular supervisory visits on Forsyth's behalf to monitor their health and whereabouts.

Cultural Opposition and Conflict

In 1991 police in New South Wales had begun a year-long investigation of The Family, code-named "Project A." A social worker, Pauline Rockley, was a driving force in this investigation. She worked with the DCS as Campbelltown's district manager and became the coordinator of the case against The Family. Rockley helped the police plan the raids on three homes in The Hills district in May (Allison 1992e).

When Rockley testified as a key witness for the custody case involving sixty-five children (held in the Cobham Children's Court), she shed light on how the raid came about. She described the confidential New South Wales (NSW) Police Service document known as "Children of God—Project A."[15] She revealed that in the mid-1970s there had been a proposal for an NSW parliamentary inquiry into the Children of God religious sect, which did not proceed because the families involved "disappeared." She discovered from reading Immigration Department files that the former NSW Minister for the Environment, Tim Moore, had pushed for the inquiry and that "some parents whose names are in those files are part of these proceedings" (Allison 1992b).

The DCS gathered its information from former members of COG ,[16] from police and immigration files, and from the group's internal literature seized during the raid of May 15. The DCS alleged that the children were "brainwashed and sexually abused." Under cross-examination in court, Rockley revealed that the allegations were based solely on COG literature (some seized from the raids) and the claims of former members who would soon give evidence in the care case.

The barrister representing parents from The Family, Robert Cavanagh, claimed that Rockley's testament was "tainted by value judgments and nonconsideration of the evidence." The judge also noted that there were "gaps and loose threads" in Rockley's testimony. Rockley claimed that "some of the 65 children of the religious sect . . . probably took part in oral and vaginal sex with their peers, adolescents and adults" and that it was "probable" that young boys and girls had been involved in such sex, although the department did not believe that anal sex had occurred. Rockley admitted, however, that there was "no specific evidence" of rape, pedophilia, homosexuality, or incest.

Rockley was described as breaking down twice under cross-examination. When asked to specify which children had been sexually abused and by whom, she said that, considering the sexual beliefs and practices of the sect, the department believed that all the children had been sexually abused and that the abuse would continue. She did admit, however, that when the department met on May 14 and decided to seize the children, it only had general information, nothing specific.

The barrister for the children, Mark Trench, dismissed the former members as "disgruntled" ex-members who tried to "set up" parents of The Family (Allison 1992d). He asked Rockley to produce specific evidence covering every possible form of sexual abuse as applied to the children under the Child Care and Protection Act of 1987.[17] She replied: "No specific information . . . we're talking of subtle sexual abuse in some cases. I'm not implying that all these children have had sexual intercourse with someone. We're saying it begins with children being taught at an inappropriate age of sexual contact and sexual practices, and this can lead up to other forms." She concluded by saying it was "probable" that some children had been involved in sexual intercourse, had been sexually assaulted by indecent touching, or had been subjected to oral sex (Allison 1992b).

On May 21 Justice Gray of the Supreme Court of Victoria at Melbourne ordered the sect children released into the custody of their parents until the determination of the Protection Applications (Nicholas 1999).

The Aftermath

Seven years later, in April 1999, Justice John Dunford of the New South Wales Supreme Court ruled that the seizure of sixty-five children in the Sydney homes had been illegal. Justice Dunford ruled that the officer named on the warrants, Sergeant Gregory Sullivan, was required to attend the raids but had never left Castle Hill police station. "(B)eing in a radio control room in touch with the people who were at the premises is not in my view taking part in the execution," Justice Dunford noted. This meant that the police and the DCS were trespassing when they broke into the homes in Cherrybrook, Kellyville, and Glenhaven and "rounded up" the children on May 15, 1992 (Allison 1992a).

In August 1992 fifty-seven children subsequently launched a suit against the State of NSW, asserting that they had suffered psychological damage after the raids on The Family's homes. The NSW Supreme Court found that the children were entitled to seek damages from the NSW government because search warrants used in the raids had been worthless (Allison 1992c).

The children argued in court that they were unlawfully arrested and falsely imprisoned. They complained that they had been lied to by the Department of Community Services (DOCS). One boy reported that they had been told they were going on a three-day holiday and that the officers were friends of their parents (Allison 1992c). Instead they were taken to state institutions where they were detained for six days until court proceedings ruled that they could return home (Nicholas 1999).

The children's solicitor, Greg Walsh, called on Attorney General Shaw to settle the case immediately, protesting that the children "had been through enough!" He complained that "they were branded when they were taken as having been sexually abused, each and every one of them. That's something which is ringing in their ears today as it was then, and they want the matter resolved and they want justice to take place. Many of the children continue to wet their beds, have nightmares and live in fear the incident could happen again" (Allison 1992c).

Spokespersons from The Family offered an insightful comment on the aftermath of another raid in Argentina:

> Because the system is not equipped to deal with the sheer scale of the problems generated by a mass raid—the authorities are tempted . . . forced to cut corners . . . to make decisions under desperate circumstances that ignore, violate human rights. They are put in an embarrassing position where they must break their own rules because of the unwieldy situation, where their chief concern is to save face, cut down expenses.[18]

Family leaders estimate that, worldwide, six hundred children of the Family have been examined by court-appointed officials, but no evidence of abuse has been found.

Ogyen Kunzang Choling

Ogyen Kunzang Choling (OKC) is a Tibetan Buddhist community that is housed in a French chateau, known as "Chateau Soleil" near the town of Castellane in the French Alps where members built a temple and a residential school for their children.[19] On May 30, 1997, the members of OKC awoke to find that they were the target of a government raid. One eyewitness mistakenly thought that the legion of gendarmes that suddenly appeared were chasing an escaped inmate from a nearby prison.

> Early in the morning, over a hundred gendarmes descended on us, with many vans and a helicopter. At first we thought a dangerous criminal had escaped from the nearby prison and was hiding in the woods, and that was why they were here. But we realized they came for us![20]

The raid team was composed of 130 gendarmes from Castellane, policemen from the city of Digne, and around 20 paramilitary GIGN[21] from Perpignon. They arrived in fourteen vans and a helicopter. First the police secured the perimeter, and then they served a warrant and searched the premises. The GIGN soldiers were stationed in front of every door for two hours, holding "big guns."[22]

The purpose of the raid was to investigate three complaints: nonassistance to a person endangered; involuntary injury; and the unlawful practice of medicine. The judge at the nearby town of Digne had issued the search warrant. Although the authorities had received no complaints concerning child abuse, it appeared that one of the main purposes of the raid on OKC was to examine the thirty-two children who were enrolled in the Chateau Soleil boarding school. The raid team was accompanied by doctors, nurses, and psychologists who examined the children for signs of sexual abuse or medical neglect. According to the same eyewitness, these children were treated in a callous fashion during the examination:

> All the adults and children had to go one by one for interrogation. The psychiatrist questioned the 30 children. They recorded their height, their weight, and one doctor did sexual and gynecological examinations in a police van. One little girl screamed "No! No!"—so the doctor threatened to slap her! At first, we did not realize what they were doing, then we insisted that—at least for the little girls—their mother or an older woman should be there to explain to them what was going on—but they refused. One girl, who is twelve and is very strong, said "No!"—and they let her alone. The doctor was very unkind, very brutal! My husband wrote a complaint to the judge, but nothing happens.[23]

It appeared that the investigation of the children was just part of a much broader strategy, operating under the code name, "Operation Soleil." On that same day of May 30, 1997, seventeen raids were carried out simultaneously on OKC centers in France and Belgium. The Belgian raids had been authorized by a Brussels Juge d'instruction, Jean-Claude Leys, who authorized a raid force of approximately two hundred gendarmes and investigators. Police proceeded to raid all the OKC properties, with a view to discovering various forms of financial abuse and fraud. The investigators were accompanied by a psychologist, an expert accountant, a mathematician, and a work inspector, since OKC was suspected of exploiting the labor of illegal immigrants ("Le secte belge-tibetaine de Castellane" 1996). Robert Spatz, the group's Lama and spiritual leader, was arrested on the street in front of OKC's vegetarian restaurant in Brussels. Six others were arrested (his wife, his accountant, and four administrators) and charged with complicity in the leader's alleged crimes. Fifty other members were taken in for questioning.

The investigators reported to the press that they had discovered "cells" at Chateau Soleil. These "cells" were constructed with soundproof walls, and journalists speculated as to whether they were used to isolate children from their parents and stifle the children's screams. OKC spokespersons told the journalists that the cells were traditional Buddhist meditation chambers, but the news reports noted that investigators suspected that they had been used for the *sequestration* of children, and investigators were looking into whether people entered them voluntarily and whether they had been used for human trafficking. At the Belgian court hearing, however, the expert surveyor appointed by the judge stated that it was impossible to "sequester" anyone inside these cells, because they opened from the inside (Allard 1997).

The investigators also noted that they had found some curious hermetic objects: Tibetan Buddhist prayer wheels, flags, incense holders, and tiny statues of Buddha. These were described in the media as sinister clues denoting *secte*-like activities.

Origins

Ogyen Kunzang Choling was founded in 1972 by Robert Spatz (b. 1944) and was the very first Buddhist center to open up in Brussels. A Belgian citizen, Spatz had traveled in India during the 1960s, where he studied for six years under a Tibetan master, Kyabjé Kangyour Rinpotché (1895–1975), who initiated him into the higher levels, awarded him his spiritual title of "Lama Kunzang Dorjé," and entrusted him with the mission of opening a Buddhist center in Europe.

OKC also established Tibetan Buddhist centers in Portugal and Tahiti. In 1974 Lama Dorje set up Chateau Soleil, a monastery in the French Alps with a temple and a residential school for the children of the adepts. The Dalai Lama visited the OKC center in Brussels in 1990. OKC belongs to the Red Hat, Nyingmapa lineage of Tibetan Buddhism. It emphasizes the worship of Tara, the spiritual mother of Buddha."[24]

Robert Spatz was soon labeled as a "gourou [guru]" in the French-speaking media. Media reports described him as a "soi-disant [self-styled]" Lama, whose spiritual credentials were in question simply because he is a Belgian and a former TV repairman. His disciples protested that he was given his honorific title by an authentic Tibetan spiritual master, part of the ancient lineage of Tibetan spiritual masters going back to Kagyur Rinpoche, H. H. Dudjom Rinpoche, and H. H. Khentse Rinpoche (a teacher of the Dalai Lama).

Cultural Opposition and Conflict

OKC's troubles may be traced directly back to the rise of a government-sponsored anticult movement in France. A series of mass suicides in the Solar Temple, between 1994 and 1997, in Quebec, Switzerland, and France, stimulated a widespread fear about the dangers of *sectes*. The French National Assembly appointed a commission to study the problem of *sectes* in France, the 1995 Guyard Commission, which produced a list of 173 religious or philosophical groups in France labeled as "sects"; all were viewed as potentially dangerous. OKC was one of the 173 groups on this list, although there were fewer than five hundred adepts in France. Jean-Louis Corne, the chief administrator of Chateau Soleil, explained how his attempts to correct the situation were foiled:

> I wrote to M. Gest regarding the list of sects, wanting to know what the *renseignement generaux* [secret police] file was on us. Their response was that the Guyard Commission had dissolved; it finished its job once the Guyard report and list were published, so now they had no more responsibility. So, there was no one to respond. So, we were stuck with our name on the list! Also, Alain Gest is a deputy, therefore he has diplomatic immunity, and one cannot pursue him with lawyers.[25]

In the French government reports, OKC was described as a *secte Orientaliste* that fulfilled at least one of the criteria named by the Guyard Commission—that of *l'embrigadement des enfants* (indoctrination of children). Moreover, according to the 1999 government report ("Sects and Money"), OKC was considered to be one of the richest *sectes* in France.[26]

The Belgian government soon followed France's example, and by April 1997 had appointed the Moureaux Commission, which duly produced a list of 189 *nuisibles*[27] groups, considered to be *sectes*. OKC was featured on this list, and the investigation into OKC began in April 1997, right after the Belgian report was published.

A second source of opposition came from several former OKC members, who expressed their grievances to the press or in court. According to a member of Chateau Soleil, their troubles started with a complaint from a mother who came to visit her forty-four-year-old daughter:[28]

> She came here to persuade her daughter to leave and go home with her. The daughter refused, so she called the police. The police chief from Cas-

tellane arrived with a doctor, who concluded she was well cared for and was taking the medicine that he would have prescribed. But then it was discovered that our doctor, who lived in Belgium and came here regularly for retreats . . . he had to pay a big fine, because he was not registered with *l'ordre des médecins français*. We also had grandparents come and take away their grandchildren, whose parents lived here.[29]

Later this woman's daughter was diagnosed with cancer. During the eighteen months preceding the cancer diagnosis she had been seen by two expert physicians and a psychiatrist, and after the cancer was found, she was seeing a physician chosen by her family. When she died a year after she had been diagnosed, OKC officials were charged with manslaughter. But when the case went to trial in Digne-les-bains on November 8, 2001, the charges were dismissed.

A common criticism leveled against OKC was that the parents were overworked and that their children followed a spartan regimen. Former members claimed that the children could be shut up for several days or a week in a wooden hut without light or food, and that the children were beaten and were washed only once a week.

These assertions were contradicted by a 1996 investigation into the wellbeing of thirty-two children living at Chateau Soleil, ordered by the juvenile judge at Digne. The investigators found that the children were in school for four hours daily, studying general courses, and their other activities included Buddhist rituals, martial arts, Tibetan horticulture, dance, and handicrafts. They read widely and were allowed to watch television, and they appeared to be healthy and energetic. The result was a favorable report.

It is noteworthy that favorable legal results of OKC's court cases were consistently ignored in media and government reports, where only the "bad news" was featured. For example, the 1997 Belgian Parliamentary Commission stated that OKC children were cut off from society and would be forced to remain in the community once they reached adulthood. It ignored the findings of the 1996 investigation and the judge's conclusion that the children's conditions were "highly privileged." A judgment of dismissal to the motion that the children be taken out of their parochial school and enrolled in the local public school was delivered on January 23, 1997, by the same judge, following the prosecutor's submissions. The report of the 1997 Belgian Parliamentary Commission also failed to mention the ruling of noneducational assistance to be delivered by the judge at Digne, on January 23, 1997, although a copy was delivered to the Commission by OKC officials.

Other complaints were those typically leveled against communal societies—that OKC demanded voluntary labor from its members, and provided only food, lodging, and Buddhist instruction in exchange. At the OKC center in the Dordogne, two families lived together, practiced Tibetan Buddhism, and ran a *chambre d'hote*—"and they were accused of being in a *secte*—just because they all lived together!"[30] The vegan and macrobiotic diet of OKC members was interpreted as a brainwashing technique, "used to psychologically bind new disciples to the group."[31]

Aftermath

Leaders of Chateau Soleil were charged with depriving children under the age of fifteen of food and care. This charge included five children of Portuguese origin, who were very short compared to French children their age. But all the charges were dismissed when the cases appeared before the tribunal at the Court of Digne. On November 8, 2001, the Criminal Court of Digne acquitted all French defendants of the charges of "unauthorized and/or illegal practice of medicine, or failure to assist a person in danger" ("L'OKC Devant le tribunal," 2008). The juvenile court judge at Digne had already issued a *non-lieu* [dismissal of charges] on October 12, 1999.

But in Belgium the legal situation was far more complex. On June 4, 1997, Robert Spatz and five associates were indicted for "conspiracy, money laundering, sequestration, failure to assist a person in danger and aggravated unlawful detention beatings." By the end of June the *juge d'instruction* in Brussels had outlined an impressive list of the kind of charges often leveled against *sectes*: charges of *abus de confiance, faux et usage de faux*, extortion of salaries and important gifts/donations, nonassistance to a person in danger, and the *sequestration* of children. Social legislation infractions, such as working "under-the table" and exploiting the labor of immigrants, and complaints of capturing inheritances were also mentioned ("Une secte bruxelloise" 1997).

In 1999 Robert Spatz was charged with fraud because he allegedly owed fifty million Belgian francs to the ONNS (Social Security). In 2001 Spatz went before the *tribunel correctionel* at the parquet of Bruxelles charged with "obtaining the complete submission of members of the community by fraudulent maneuvers between 1975 and 2008." Spatz was also charged with "social fraud" (fraud, falsifying documents, extortion, abuse of confidence, and money laundering) and he and one of his disciples were charged with using a false name (their Tibetan titles) ("L'OKC Devant le tribunal" 2008). The legal process is still ongoing as of this writing.

The lawyer who is defending OKC, Maitre Inez Wouters, explained in an interview that when the government wants to get rid of a *secte*, the prosecutor's typical strategy is "to throw a whole bunch of vague charges at the group and then the group will be bankrupted trying to prove its innocence."

In an amusing story told by Mme Corne, it appears that even a government raid has a human or, more specifically, humorous side:

> At the beginning, the police were very stern. They said, "you are not allowed to take photographs!" But, by the end of the day, our boys were very curious about the guns, and they were running in and out of the vans, and the police were giving them biscuits. The boys wanted to take photographs of their friends standing beside the soldiers, or holding their guns, so they let them. So, we have many, many photos of the police and soldiers smiling with our children. At the end of the day, the GIGN told us, "We are hungry!" They had risen at 2:00 am and driven all the way to Castellane from Aix-en-Provence! So we invited them to have soup in the kitchen (but they were not allowed). My son was fourteen and very interested in the GIGN. He took photos with them and gave them his address to write. "Your children are so great!" their chief told us.[32]

Maitre Inez Wouters added these comments during the interview: "They examined all the children for abuse, and they found the children had *not* been abused—but, of course, by the end of the examination, they were!"

Conclusion

All these case studies have common features. Most striking is that authorities failed to unearth evidence of the widespread abuses of children that were claimed in each case. Certainly there have been cases in which children in new or unconventional religions were starved to death, died of medical neglect, or were included in a mass suicide or homicide. However, these are quite rare. Moreover, I am not aware of a single case in which a child was actually rescued from harm by a government raid.

There appear to be four common patterns in the raids discussed here. These can be summarized as follows.

The Influence of a Network of Cultural Opponents

In every case except the Doukhobors, it is fair to say that the raids were prompted by former members, anticult activists, and social workers who collaborated to oppose the "sect" or "cult" and to save its children. These different interest groups pooled information and cooperated with law enforcement and governments in a concerted effort to oppose what they perceived to be a harmful "cult."

As Stuart Wright (1995) found in his analysis of the Branch Davidian tragedy at Waco, such networks can have a powerful impact on the perceptions of government authorities and give impetus to state control actions such as raids. In the raids on the AIL, The Family, and the OKC we find that apostates played an active role in organizing a coalition of interest groups that formed to oppose the local "cult." Similarly, in the case of the FLDS, apostates Flora Jessop, Becky Musser, and Carolyn Jessop played key roles in forming an oppositional alliance, as others have documented in this volume. I will not belabor this point, as several chapters in this book offer detailed analyses of the role played by cultural opponents.

The Complicity of Media

In many cases we find the media cooperating closely with secular authorities, both before and after the raids. News reports manifest a heavy reliance on "official stories"—from law enforcement, social workers, or local politicians—inflaming the public's "low level prejudice towards 'cults'" (Beckford 1999, 119).

In the AIL case, TV crews actually accompanied former members to the front gate of the monastery and filmed their conversation with the monks who, in turn, refused them entry or turned down their urgent requests to see their relatives. The Apostles claim that from 1970 to 1983 alone the AIL was the subject of more than four hundred reports on radio and television, and sixteen hundred reports in newspapers.

Striking discrepancies between media accounts of the raids and the accounts of eyewitnesses may be found. The news reports on the raids at Chateau Soleil, AIL, and FLDS, for example, offered highly selective information that justified the government's decision to conduct a raid and conveyed the notion to the public that a dangerous "cult" had finally been busted for perpetrating heinous crimes. The sheer volume and breadth of unsupported allegations chronicled in these news stories lend an appearance of authoritative fact. But what these news reports often fail to mention is the dearth of incriminating evidence, whether concerning child abuse, illegal drugs, or firearms. They usually fail to comment on the excessive force and military hardware deployed, and the unpleasant gynecological examinations to which the children are subjected.

It is clear that in most of the cases I have studied (Palmer 1998, 1999, 2010), journalists were partisans, siding with law enforcement, neglecting to present the targeted groups' perspectives, and preparing the public to accept these expensive "fishing expeditions" or overreaching militarized raids without questioning their initial purpose or reporting their eventual results.

An unexpected twist occurred in the case of the Texas FLDS. The April 2008 raid on the FLDS in Eldorado, Texas, sparked international media coverage. The initial reaction of journalists was to present the women and girls as victims, the polygamous leaders as pedophiles and abusive husbands, and the young boys as future patriarchs and sexual predators-in-training. Only in a few cases were FLDS women's accounts of proactive involvement or sincere convictions taken seriously. That journalists largely dismissed the accounts of FLDS women who did not validate the "victim" narrative probably tells us more about mainstream media than it does about women in insulated religious communities.

Interlocking Allegations

In most cases we find that the child abuse allegations are often intermingled with allegations or concern over crimes of quite a different nature or other forms of social deviancy. The tactic of using a barrage of interlocking allegations tends to exacerbate the ability of NRMs to defend themselves against a chaotic array of charges. The claims and allegations made against the OKC, AIL, Doukhobors, and FLDS were "bundled" so as to suggest a plethora of interrelated kinds of deviant behavior. In the FLDS case, for example, the issue of polygamy was cast as part of a reticulate structure of sinister and connected behaviors (child abuse, slavery/servitude, "brainwashing," stockpiling weapons, terrorism, possible mass suicide).[33]

Cultural Tension and Intolerance

One finds in the reports of social workers, law enforcement agents, and other state officials (who were supposedly "investigating" the group) a conspicuous absence of empathy and information concerning the religious worldviews of these minorities. Surely an understanding of the religious beliefs and traditions of the FLDS, as well as the other targeted groups discussed here, might have been informative, providing some historical context. Occasionally an odd, distorted fragment of the group's theology surfaces in government reports, the courts, or in the media, cited as evidence of pathology in the leader or the group, but in general there appears to be very little effort to engage in what Ninian Smart (1999) called "moccasin walking."

Although a more intimate acquaintance of the theology of these unconventional religions would not necessarily have improved their legal situation (though they certainly provide mitigating evidence), at least it might have encouraged dialogue between the agents of the state and the group leaders, and perhaps helped to avoid the excessive use of force and potential danger of a raid.

Behind the tortured logic of the raid strategy, there is a mission to rescue the children in order to "save" them, to resocialize the "cult's children" so that they may have a greater range of choices—in future professional life, values, and modes of living. The critique is that they are trapped, indoctrinated in a limited and unrealistic world. The assumption is that once they encounter the "real world" they will never choose to return to the "unreal" one. There is a value-laden judgment here that would be unacceptable to cultural anthropologists—a judgment that is highly selective. It would be unthinkable for the U.S. or Canadian government to raid a Chassidic community, claiming that the bris is child abuse, to seize its children and place them in a Christian or secular foster home in order to allow them greater "choice"; nor would it be prudent to remove children from a Mohawk, Cree, or "fundamentalist" Muslim community, where life is a "one-possibility thing" (Bellah 1964), in order to liberate their offspring from a culturally disfavored group or minority faith.

The notion of children growing up in "cults" evokes a strange admixture of fear and fascination in the public mind, and the reactions range from benign curiosity to full-blown, state-sponsored rescue operations. In order to understand these ambivalent responses, it is useful to consider what Schlissel, Gibbens, and Hampsten (1989) refer to as "two mutually conflicting obsessions" in North American culture—"the frontier and the family." "The field between them becomes charged," these authors note, "for the frontier suggests that which is expansive and unlimited, and family implies boundaries and a safe homecoming; thus there is a tug-of-war in two directions." This statement aptly captures the cultural tension surrounding the reactions of a host society, and it helps explain the often ill-advised efforts at social control aimed at minority faiths.

New or unconventional religions might best be understood as voluntary families camping on the frontiers of orthodox religion and conventional society. Their members inhabit volatile, rapidly changing environments, owing to the forces of charisma, prophecy, poverty, and persecution that shape their futures. "Why would sensible Americans venture out into these wild, disorderly spaces," the public might wonder, "and what will happen to the children born on these new spiritual frontiers?"

I have argued elsewhere that the intense concern over the fate of children in unconventional religious communities is rooted in this familiar cultural tension (Palmer 1998, 1999). The human family has always been composed of a fragile and ephemeral aggregation of needs, but within religious bodies the family is socially constructed as a "reality" that implies solidity and permanence. In the LDS and FLDS, and in other groups such as the Twelve Tribes (Palmer 1999), there is even the eschatological promise of physical immortality and an eternal togetherness. Thus, in these government raids and struggles over the custody and ownership of children, we find a powerful mythic quality that reveals a timeless conflict pitting religious believers against an unbelieving and inimical world with regard to the essential value of the family. The actions of the state to exercise social control over unconventional religious communities guarantee good news copy and excite suspense. But these efforts which are framed as benevolent and carried out sometimes by well-intentioned state actors, imprudently allied with opponents of these religious communities, are too often plagued by poor judgment and cultural misunderstandings that are dangerous and ultimately counterproductive.

It would appear that the overriding aim of these government raids was to exhibit the state's control over groups perceived as deviant and as constituting a threat to the moral order. In the process the state's actions severed the most intimate and tender of human bonds, that between parent and child. Officials expressed frustration because of the lack of evidence that abuse was taking place. From their perspective, the inaccessibility of the commune, because of "cultic secrecy" and the supposedly collective nature of the abuse, impeded their progress. Current laws are based on the assumption that claims can be readily investigated through talking to teachers, neighbors, and family doctors—a situation that does not apply to insulated religious communes. From their perspective, this situation justified bending the law.

This social control strategy is based on an ethnocentric assumption that our contemporary, competitive, materialistic, and secular society offers a paradigm for normalcy concerning the family, gender roles, and the education of children, and that groups that do not conform to this model should be compelled to do so. Different notions of abuse or danger prompted these raids, but in each case the official rationale given by public authorities to explain and justify the raid was to "protect the children." By framing the problem as child abuse requiring state intervention, state officials could use this effective legal mechanism to exercise social control over disfavored and controversial religious groups. Child abuse claims made by apostates and opponents drew the attention of authorities and were made more actionable precisely because the groups in question were seen as "cults." What all these cases reveal is that illegal and overreaching actions by the state against minority religious communities seem to repeat themselves over time and across cultures. It matters not that these cases occur in Western countries with relatively strong constitutional protections and religious freedoms. Government authorities appear to be more willing to dispense with legal precautions and ignore equal protection safeguards using child-saving claims to cloak state-sanctioned violence aimed at unpopular religious groups.

NOTES

1. http://www.ombud.gov.bc.ca/resources/press_releases/.../PR99-005.html.

2. Because they did not write accounts of their history, their origins are poorly documented.

3. In 1974 Simma Holt was elected as a Liberal candidate to the Canadian House of Commons. The influence of Holt and other politicians in the Social Credit Party in the decision-making process behind the raids was significant.

4. The Sons of Freedom might be compared to the Lakota Sioux ghost dancers of Wovoka, who sought to escape the white man's tyranny by wearing ghost shirts and circle dancing in the apocalyptic expectation of a supernatural intervention.

5. See the New Denver Survivors Collective home page; "Is There Justice after Half a Century?" Accessed online at http://www.newdenversurvivors.tk/.

6. Accessed online at http://www.jdkoftinoff.com/main/Information/About_Jeff_Koftinoff/The_Doukhobors/.

7. His honorific title is Pope Gregory XVII.

8. St. Jovite has since been renamed "Tremblant."

9. This is a crime in the Napoleonic Code, a notion similar to unlawful imprisonment, retaining the child against the other parent's will. See *"Justice" Put on Trial* 1984.

10. Michel Collin was a Catholic priest from Lille, France, from the Congrégation du Sacré Cœur. Inspired by the secrets of Fatima, in 1950, Collin experienced an apparition in which Jesus appeared and anointed him as Pope Clement XV (See Cuneo 1998).

11. Interview with Father Simon, June 20, 1995. The AIL also established sister communities in St. Veronique, a nearby village in Quebec, as well communities in Guadalupe, Puerto Rico, Guatemala, Mexico, and the Dominican Republic. The monks also keep a low- key presence in France and Italy.

12. "Sequestration" has the connotation of hiding, holding in captivity, or even kidnapping.

13. Interview with Father Simon, July 16, 2008.

14. Ibid.

15. Compiled by the Organized Crime Section of the Police Task Force Group, the paper sets out thirty-two alleged practices of the Children of God, which the police and the department claim went underground "about 1978" and emerged as The Family. The document was a point of discussion on the evening of May 14 when senior departmental executives, including Miss Rockley, and the police were deciding if and when to raid the homes.

16. The Children of God changed its name to "The Family of Love" in 1978.

17. Trench asked: "Did, for instance, Miss Rockley have any specific information that any of these children had been threatened in any way immediately before, during or some time after, as some act of indecency was taking place in his or her presence? Was there any specific evidence that any person had attempted to have intercourse with children under the age of 10? Or between 10 and 16?"

18. Interview with Lonnie and Claire Borowick at the Annual Meeting of the Society for the Scientific Study of Religion (SSSR), Louisville, Kentucky, October 2008.

19. "Ogyen Kunzang Choling" is translated in the group's literature as "Domain of the Clear Light."

20. Interview with Madame Corne, eyewitness to the event and the wife of the monastery's chief administrator, Jean-Louis Corne, June 9, 2009, at Chateau Soleil in the Verdon Gorge.

21. GIGN stands for the Groupe d'Intervention de la Gendarmerie Nationale (National Gendarmerie Intervention Group). It is the French Gendarmerie's elite Special Operations counterterrorism and hostage rescue unit; part of the military force called the Gendarmerie. GIGN units are closer to enhanced SWAT teams than to pure military units. Its missions include arresting armed criminals, those taking hostages, in particular; counterterrorism; dealing with aircraft hijacking; and preventing mutiny in prisons.

22. Interview with Madame Corne.

23. Ibid.

24. Tara was described as "a very important divinity, like a bodhisattva, except she was never born. She gives very fast blessings." Interview with a young monk, a teacher at Chateau Soleil, Khenpo Tsheten from Bhutan, sent to France by H. E. Shechen Rybjam, the grandson of Khentse, his spiritual master in Nepal, June 9, 2009.

25. Telephone interview with Jean-Louis Corne, administrator of Chateau Soleil, June 9, 2009.

26. Report No. 2468, December 1995; and Report No. 1687, June 1999.

27. *Nuisible* can be translated as "harmful," but as I was told by a woman who works in the Belgian CIAOSN (Le Centre d'information et d'avis sur les organisations sectaires nuisibles [Center for Information and Advice on Harmful Sectarian Organizations]), "*nuisible* is an adjective we usually apply to small, feral, biting animals."

28. This mother had complained to the authorities that her forty-four-year-old daughter, who was suffering from nervous depression, was not receiving adequate medical care at Chateau Soleil

29. Interview with Madame Corne.

30. Ibid.

31. Le Commission parlementaire belge, p. 158.

32. Interview with Madame Corne.

33. I am indebted to Jessica Authier, a student in my class at Concordia University in Montreal, for her media search and critique of news reports relevant to the FLDS raid.

REFERENCES

Allard, Philippe. 1997. Vaste opération policière dirigée contre l'OKC." *Non aux sectes,* May 30.

Allison, Col. 1992a. "Sect Warns of $10M Damages Claim over Raids." *Sydney Morning Herald*, July 27.

———. 1992b. "Sex Abuse Was Subtle, Court Told." *Sydney Morning Herald*, August 4.

———. 1992c. "Magistrate Slams Sect Case Lawyers." *Sydney Morning Herald*, August 19.

———. 1992d. "Child Sex Evidence Queried." *Sydney Morning Herald*, August 25.

———. 1992e. "Testimony against Sect Tainted, Court Told." *Sydney Morning Herald*, August 28.

Beckford, James A. 1999. "The Mass Media and New Religious Movements," pp. 103–20 in Bryan Wilson and Jamie Cresswell (eds.), *New Religious Movements: Challenge and Response*. London: Routledge.

Bellah, Robert Neeley. 1964. "Religious Evolution." *American Sociological Review* 29 (3): 358–74.

Chambre des Représentants de Belgique. 1997. Rapport d'Enquête Parlementaire visant à élaborer une politique en vue de lutter contre les pratiques illégales des sectes et le danger qu'elles représentent pour la société et pour les personnes, particulièrement les mineurs d'âge, (Documents parlementaires de la Chambre des Représentants; Législature 49, document 0313: 007 et 008) April,28, 1997 (http://www.dekamer.be/FLWB/pdf/49/0313/49K0313007.pdf partie 1: 3330 Kb) (http://www.dekamer.be/FLWB/pdf/49/0313/49K0313008.pdf partie 2: 2649 Kb).

Cuneo, Michael W. 1998. *The Smoke of Satan: Conservative and Traditionalist Dissent in Contemporary American Conservatism*. New York: Oxford University Press.

Father Jean de la Trinité and the Hidden Children of St. Jovite. 1971. St. Jovite, Quebec: Editions Magnificat.

Holt, Simma. 1964. *Terror in the Name of God: The Story of the Sons of Freedom Doukhobors*. Vancouver, B.C.: Crown.

Huxley, John, 1992. "Sex-Cult Children Held—Children of God." *Sunday Times*, May 17.

Janzen, William. 1990. *Limits on Liberty: The Experience of Mennonite, Hutterite and Doukhobors Communities in Canada*. Toronto: University of Toronto Press.

"Justice" Put on Trial. 1984. St. Jovite, Quebec: Editions Magnifcat.

Keiran, Simone. 2008. "When Commemorative Statues & Public Art Offends." New Denver & Nelson, BC: Lessons on Homage, Pilgrimage & Sensitivity." Accessed online at http://www.modern-art.suite101.com/ (September 11, 2008).

"Le secte belge-tibetaine de Castellane." 1996. *Le Figaro*, December 3.

"L'OKC Devant le tribunal." 2008. *La Dernière heure*, August 30.

Nicholas, Grace. 1999. "Seizure of Sect Children Ruled Unlawful." *Sidney Morning Herald*, April 1.

Palmer, Susan J. 1998. "Apostates and Their Role in the Construction of Grievance Claims against the Northeast Kingdom/Messianic Communities," pp. 191–208 in David G. Bromley (ed.), *The Politics of Religious.* Westport, CT : Praeger.

———. 1999. "Frontiers and Families: The Children of Island Pond," pp. 153–71 in Susan J. Palmer and Charlotte Hardeman (eds.), *Children in New Religions.* New Brunswick, NJ: Rutgers University Press.

———. 2010. *The Nuwaubian Nation: Black Spirituality and State Control.* Burlington, VT: Ashgate.

Palmer, Susan J., and Stephen Luxton. 1998. "The Ansaaru Allah Community: Postmodernist Narration and the Black Jeremiad," pp. 353–70 in Peter B. Clarke (ed.), *New Trends and Developments in the World of Islam.* London: Luzac Oriental.

Palmieri, Aurelio. 1915. "The Russian Doukhobors and Their Religious Teachings." *Harvard Theological Review* 8, no. 1 (January).

"The Religion Report." 1993. Australian Broadcasting Corporation, September 10.

"Righting the Wrong: The Confinement of the Sons of Freedom Doukhobor Children." 1999. Ombudsman, British Columbia. Report No. 38, April.

San Pietro, Michel. 1991. *Saul, Why do you persecute me?* St. Jovite, Quebec: Éditions Magnificat.

Schlissel, Lillian, Elizabeth Hampsten, and Byrd Gibbens. 1989. *Far from Home: Families of the Westward Journey,* Albuquerque: University of New Mexico.

Smart, Ninian. 1995. *Worldviews: Crosscultural Explorations of Human Beliefs.* Englewood Cliffs, NJ: Prentice Hall.

"The Religion Report." 1993. Australian Broadcasting Corporation, September 10.

"Une secte bruxelloise d'aspect bouddhique soupçonnée d'escroquerie et de maltraitance." 1997. *La Libre Belgique,* May 31.

Woodcock, George, and Ivan Avakumovic. 1977. *The Doukhobors.* Toronto: McClelland and Stewart.

Wright, Stuart A. 1995. *Armageddon in Waco: Critical Perspectives on the Branch Davidian Conflict.* Chicago: University of Chicago Press.

3

The Struggle for Legitimacy

Tensions between the LDS and FLDS

RYAN T. CRAGUN, MICHAEL NIELSEN,
AND HEATHER CLINGENPEEL

The Church of Jesus Christ of Latter-day Saints (LDS) has spent a considerable amount of time, money, and effort to distance itself from polygamy and those who continued the practice since it stopped performing plural marriages in the early 1900s (Cragun and Nielsen 2009). Those efforts were redoubled as a result of the Texas state raid on the Fundamentalist Latter Day Saints (FLDS) in April 2008. Herein we describe the efforts, measures, and strategies employed by the LDS to marginalize the fundamentalist Mormons following this incident.

The reason why the LDS has spent so much time and capital to distance itself from the FLDS is best understood as an issue of legitimacy. Legitimacy is defined in various ways; however, in reference to organizations (as opposed to individuals or beliefs), it generally implies the organization's cultural acceptance or "taken-for-granted" status. To a religious organization, legitimacy is important because it translates into social acceptance, which, in turn, means a reduction in persecution and unfavorable treatment (Lythgoe 1968). Establishing legitimacy is a fundamental process that is basic to social organization. All organizations intending to survive or grow require widespread acceptance and some degree of congruence with the surrounding culture (Johnson et al., 2006). The pursuit of legitimacy is what drove the ordination of women in mainline Protestant churches in the United States (Chaves 1997), and it is also the underlying motivation as religions transition from cult or sect to denomination (Johnson 1957, 1963; Lawson, 1995a, 1995b).

In Stark and Finke's (2000) model of religious economies, religions and societal religiosity cycle over time; large churches lose their appeal, opening the religious marketplace to smaller, more motivated competitors (sects and cults). The smaller sects and cults eventually become churches, and the cycle repeats. Inherent in this model, although not generally discussed by its advocates, is the process of legitimation (Cragun and Nielsen 2009). In order to become widely accepted and to grow, sects and cults must legitimize to some degree or remain too esoteric to have broad appeal. However, they must also balance that legitimacy with niche appeal—they must distinguish themselves from religious competitors. Thus both legitimacy and niche appeal are essential components of religious evolution. Mauss (1994) describes the legitimation of sects and cults as a process of "assimilation" or "accommodation," which he phrases as a "quest for respectability." Cragun and Nielsen (2009) describe attempts by religions to appeal to specific religious market niches as religious "differentiation."

One important goal of religions is to increase membership (i.e., market share). Increasing membership requires an accurate estimate of consumer demand and the product being sold; thus both must be evaluated. Religions, like corporations, evaluate consumer demand and their product, changing each based upon the goal of increasing membership, as depicted in Figure 3.1. For example, expanding priesthood to African Americans could be seen as product innovation within Mormonism, and modifying temple garments and clarifying questions to be asked in temple-recommended interviews could be seen as responding to consumer demand (Buerger 1994). Religions grow by increasing legitimacy but simultaneously by illustrating how their "product" is better than another, particularly for specific consumers.

The aim of this chapter is to illustrate how the LDS has been and continues to be engaged in a struggle for legitimacy with a dissident sect that significantly threatens its hard-earned legitimacy: polygamists in general and the FLDS in particular. The very presence and occasional notoriety— for instance, the raid in Texas—reawaken in the public mind the issue of polygamy which is intimately tied to the history of the LDS. To illustrate the struggle for legitimacy between the LDS and FLDS, we first outline why the LDS cannot return to polygamy as a practice. We then examine efforts by the LDS to distinguish itself from the FLDS and other polygamists prior to the raid in 2008. The final section of this chapter examines efforts by the LDS to distinguish itself from the FLDS after the raid.

Modernization of the LDS

Many advocates of religious economies models, when discussing the religious marketplace, fail to note that the demands of religion consumers change over time (Bruce 2002; Stark and Finke 2000). Although the model of religious marketplace adaptation outlined above suggests oscillation between differen-

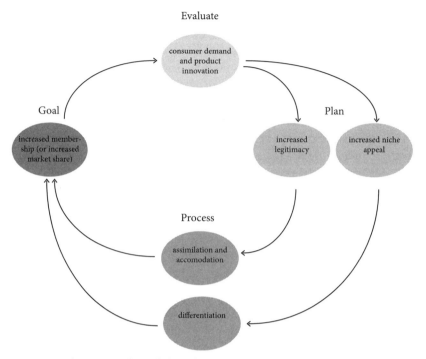

Figure 3.1. Religious growth as a balance between legitimacy and niche appeal.

tiation and legitimation, it is important to keep in mind that such oscillations occur as a result of changing demand. In other words, religions (the suppliers of religious goods) are responding to religious adherents (those demanding the goods). A substantial body of sociological literature suggests two trends among consumers of religion in the United States (and in other parts of the world; see Norris and Inglehart 2004). First, many people are leaving the religious marketplace altogether, becoming irreligious or secular (Kosmin and Keysar 2006). Second, those who remain in the religious marketplace no longer want orthodox or traditional religious goods (Bruce 2002). As a result, religions are decreasingly focusing on sin, misbehavior, and punishment (Bruce 2002; Hunter 1983). There is also less discussion of heaven and immortality. What religion consumers want is a "softer," more this-worldly religion. A good illustration of this cultural accommodation in the nature and message of religion is the recent bestselling book by one of the most popular pastors in the United States, Joel Osteen. In his book, *Become a Better You* (2008), no attempt is made to use hell as a threat to avoid sin. Instead, the book focuses on steps to improve one's life in the here and now, today.[1]

RYAN T. CRAGUN, MICHAEL NIELSEN, AND HEATHER CLINGENPEEL

Thus the model of religious markets outlined above has to be situated within a changing social context. Figure 3.2 illustrates this idea with the LDS. The y-axis depicts religious distinctiveness or the defining characteristics of a sect (what fundamentalists strive toward when they encourage fundamentalism). The x-axis depicts the passage of time in modern, rationalizing societies. The decending broken line suggests a trajectory away from religious distinctiveness and toward modernization (or less religious distinctiveness). The brackets are a continuum from differentiation to legitimation: religions can legitimate or differentiate to a greater or lesser extent. The continuum between legitimation and differentiation modernizes over time, following the "Conventional Religiosity" line. As the LDS legitimizes, it pushes the continuum to the right. When major legitimacy milestones are passed, like repudiating polygamy, giving blacks the priesthood, removing the penalties from the temple ceremony, and accepting celibate gays, the religion has shifted the acceptable parameters for what it can and cannot do to differentiate itself from other religions. As a result, even when the LDS enters into a differentiation phase (what Mauss [1994] calls "retrenchment"), it can only differentiate so far—it cannot undo the modernization that has already taken place. It can only go back as far as its last major legitimation shift. In other words, the LDS is modernizing in the pursuit of legitimacy.

Thus one can think of the competing forces leading to changes in the LDS (and other religions) as moving targets. The LDS does shift between legitimation and differentiation, but while it shifts along that continuum, the continuum itself shifts. The second shift is the underlying process of modernization. What it means to be "legitimate" in a given culture is not static. Thus the legitimate LDS of 1830, which included glossolalia, visions, and supernatural visitations, is not the legitimate LDS of 2008, which does not include any of those features (at least, not nearly as frequently, if ever; see Bushman, 2007).

A particularly appropriate illustration of the modernization of the LDS can be shown by asking the following question: What would happen to the LDS if it were to revert back to what it was in the 1860s? The answer is that it would likely experience a quick and ignominious demise. Changing social norms demand accommodation to those norms in order for a religion to be seen as legitimate (Chaves 1997; Hunter 1983; Mauss 1994).

The LDS of the 1860s is, in many ways, more akin to the present-day FLDS than to the present-day LDS. It is precisely that dilemma that has led the LDS to engage in a concerted effort to differentiate itself from the FLDS. The pursuit of legitimacy and organizational expansion has led Mormonism to modernize. Now that it has, it must distance itself from groups that represent

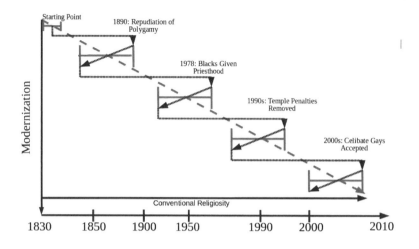

Figure 3.2 The subtle modernization of Mormonism.

the less legitimate past and threaten the legitimacy that the LDS has worked so hard to attain. To do that, the LDS uses the courts, government, laws, and the media in an effective campaign of differentiation.

Building Legitimacy before the 2008 Raid

Since the mid-nineteenth century, when the Mormon practice of polygamy and slavery was labeled by the Republican Party as the "twin relics of barbarism" (Hardy 1992), polygamy has impeded the efforts of Mormonism toward legitimacy in the broader culture (Bradley 1993; Van Wagoner 1992). A complete recounting of this history is beyond the scope of this chapter, but a brief summary is instructive. Polygamy stirred anti-Mormon sentiment in Nauvoo, which eventually contributed to the martyrdom of Joseph Smith and the LDS migration westward (Altman and Ginat 1996; Bushman 2007; Shipps 2006). Intensifying federal pressure resulting from the open practice of polygamy disincorporated the Church, created administrative chaos by forcing leaders underground, and inflicted economic and psychological suffering on families by the incarceration of thousands of fathers. The federal government threatened to confiscate the temple and persistently withheld statehood, with its promise of greater autonomy, until Church president Wilford Woodruff issued the Manifesto in September 1890 withdrawing the Church's support for new plural marriages. The Manifesto signaled the beginning of a permanent retreat from the practice. After the disbanding of the Mormon People's Party and the dissolution of its cooperative economic system, statehood followed in 1896. Considerable confusion reigned about whether the Manifesto should be interpreted to include the continuation of formerly contracted plural marriages. Perhaps more important, new plural marriages authorized by General Authorities and Joseph F. Smith's continued cohabitation with his own plural wives contributed to the confounding state of affairs.

When Apostle Reed Smoot was elected to the U.S. Senate in 1902, the Church came under close scrutiny and accusations of bad faith. President Joseph F. Smith issued a "Second Manifesto" in 1904, threatening to take action against polygamists. In 1905 the Church disciplined two of its twelve apostles who had been advocating and performing plural marriages (Hardy 1992; Quinn 1985, 1998). A series of such actions and public declarations over the next decade firmly moved the LDS away from its polygamist past and apart from those who advocated or engaged in polygamy. Before he died in 1918, President Joseph F. Smith issued nine public statements against polygamy and instructed stake presidents[2] to bring polygamists before church courts (Bradley 1993). In 1933 an "official statement" on polygamy (the "Final Manifesto") was printed in the *Deseret News* to denounce some polygamists who claimed that the Church continued to secretly endorse polygamy. Two years later the Church guided a bill through the state legislature upgrading polygamy from a misdemeanor to a felony (Bradley 1993). That same year members of the Zion Park Stake in southern Utah were forced to take a loyalty oath declaring their support for the LDS First Presidency and condemning plural marriage; members who refused were excommunicated. When government officials raided the polygamists of Short Creek in 1935, the local stake president offered his assistance in the prosecutions. Anti-polygamy raids followed in 1944 and 1953. Also during this period J. Reuben Clark, a counselor in the First Presidency, and Apostle Melvin J. Ballard spearheaded efforts to reduce polygamy in Utah and the Intermountain West, highlighting the distinction between LDS Mormons and polygamist Mormons. Following the 1944 raid Elder Mark E. Petersen wrote a letter to the UPI news service distancing polygamists from the LDS and stressing LDS cooperation with government efforts to eliminate polygamy (Van Wagoner 1992). Governor Howard Pyle of Arizona said of the 1953 raid, "We didn't make a single move that we didn't clear with the Council of the Twelve. They were one thousand percent cooperative, a hundred percent behind it" (Bradley 1993, 125). Excommunication of polygamists has continued; polygamists with Mormon roots, however, remain committed to living "the Principle," which they believe the LDS discontinued only for reasons of political expediency.

By 1950 LDS leaders largely ignored polygamy publicly, while continuing quietly to excommunicate those who confessed to engaging in polygamy or against whom they had evidence (Bradley 1993). Except when polygamy captures media attention, this policy seems to have persisted in Utah (Van Wagoner 1992). Polygamy is downplayed within the Church despite the fact that the earthly practice was "discontinued" rather than "repudiated" (White and White 2005). For instance, although references to polygamy were omitted from the 1998 manual of Brigham Young's teachings used in Melchezidek Priesthood and Relief Society classes, "the original spelling and punctuation have been preserved," apparently "to convey a sense of historical accuracy to altered texts" (White and White 2005, 176).

These efforts notwithstanding, polygamy has continued to flag the LDS. Nearly every time polygamy or a polygamist enters the mainstream media, the LDS issues a press release encouraging media outlets to distinguish between the LDS and the polygamist(s) of interest. Between 2002 and March 2008 (the month before the raid) the LDS issued 29 press releases on its website (http://newsroom.lds.org) concerning polygamy (an average of 4.8 per year). At least one press release was issued for every major polygamy story during that period: *Newsweek*'s coverage of Polygamy Porter Ale (The Church of Jesus Christ of Latter-day Saints 2002a), polygamist Tom Green's defiance (The Church of Jesus Christ of Latter-day Saints 2002b, 2002c), Elizabeth Smart's kidnapping by polygamist Brian David Mitchell (The Church of Jesus Christ of Latter-day Saints 2003b), the release of John Krakauer's book, *Under the Banner of Heaven,* that attacked polygamy (Otterson, Turley, and Millet 2003), Warren Jeffs's flight from the FBI (The Church of Jesus Christ of Latter-day Saints 2006a), HBO's series *Big Love* highlighting polygamy (The Church of Jesus Christ of Latter-day Saints 2006b, 2006c), Warren Jeffs's arrest (The Church of Jesus Christ of Latter-day Saints 2006d, 2006e, 2006f), the release of the PBS film on Mormonism (The Church of Jesus Christ of Latter-day Saints 2007a, 2007b, 2007c, 2007d), and a preemptive press release the week before Warren Jeffs's trial (The Church of Jesus Christ of Latter-day Saints 2007e).

Many of these press releases contain canned text, reflecting the increasingly corporate, public relations nature of the LDS Media Affairs Division. Of the twenty-nine articles, ten note that "the Associated Press style guide tells its reporters that the term Mormon 'is not properly applied' to the other churches that resulted from the split after Joseph Smith's death." Another seven articles repeat a quote by Gordon B. Hinckley, former president of the Church. In 1998 President Hinckley said:

> I wish to state categorically that this Church has nothing whatever to do with those practicing polygamy. They are not members of this Church. Most of them have never been members. They are in violation of the civil law. If any of our members are found to be practicing plural marriage, they are excommunicated, the most serious penalty the Church can impose. Not only are those so involved in direct violation of the civil law, they are in violation of the law of this Church. (Hinckley 1998)

Additionally, there are six items on the LDS Newsroom website that are not press releases but provide historical background about the LDS that clarify policies on polygamy. All of them include disclaimers about present-day polygamy (e.g., articles on Brigham Young and Joseph Smith and the Restoration). In short, the LDS has engaged in a meticulous effort to differentiate itself from polygamist groups, both through the media it controls and by trying to compel the mass media generally to report about polygamists in ways that completely disassociate them from the LDS.

Maintaining Legitimacy after the Raid

If the LDS made modest efforts to distance itself from the FLDS before the raid, these efforts were redoubled afterward. Immediately following the raid on the Yearning for Zion (YFZ) Ranch at Eldorado, the LDS released a press statement "reiterat(ing) that it has nothing whatsoever to do with any groups practicing polygamy" (The Church of Jesus Christ of Latter-day Saints 2008b). This claim, of course, ignores the groups' shared heritage in favor of focusing on the Church's current views regarding contemporary polygamy. Joe Cannon, publisher of the *Deseret Morning News*, has maintained that the LDS and FLDS are "utterly different in . . . beliefs and practices" (Cannon 2008). This assertion is clearly inaccurate, as both groups hold the Book of Mormon and other texts to be sacred scripture and share a number of beliefs that distinguish them from historic Roman Catholic, Orthodox, and Protestant beliefs (their niche appeal). Assertions that the LDS and FLDS are distinct, though hyperbolic, must be understood in the context of a search for legitimacy. Both Fundamentalist and non-fundamentalist Mormons seek to enhance their claims to legitimacy. Fundamentalist Mormons do so by emphasizing their true "Mormonness" and non-fundamentalist Mormons by emphasizing their essential "Christianness."

In the months following the raid on the FLDS in Texas, the LDS began a campaign to distance itself as much as possible from the many polygamous groups that broke from the mainstream Mormons over the years (Adams 2008; The Church of Jesus Christ of Latter-day Saints 2008a, 2008b; Winslow 2008). The formal initiative, begun in June 2008, appears to be a continuation of an earlier, informal effort begun in April 2008 to distinguish between the different branches of Mormonism in a series of statements released by Church leaders (Cannon 2008; "LDS Apostle Lists Differences with FLDS Sect" 2008; Winslow 2008b, 2008c, 2008d, 2008e, 2008f). These initiatives provide compelling support for our thesis that the established Church has worked to marginalize dissident sects in order to preserve exclusive claims to legitimacy.

As part of the formal initiative, the LDS chronicled a list of errors compiled by researchers whom it employed to monitor mass media coverage. The effort was undertaken in order to challenge connections between the FLDS and LDS. For instance, the LDS asserted that "Russian and Mexican media outlets . . . incorrectly referred to the FLDS Church as being the LDS Church" and were also critical of the Agence France-Presse for running a picture of an LDS temple in a story on the FLDS (Winslow 2008d). Elder Quentin L. Cook, of the Quorum of the Twelve Apostles, argued that the media's use of the word "Mormon" was confusing for the general public because it erroneously linked the LDS with the FLDS ("LDS Apostle Lists Differences with FLDS Sect" 2008). Elder Cook also noted that LDS members were experiencing "fallout" from the raid on the FLDS; LDS missionaries and members were mistakenly associated with the FLDS and allegedly experienced mild persecution as a result (Winslow 2008g). The LDS investigators who monitored media coverage of the raid reported that, of more than fifteen thousand articles about the event during the first month and a half of coverage, only about "5 percent of articles accurately reported on the distinction between the two faiths" (Wickman 2008).

What the LDS saw as a disturbing conflation produced a rapid response by officials to conduct a nationwide survey. The intent of the survey was to determine the public perception of the link between the LDS and FLDS. The survey found that 91 percent of the one thousand respondents had heard about the raid on the FLDS in Texas, and 36 percent believed that the FLDS in Texas was part of the LDS headquartered in Utah. Only 29 percent of the survey respondents said that the FLDS and LDS were not connected at all, and 44 percent were unsure to which religion the FLDS group in Texas belonged (The Church of Jesus Christ of Latter-day Saints 2008a).

These results, in concert with the previously reported connections made in news reports, prompted the LDS to mail letters to major media outlets demanding clarification of the LDS/FLDS distinction (Wickman 2008). The LDS-employed researchers saw these combined initiatives as contributing to an improvement in the reporting. According to one news release, "After the Church began to push for more clarity, the media dramatically improved its reporting, with over 60% of articles accurately reporting on the distinction," and a second news release also reported favorable reception to the letter and an improvement in coverage (The Church of Jesus Christ of Latter-day Saints 2008b, 2008c). An independent study designed to test media coverage found even more cautious reporting on the distinction—less than 1% of news articles confused the two groups (Cragun and Nielsen 2009).

The public relations effort of the LDS to clarify the differences between itself, the FLDS, and other polygamist groups was not received uncritically, however. The LDS had applied in 2005 to trademark the term "Mormon" (Cragun and Nielsen 2009; U.S. Patent and Trademark Office 2005). Although its petition was denied, Elder Lance Wickman, who heads the Legal Department of the LDS, asserted in his letter to the media, in June 2008, that the media should use the term "Mormon" exclusively to refer to the mainstream LDS (Wickman 2008). He specifically discouraged the use of "fundamentalist Mormon" in reference to groups advocating polygamy. Principle Voices Coalition, an advocacy organization representing fundamentalist and polygamist Mormon groups, responded with a denunciation: "We strenuously object to any efforts to deprive us and others of the freedom to name and describe ourselves by terms of our own choosing" ("The Principle Voices Coalition Statement" 2008). Principle Voices argued that they were entitled to call themselves whatever they liked. They also maintained that "polygamist sects," the term Wickman's letter encouraged the media to use for fundamentalist Mormon groups, was not the term preferred by polygamists: "In the recent past, the Church has insisted that we instead be defined as 'polygamous sects,' even though most of us are not (and do not refer to ourselves as) polygamists." Rather, they insist on being called "fundamentalist Mormons," pointing out that the LDS itself had first used this descriptive term in referring to them (Driggs 2001, Quinn 1998).

The Legitimacy Frontlines

In order to examine some of the ways in which the LDS has attempted to separate itself from the polygamous splinter sects, we conducted extensive in-depth interviews with six people who have been on the frontlines in the struggle for legitimacy. These included John and Esther,[3] a man and a woman who recently left the FLDS; Anne Wild and Mary Batchelor, two women involved in the Principle Voices Coalition; Alma Allred, an LDS member who teaches college-level courses at an LDS Institute of Religion in Utah and whose extended family includes polygamists; and Kim Farah, an official LDS spokesperson. Their comments and experiences illustrate the ongoing efforts to draw distinctions between mainstream Mormonism and its fundamentalist varieties.

In her role as an official spokesperson for the LDS, Kim Farah has focused on educating the media in order to convey the message and image that the Church wishes to represent to the world. Control over the term "Mormon" was an important part of this effort. According to Farah, "Polygamists cannot be Mormon. The Church of Jesus Christ of Latter-day Saints does not practice polygamy, and anyone found practicing polygamy is excommunicated; therefore they are not members of our faith. And we, by saying that, are 'owning' the word Mormon. That can be problematic—who owns the word 'Christian,' you know—but for us, we own the word Mormon in relation to our faith." As noted earlier, the LDS filed a trademark claim for the term "Mormon," but it was rejected. Nevertheless, it is clear that LDS leaders and representatives seek to control the language as part of an organized effort to manage its image. Farah offers the following explanation:

> We work with media on a case-by-case basis. When situations arise, we may modify what we send out depending on the situation. But I would say that the policy, for want of a better word, is education. . . . Clearly, the journalists are working in what can be a very murky situation when trying to talk about polygamy in a fair and accurate way, and so we educate our side of the story and let it go from there.

This task, she went on to say, "becomes difficult when other groups self-identify that way [as "Mormon"], and that's where it becomes very difficult for journalists. We try and work with journalists to help them make that distinction." The LDS policing of media language by public relations managers with regard to polygamy is a critical enterprise. Farah insisted that when the word "Mormon" is used to describe groups practicing polygamy, it creates "unnecessary and unwanted confusion" because,

> in the public's mind, Mormon is the Mormon Tabernacle Choir, the Mormon Trail, the Mormon Pioneers, Salt Lake City. And for a faith that has not practiced polygamy for over a century, that is problematic; it feeds into a stereotype. So, we try and say who we are without making a judgment on a polygamous sect whose practices and beliefs are different [from ours].

The financial resources of the LDS give it the ability to use paid professionals to help steer and manage its media image. As such, the LDS wields substantial control over public perception. This stands in sharp contrast to the resources of smaller polygamous sects which, for the most part, lack professional public relations staff and have diverse beliefs and practices (Wilde 2007). Consequently the dissociation sought by the LDS from its polygamist progeny, in terms of the media coverage, has been successful.

Membership Control and Exclusion

Strict control over the composition of membership is another means by which churches manage their public image. Membership and its related processes clearly illustrate efforts by the LDS to restrict and exclude fundamentalists. This became clear as our interviewees described the experiences of former polygamists who tried to join the LDS. The baptismal rite acts as a formal gateway by which the LDS admits newcomers. The typical process by which someone joins the LDS is as follows: people seeking to join complete a series of lessons with LDS missionaries, which are followed by an interview with a senior missionary and a local leader (typically a bishop), before they are baptized.

Alma describes a more demanding and rigorous process for former fundamentalists who wished to be baptized into the LDS: "You can't be baptized if you were raised in fundamentalism without permission from the president of the church. My [fundamentalist] cousin . . . talked to me and he said he wanted to join the Church. I told my supervisor at the institute, who said I needed to talk to a member of the Quorum of the 12." Alma, through his connections in the LDS, knew one of the apostles, Joseph B. Wirthlin. Alma contacted the apostle and remembered very clearly what Elder Wirthlin told him:

Brother Allred, this is Elder Wirthlin. Let me tell you how it works. This is missionary work, and missionary work goes under the direction of the mission president, so you really should tell the mission president what you are doing. You do what he tells you to do, but they still can't be baptized until the mission president interviews them, and a member of the twelve interviews them. We—if we think they should be baptized—we submit their names to the prophet, and he makes the decision.

Thus, unlike the process for the typical convert, former polygamists require special interviews with General Authorities, who then make a recommendation to the highest authority in the religion—the Prophet himself.

That former fundamentalists require approval of the Prophet, the highest authority in the Church, suggests that such decisions are not made lightly. The implication is that the LDS makes membership difficult for polygamists even after they have renounced polygamy. John, a former FLDS member, noted in his interview that those in the LDS who have contact with fundamentalist Mormons are carefully scrutinized to insure that they are staying true to the teachings of the Church. John works in a factory owned by a former FLDS man, but the factory employs people of various faiths, including members of the LDS. He described how the Church monitors members' contacts with polygamists.

Some of the Mormons there told me that they've been questioned by their bishop; they've just basically been double-checked to make sure they're not sympathetic . . . They [the bishops] just want to make sure that they are not becoming sympathetic towards polygamy because it's not a part of their religion . . . Thing of it is . . . I loaded one guy up with some questions to go ask his bishop. His bishop wouldn't answer them. He's like, 'We've been instructed not to discuss that. All we've been instructed is we're not to be sympathetic. They're not Mormons; they're polygamists. And we don't live polygamy.' They won't talk about it. They won't discuss the subject.

This same kind of screening is also exercised over the LDS practice of performing posthumous ordinances, which all Mormons believe to be essential for the afterlife. Alma describes one of his experiences with his extended family:

Two of my uncle's widows joined the church before they died. They wanted to be sealed to him, but the church said, 'No, we can't authorize it.' Did you see the item in the news a couple weeks ago about posthumous sealings for fundamentalist leaders? Somebody had been doing it without authorization. LDS people can do it, but it has to be authorized by the President of the Church.

In effect, both living and deceased former polygamists require special approval for admission into the religion by the highest authority in the Church, showing the carefully drawn lines between the two groups. Despite a procedure in place to allow living and deceased former polygamists into the LDS, church leaders are very reticent to allow such conversions. Alma explained that his grandfather was excommunicated for polygamy and has not been re-baptized, even though his family has petitioned the Prophet.

My dad wanted his father's (temple) work to be done, because his father was excommunicated for apostasy. He had me write a letter for this to the prophet. So, I wrote a letter to President Hinckley and, basically, I got a letter back saying, 'Can't help you.' So, if my grandfather, who was excommunicated in 1932; if he can't be baptized posthumously, they aren't going to let Rulon—who died some 40 years later—they aren't going to let more recent fundamentalists be baptized. It gives you an idea of what they think of the fundamentalists. We're baptizing everyone we can, but not them [the fundamentalists].

Alma's account illustrates the antipathy of the Church toward the polygamists. Temple rites, which Mormons believe are essential for advancement in the afterlife, represent an important vehicle by which the LDS exerts its control over competing claims of legitimacy.

The LDS and Law Enforcement

In the past, LDS officials and members took it upon themselves to inform legal authorities about polygamous activities (Bradley 1993). Although these efforts may have been part of a formal effort by the LDS to control its identity and marginalize fundamentalists, the LDS now claims that any such collaborative efforts with law enforcement are in the past. The Church claims not to be involved in identifying and turning over fundamentalists to legal authorities. Kim Farah states, "We are very, very careful not to get involved [with law enforcement]. I cannot speak to what happened in the 50s, 60s and 70s, and I don't know if we could even confirm those [allegations]. I just know the policies of the Church and how we work today, and we don't have anything to do with [Utah Attorney General] Mark Shurtleff."

Recognizing that fundamentalists might be skeptical of such claims, Farah clarified the Church's position as follows:

> I'm not discounting that there might be those in polygamous groups that feel that we work with law enforcement, but from our end, we don't. We don't work with law enforcement at all. We don't feel it's our role. We're a religious faith; we aren't involved with how to enforce civil laws, and we don't. And we wouldn't have knowledge of [fundamentalists], because we don't have a relationship with them.

Farah also added that the Church adheres closely to the law: "We believe in being subject to kings, presidents, rulers, and magistrates and obeying, honoring and sustaining the law. One cannot obey the law and disobey the law at the same time." This statement serves both to differentiate the Church and to suggest that fundamentalists violate the law at their own peril.

Church-state relations are delicate in Utah, and the state's policies toward polygamy continue to bring the LDS under scrutiny. The tension surrounding church-state issues continues to affect the prosecution of polygamy. In the early 2000s Utah county attorneys were not actively prosecuting polygamy. However, after receiving public pressure surrounding polygamist Tom Green's flouting of polygamy laws openly in national news media, Utah State Attorney General Mark Shurtleff decided to take action. Before doing so, he contacted an LDS apostle to alert the Church of his intentions. "I knew that every story coming out about polygamy would draw a connection between the practice and the LDS Church. There was going to be an impact, and not a positive one," Shurtleff recalled (Dark 2007). Thus, although he may not have asked for direction or permission to prosecute polygamy, Shurtleff felt obligated to notify LDS officials about forthcoming law enforcement actions. Such a gesture by Utah's attorney general reveals a powerful connection between the state and the LDS. Thus Farah's disclaimer that "we don't work with law enforcement at all" is somewhat misleading. The Church's influence in matters of state is profound, even if indirect. The majority of the state's elected officials are LDS members; state policy makers and officials are in positions of power to shape and affect laws and the enforcement of laws. In short, although the LDS may not be directly involved in efforts to prosecute polygamy, many LDS members are part of the state's legal machinery.

The Effects of the Texas Raid on the FLDS and the LDS

John and Esther were in positions to observe the effects of the Texas state raid on the FLDS. John actually served as a consultant to state officials. In that capacity John recalled telling them, "I'm just going to warn you that Warren [Jeffs] predicted judgments, judgments, judgments, raid, raid, raid and all this. . . . Whatever you guys do, don't go in there with any more than about 6 officers at a time, because they'll call it a raid." A state official, he recalls, replied, "Believe me I'm not in the business of fulfilling prophecies, especially Warren's." This advice went unheeded as Texas officials descended en masse upon the FLDS community in Eldorado. As Martha Bradley Evans points out so eloquently in her chapter in this volume, the Texas state police repeated the same mistakes that the Arizona police made fifty-five years earlier. The Eldorado raid had a counterproductive effect on the FLDS community. Living in the Colorado City/Hildale area at the time of the raid, Esther confirmed John's warning. "[The raid] actually strengthened the FLDS beliefs a lot. I noticed in our town it did that a lot . . . After the raid everyone always had an eye on their children [fearing another raid]." Evidently the Texas raid only confirmed the Prophet's warnings in the minds of FLDS members, bolstering their faith and engendering a shared sense of persecution.

The general public became more inquisitive following the raid as well. For example, Esther reports that strangers began asking questions about her religion. "When I was in the FLDS after the raid in Texas, there were a lot more questions being asked. When I went to other towns and I wore the [FLDS] dresses, [people] would ask different questions about the religion and some people even asked how they would be able to talk to one of our leaders to see if they could get in."

Esther reports that FLDS members saw the raid as another despotic act of the state which followed the disturbing arrest of their Prophet, Warren Jeffs, two years earlier. However, FLDS members chose to interpret these events as a test of faith.

> When Warren did get caught, [FLDS believers] said, "This is just a test to see if we can get him out by our faith and prayers." We would fast for four days straight. You could have water and clear juice. Everybody fasted for four days at a time to help the Prophet, except for the men who went out to work. They could have snacks, but lots of people just went with water and juices and stuff. Sometimes they would say you could have one meal out

of the four days just so you don't die, but it was really interesting. I even believed that if we fasted and prayed enough, he would be released.

Maggie Jessop, an FLDS woman who was living at the YFZ Ranch at the time of the raid, also described the raid as a kind test of faith but indicated that she expects the perpetrators of the raid to face divine judgment.

Our Father in Heaven knows the answers, and He will provide the tools of rehabilitation. He alone can heal all wounds, mend broken hearts, revive tattered feelings, and replenish sinking spirits. This He will do as we turn to Him in gratitude, trusting in Him to assist us in returning to innocence once more. Truly, the Lord has watched over us, continually providing His protection, though He has required intense experience of us. . . . History does indeed repeat itself, and anyone who will study it can see that those who claim to be true followers of the Lord, Jesus Christ must and shall suffer persecution from those who are in opposition to Him. When the Cup of Iniquity of the unrighteous is filled, He will come out of His hiding place and right all wrong. He shall deliver the innocent and bring judgment upon their oppressors. (Jessop n.d.)

Following the raid in Texas, LDS members were mistakenly identified by the public as being polygamists. In one case, a man who had been considering joining the Church returned his Book of Mormon to the missionaries, believing that the LDS was the group raided by Texas authorities (Winslow 2008g). Stories such as these were widely reported in Utah. In order to address the misreporting, the LDS mobilized its public relations operations to leverage distance between itself and the FLDS, not only by issuing press statements but by developing and distributing videos to depict how ordinary LDS members in Texas lived and practiced their faith. This was important, Farah stated, because "that particular story [the raid] received so much attention internationally as well as nationally that we felt it was important to say who we are, not who we were not. So you'll see that in the things we posted on the website, we don't talk about polygamy, we talk about who we are in relation to Texas and Texas Mormons." To help clarify the distinction for the public, Farah and her staff filmed LDS members living in Texas,

I was the one who did the filming in the course of seven days, and we just plucked members from various congregations, there was no screening, and they were just themselves. We thought that that was the most important thing to do, to show who we are, and people can draw those distinctions in their minds between what we put on our website and what they were seeing on the evening news.

Although the impact of the raid on the LDS may have been minimal, the Texas raid did apparently affect independent polygamists living in Utah. Mary Batchelor's efforts to present polygamy as something more than a caricature made her a highly visible figure. After the raid in Texas Mary reports that her family began experiencing difficulties. One incident, in particular, involved her daughter.

I started having problems in my new neighborhood because I'd only lived there for a couple of months . . . Pretty soon my kids came to me with problems at school, with teachers, with students . . . One teacher actually flat-out asked my daughter, right in front of the whole class, "Is that your mother on the news who is the polygamist lady dealing with all that polygamy stuff?" My daughter was embarrassed, but answered bravely, "Yes, that is my mom and I am not going to talk about it with you in front of this class." She was in middle school at the time. She was taunted after that by other students who said nasty things about her "plyg father" or "plyg parents."[4]

The teacher who had singled out Mary's daughter in the classroom was a devout LDS member.

Anne and Mary also described a general sense of anxiety among the Mormon fundamentalists they knew. The raid in Texas had an impact on polygamists in Utah and throughout North America, they said, heightening suspicion and fears of retribution. Incidents such as the one described above reveal that the quest for legitimacy is not without costs. Polygamy advocates working to increase society's acceptance of plural marriage, or fundamentalist Mormon adherence to "the Principle," risked formal and informal sanctions as a result of their beliefs.

LDS Use of Economic Resources to Oppose Polygamy

Our interviews revealed another instance of the LDS using its power to marginalize and exclude fundamentalists by reducing its business dealings with the suspected groups. According to Mary,

There have been several issues in the last couple of years, one of which was that there was an edict that went out where the LDS Church was encouraging their members not to do business with any fundamentalist Mormon or polygamist. That is very, very harmful. We are talking about economic consequences on our families.

Anne added that "there was at least one community where they [the LDS] were telling people not to patronize [fundamentalist-owned] businesses. This was just a couple of years ago." Although Anne and Mary did not suggest that such efforts by the LDS were common, they were aware of situations in which fundamentalist Mormon businesses were excluded. According to Mary,

> A lot of polygamist people own their own businesses and a lot of them are in woodwork and building, construction; those kinds of things. Cabinet makers and construction workers suddenly lost contracts where they were working on temples or church buildings. They were doing all the woodwork and the furnishings and they lost contracts, massive contracts. They had been doing this work for years and years, this was the lifeblood of their business. The LDS Church did not want to fund any polygamist family through their businesses.

Another example of the LDS using financial means to attack polygamy was more direct. According to one news report, a few years ago the LDS made a donation to Tapestry Against Polygamy (TAP), an anti-polygamy organization with the explicit aim of assisting women to leave polygamous lifestyles (Stack 1999).[5] Mormon fundamentalists saw the donation as a direct assault on them and their most foundational beliefs. Here is how Mary described the donation:

> That was offensive to all of us. . . . [Tapestry Against Polygamy] was created by people that had left polygamy. [The LDS] didn't disclose how much, but our understanding is that [they donated] more than $10,000. . . . [Tapestry] had made comments that were anti-Mormon; not just anti-polygamy, but public anti-Mormon, anti–Joseph Smith comments, [yet] the church donated to Tapestry.

For fundamentalist Mormons, the LDS could not have made a clearer statement about their position toward polygamy by funding an anti-polygamy group. This gesture was seen as the LDS reaching beyond a mere statement of difference to an overt act of antipathy toward polygamists. Whether such antipathy was rooted in the LDS's ongoing struggle for legitimacy or in its view that polygamy is illegal and often abusive to women and children is unclear. In either case, it was an indication of the Church's determination to delegitimize its fundamentalist branches and weaken rival assertions of religious authority.

Conclusion

In this chapter we have used the FLDS raid in Texas as a way to highlight how the LDS has used the legal system, media, Church policies, and its resources to reinforce its claims to legitimacy while distancing itself from fundamentalist Mormon sects. In its ongoing quest for growth and acceptance, the LDS has altered policies to conform more to those of the broader society. This process of modernization is ongoing as social norms and the demands of religious consumers continue to change. The process of adapting and conforming to broader cultural norms is best understood as an attempt to be seen as a legitimate competitor in the religious marketplace. But conforming to social norms has to be carefully balanced with maintaining a unique niche, allowing the religion to differentiate itself from other competitors.

The quandary of modernity for the LDS was brought into sharp relief by the 2008 Texas state raid on the YFZ Ranch which focused on polygamy and underage marriage. Common religious roots and past ties between the groups threatened the public image and progress of the mainstream LDS. Much like the reaction of the Seventh-day Adventist Church to the Branch Davidians, the mainstream Church moved rapidly to mobilize resources in order to marginalize the dissident sect and preserve its own claim to legitimacy (see Lawson 1995b).[6] LDS public relations officials framed a narrative that maximized social distance from the FLDS, painted the fundamentalists as pariahs, and made no effort to defend the Principle, a central doctrine initiated by the founder and Prophet of the LDS, Joseph Smith. The unfolding of events following the Texas raid with regard to the Mormon institutional leadership can be explained in terms both of modernization theory and an understanding of the importance that institutions place on legitimacy. In the wake of sect-to-church institutionalization (Weber 1964), the LDS could ill-afford to retreat from its hard-earned "Church" status to embrace the sectarian past or those representing that past. The risk of jeopardizing its legitimacy by owning the religious origins of celestial marriage was too great for the modern Church of Latter-day Saints.

1. Indeed, most uses of the word "hell" in the book are like the following from page 238: "Understand that your destiny is not tied to what people are saying about you. Some critical people in Houston predicted that Lakewood Church would never be able to meet in the arena known as the Compaq Center. They told us we didn't have a chance. In fact, at a business luncheon attended by numerous high-level city leaders, one man told the people at his table, 'It will be a cold day in hell before Lakewood Church ever gets the Compaq Center.'"

2. A stake is an administrative unit of congregations comparable to a diocese in the Catholic Church.

3. These are their actual first names, but they wish to remain anonymous. The other interviewees are public figures and thus are not concerned with anonymity, as they regularly speak "on the record."

4. The contraction "plyg" is used as a derogatory term toward polygamists.

5. In our interview with Kim Farah we confirmed that this donation occurred, although she did not recall the amount of the donation.

6. The Branch Davidians were initially known as the Davidian Seventh-Day Adventists. Their founder, Victor Houteff, broke from the Seventh-Day Adventist Church in 1935 to form the group, settling outside Waco, Texas (see Pitts 1995).

REFERENCES

Adams, Brooke. 2008. "Fundamentalists: We're Mormon, Too." *Salt Lake Tribune*, July 9. Accessed online at http://www.sltrib.com/faith/ci_9828897 (July 13, 2008).

Altman, Irwin, and Joseph Ginat. 1996. *Polygamous Families in Contemporary Society*. Cambridge: Cambridge University Press.

Bradley, Martha Sonntag. 1993. *Kidnapped from That Land: The Government Raids on the Short Creek Polygamists*. Salt Lake City: University of Utah Press.

Bruce, Steve. 2002. *God Is Dead: Secularization in the West*. London: Blackwell.

Buerger, David John. 1994. *The Mysteries of Godliness: A History of Mormon Temple Worship*. Salt Lake City, UT: Signature Books.

Bushman, Richard Lyman. 2007. *Joseph Smith: Rough Stone Rolling*. New York: Vintage.

Cannon, Joseph A. 2008. "Adoption of FLDS Name Is Akin to Identity Theft." *Deseret News*, May 11. Accessed online at http://deseretnews.com/article/0,1249,700224488,00.html (May 12, 2008).

Chaves, Mark. 1997. *Ordaining Women: Culture and Conflict in Religious Organizations*. Cambridge, MA: Harvard University Press.

The Church of Jesus Christ of Latter-day Saints. 2002a. "Polygamy." *LDS Newsroom*, January 28. Accessed online at http://newsroom.lds.org/ldsnewsroom/eng/commentary/polygamy (May 22, 2009).

———. 2002b. "Mormon Tom Green." *LDS Newsroom*, June 3. Accessed online at http://newsroom.lds.org/ldsnewsroom/eng/commentary/mormon-tom-green (May 22, 2009).

———. 2002c. "Tom Green, Polygamist Coverage." *LDS Newsroom*, September 5. Accessed online at http://newsroom.lds.org/ldsnewsroom/eng/commentary/tom-green-polygamist-coverage (May 22, 2009).

———. 2003. "Erroneous Reporting of Elizabeth Smart Case." *LDS Newsroom*, March 24. Accessed online at http://newsroom.lds.org/ldsnewsroom/eng/commentary/erroneous-reporting-of-elizabeth-smart-case (May 22, 2009).

———. 2006a. "Fundamentalist Mormons." *LDS Newsroom*, February 3. Accessed online at http://newsroom.lds.org/ldsnewsroom/eng/commentary/fundamentalist-mormons (May 22, 2009).

———. 2006b. "Church Responds to Questions on TV Series." *LDS Newsroom*, March 6. Accessed online at http://newsroom.lds.org/ldsnewsroom/eng/news-releases-stories/church-responds-to-questions-on-tv-series (May 22, 2009).

———. 2006c. "HBO." *LDS Newsroom*, March 6. Accessed online at http://newsroom.lds.org/ldsnewsroom/eng/news-releases-stories/hbo (May 22, 2009).

———. 2006d. "Arrest of Warren Jeffs." *LDS Newsroom*, August 29. Accessed online at http://newsroom.lds.org/ldsnewsroom/eng/commentary/arrest-of-warren-jeffs (May 22, 2009).

———. 2006e. "Polygamist Sects Are Not "Mormons," Church Says." *LDS Newsroom*, October 25. Accessed online at http://newsroom.lds.org/ldsnewsroom/eng/news-releases-stories/polygamist-sects-are-not-mormons-church-says (May 22, 2009).

———. 2006f. "Use of the Word Mormon in News Reports." *LDS Newsroom*, November 21. Accessed online at http://newsroom.lds.org/ldsnewsroom/eng/commentary/use-of-the-word-mormon-in-news-reports (May 22, 2009).

———. 2007a. "Elder Oaks Interview Transcript from PBS Documentary." *LDS Newsroom*, July 20. Accessed online at http://newsroom.lds.org/ldsnewsroom/eng/news-releases-stories/elder-oaks-interview-transcript-from-pbs-documentary (May 22, 2009).

———. 2007b. "PBS Airs First of Two Documentaries." *LDS Newsroom*, May 1. Accessed online at http://newsroom.lds.org/ldsnewsroom/eng/news-releases-stories/pbs-airs-first-of-two-documentaries (May 22, 2009).

———. 2007c. "PBS Film Likely to Cause Debate." *LDS Newsroom*, April 2. Accessed online at http://newsroom.lds.org/ldsnewsroom/eng/news-releases-stories/pbs-film-likely-to-cause-debate (May 22, 2009).

———. 2007d. "Public Response to PBS Documentaries." *LDS Newsroom*, May 3. Accessed online at http://newsroom.lds.org/ldsnewsroom/eng/news-releases-stories/public-response-to-pbs-documentaries (May 22, 2009).

———. 2007e. "'Mormons' and Polygamy." *LDS Newsroom*, September 7. Accessed online at http://newsroom.lds.org/ldsnewsroom/eng/commentary/-mormons-and-polygamy (May 22, 2009).

———. 2008a. "Church Seeks to Address Public Confusion over Texas Polygamy Group." *LDS Newsroom*. Accessed online at http://newsroom.lds.org/ldsnewsroom/eng/news-releases-stories/church-seeks-to-address-public-confusion-over-texas-polygamy-group (July 13, 2008).

———. 2008b. "Protecting the Church's Identity." *LDS Newsroom*. Accessed online at http://www.newsroom.lds.org/ldsnewsroom/eng/commentary/protecting-the-church-s-identity (July 13, 2008).

———. 2008c. "Clear, Contextual Conversation Begets More of the Same." *LDS Newsroom*. Accessed online at http://www.newsroom.lds.org/ldsnewsroom/eng/commentary/clear-contextual-conversation-begets-more-of-the-same (July 13, 2008).

Cragun, Ryan T., and Michael Nielsen. 2009. "Fighting over "Mormon": Media Coverage of the FLDS and LDS." *Dialogue: A Journal of Mormon Thought* 43:65–104.

Dark, Stephen. 2007. "I, Markus." *Salt Lake City Weekly*, June 11. Accessed online at http://www.cityweekly.net/utah/article-2464-i-markus.html (August 22, 2009).

Driggs, Ken. 2001. "'This Will Someday Be the Head and Not the Tail of the Church: A History of the Mormon Fundamentalists at Short Creek." *Journal of Church and State* 43 (1): 49–80.

Hardy, B. Carmon. 1992. *Solemn Covenant: The Mormon Polygamous Passage*. Urbana: University of Illinois Press.

Hinckley, Gordon. 1998. "What Are People Asking about Us?" *Ensign*, November, 70.

Hunter, James Davison. 1983. *American Evangelicalism: Conservative Religion and the Quandary of Modernity*. New Brunswick, NJ: Rutgers University Press.

Jessop, Maggie. N.d. "Father Forgive Them." Accessed online at http://www.truthwillprevail.org/print.php?parentid=1&index=69 (February 16, 2009).

Johnson, Benton. 1957. "A Critical Appraisal of the Church-Sect Typology." *American Sociological Review* 22:88–92.

———. 1963. "On Church and Sect." *American Sociological Review* 28:539–49.

Johnson, Cathryn, Timothy J. Dowd, Cecilia L. Ridgeway, Karen S. Cook, and Douglas S. Massey. 2006. "Legitimacy as a Social Process." *Annual Review of Sociology* 32:53–78.

Kosmin, Barry A., and Ariela Keysar. 2006. *Religion in a Free Market: Religious and Non-Religious Americans*. Ithaca, NY: Paramount Market.

Lawson, Ronald. 1995a. "Sect-State Relations: Accounting for the Differing Trajectories of Seventh-day Adventists and Jehovah's Witnesses." *Sociology of Religion* 56:351–77.

———. 1995b. "Seventh-day Adventist Responses to Branch Davidian Notoriety: Patterns of Diversity within a Sect Reducing Tension with Society." *Journal for the Scientific Study of Religion* 34:323–341

"LDS Apostle Lists Differences with FLDS Sect." 2008. *Deseret News*, April 18. Accessed online at http://deseretnews.com/article/0,1249,695271743,00.html (May 13, 2008).

Lythgoe, Dennis L. 1968. "The Changing Image of Mormonism." *Dialogue: A Journal of Mormon Thought* 3:45–58.

Mackelprang, Romel W. 1997. "'They Shall Be One Flesh': Sexuality and Contemporary Mormonism," *Dialogue: A Journal of Mormon Thought* 25 (1): 59–61.

Mauss, Armand L. 1994. *The Angel and the Beehive: The Mormon Struggle with Assimilation*. Urbana: University of Illinois Press.

Norris, Pippa, and Ronald Inglehart. 2004. *Sacred and Secular: Religion and Politics Worldwide*. Cambridge: Cambridge University Press.

Osteen, Joel. 2007. *Become a Better You: 7 Keys to Improving Your Life Every Day*. New York: Free Press.

Otterson, Mike, Richard E. Turley, and Robert L. Millet. 2003. "Church Response to Jon Krakauer's *Under the Banner of Heaven*." *LDS Newsroom*, June 27. Accessed online at http://newsroom.lds.org/ldsnewsroom/eng/commentary/church-response-to-jon-krakauer-s-under-the-banner-of-heaven (May 22, 2009).

Pitts, William L., Jr. 1995. "Davidians and Branch Davidians: 1929-1987," pp. 20–42 in Stuart A. Wright (ed.), *Armageddon in Waco*. Chicago: University of Chicago Press.

"The Principle Voices Coalition Statement." 2008. *Salt Lake Tribune*, July 10. Accessed online at http://www.sltrib.com/polygamy/ci_9837877 (July 13, 2008).

Quinn, D. Michael. 1985. "LDS Church Authority and New Plural Marriages, 1890–1904." *Dialogue: A Journal of Mormon Thought* 18 (1): 9–105.

———. 1998. "Plural Marriage and Mormon Fundamentalism." *Dialogue: A Journal of Mormon Thought* 31:1–68.

Rhodes, Hillary. 2008. "Polygamist Clothing Has Roots in 19th Century and 1950s." *Deseret News*, April 22. Accessed online at http://deseretnews.com/article/0,1249,695272815,00.html (May 12, 2008).

Shipps, Jan. 2006. *Sojourner in the Promised Land: Forty Years among the Mormons.* Urbana: University of Illinois Press.

Stack, Peggy Fletcher. 1999. "LDS Church Donates to Polygamy Tapestry." *Salt Lake Tribune*, December 4, C2.

Stark, Rodney, and Roger Finke. 2000. *Acts of Faith: Explaining the Human Side of Religion.* Berkeley: University of California Press.

U.S. Patent and Trademark Office, Federal Trademark Service, "Trademark No. 78161091," November 1, 2005. Accessed online at http://tarr.uspto.gov/servlet/tarr?regser=serial&entry=78161091 (July 22, 2008).

Van Wagoner, Richard S. 1992. *Mormon Polygamy: A History.* Salt Lake City, UT: Signature Books.

Weber, Max. 1964. *The Sociology of Religion.* Translated by Ephraim Fischoff. Boston: Beacon.

White, O. Kendall, and Daryl White. 2005. "Polygamy and Mormon Identity." *Journal of American Culture* 28 (2): 165–77.

Wickman, Lance B. 2008. "Media Letter." *LDS Newsroom.* Accessed online at http://newsroom.lds.org/ldsnewsroom/eng/news-releases-stories/media-letter (July 13, 2008).

Wilde, Anne. 2007. "Fundamentalist Mormonism: Its History, Diversity and Stereotypes, 1886–Present," pp. 258–89 in Newell G. Bringhurst and John C. Hamer (Eds.), *Scattering of the Saints: Schism within Mormonism.* Ann Arbor, MI: John Whitmer Books.

Winslow, Ben. 2008a. "LDS Church Emphasizes 'Mormon' Distinctions." *Deseret News*, July 11. Accessed online at http://deseretnews.com/article/1%2C5143%2C700242231%2C00.html (July 13, 2008).

———. 2008b. "LDS Church Calls Request 'Erroneous.'" *Deseret News*, April 23. Accessed online at http://deseretnews.com/article/0,1249,695272934,00.html (May 12, 2008).

———. 2008c. "LDS Church Critical of Foreign Press Accounts of Texas Raid." *Deseret News*, April 11. Accessed online at http://deseretnews.com/article/0,1249,695269605,00.html (May 13, 2008).

———. 2008d. "LDS Church Critical of Media Reports on FLDS." *Deseret News*, April 12. Accessed online at http://deseretnews.com/article/0,1249,695269713,00.html (May 13, 2008).

———. 2008e. "LDS Church Responds to Request to Monitor FLDS Prayers." *Deseret News*, April 22. Accessed online at http://deseretnews.com/article/0,1249,695272878,00.html (May 12, 2008).

———. 2008f. "Name Raising Eyebrows." *Deseret News*, April 7. Accessed online at http://deseretnews.com/article/0,1249,695268134,00.html (May 13, 2008).

———. 2008g. "Texas LDS Deal with Confusion." *Deseret News*, April 21. Accessed online at http://deseretnews.com/article/0,1249,695272400,00.html (May 12, 2008).

Social and Cultural Dimensions

Reader Responses to the Yearning for Zion Ranch Raid and Its Aftermath on the Websites of the *Salt Lake Tribune* and the *Deseret News*

MICHAEL WILLIAM HAMILTON

While national media provide broad-based and politically astute perspectives for readers and audiences, they sometimes fail to fully understand local or regional cultural nuances that affect a story. The 2008 Texas state raid on the Fundamentalist Church of Jesus Christ of Latter Day Saints (FLDS) is a case in point. There is a long-standing and deep-seated ambivalence among residents of Utah about the issue of polygamy and the fundamentalist Mormons who continue to practice "the Principle." One can find this ambivalence embedded in the regional media coverage of, and reader responses to, the FLDS raid. In the following pages reader reaction to the 2008 Texas state raid on the FLDS at the Yearning for Zion (YFZ) Ranch is examined in two key Utah newspapers, the *Salt Lake Tribune* and the *Deseret Morning News*. These newspapers are highly sensitive to polygamy issues arising from the historical doctrines of the Church of Jesus Christ of Latter-day Saints (LDS) and its founder, Joseph Smith, for reasons discussed below. The intent of the analysis of reader responses to regional news coverage is to explore how the LDS and Utahans interpret and frame polygamy in light of their own history, sacred experience, and collective identity, and to examine the implications of these.

The *Tribune* and the *News* have both covered the FLDS community (in Arizona and Texas) and the recent YFZ raid with alacrity. There are distinct differences in approach, however, that are related to the papers' unique histories. The *Salt Lake Tribune* is an independently owned newspaper founded by ex-Mormons that strives to achieve a balance in its reporting about LDS. The *Tribune* has always endeavored to remain independent of LDS control and influence, making news coverage of polygamy a particularly challenging charge. *Tribune* reporter Brooke Adams is assigned full-time to the polygamy beat, writing stories and blogging. The paper's Web page features a "Polygamy" tab (http://sltrib.com/polygamy) under Utah News, alongside Politics, Education, Columns, and Photos. Ms. Adams is the only American newspaper journalist exclusively covering polygamy, and her articles and the associated archives are a comprehensive and up-to-date source of news and analysis on the subject.

The *Deseret News*, on the other hand, is owned by LDS and has a high spiritual and cultural stake in the coverage of the polygamy-prone FLDS, their imprisoned Prophet, Warren Jeffs, and the raid on the YFZ Ranch. Editorial decisions on the degree of attention to give polygamists is reflected in the way that the *Deseret News* covers the FLDS. *Deseret News* reporter Ben Winslow chronicles the unfolding polygamy saga as part of his broader law enforcement beat. The well-designed Web page of the *Deseret News* has no equivalent to the Polygamy tab of the *Tribune*. However, a quick search on "polygamy," "FLDS," or "YFZ" in the Archives yields multiple hits, leading to well-researched, well-written stories, often by Winslow.

Historical Background of Utah's Foremost Newspapers

The history of the papers in which these conversations between strangers take place provides a significant prologue to the reader feedback. The *Salt Lake Tribune* (Sunday circulation: 130,000) and the *Deseret News* (Sunday circulation: 79,000) dominate the print news media in Utah ("Only Sunday News Bucks Record Drop" 2009). Claudia Bushman (2006, 168–70) gives a fascinating sketch of the intertwined histories and rivalries of these two newspapers in her helpful *Contemporary Mormonism*. The papers reflect the religious fault lines that have dominated Utah for almost 150 years.[1] The ex-Mormon founders of the *Salt Lake Tribune* set up in 1870 in opposition to LDS hegemony in Utah Territory, personified by Church President Brigham Young. The *Deseret News*, on the other hand, is Mormon founded and Mormon funded since 1850 and has generally defended the Church and its practices. But the *Deseret News* could not match the *Tribune*'s outsider voice or its unique perspective. Over time, as Utah developed and diversified, the two papers broadened their constituencies.[2] Both came to understand themselves as broader-based "real" newspapers, not simply partisan mouthpieces. As Utah tended to be more Republican in the post–World War II twentieth century, the two newspapers further distinguished themselves: the *Salt Lake Tribune* as a liberal-centrist voice and the *Deseret News* as a dependably conservative one.

Mormonism before 1960 existed as a smaller-scale, geographically isolated, regional religious culture that looked with suspicion on the Eastern establishment, as did much of the West. The *News* did not hire a non-Mormon editor until 1997. John Hughes, the British-born former editor of The *Christian Science Monitor,* served as its editor until 2006. The convoluted sale of the *Tribune* in 2000 raised fears among its readership of an LDS takeover of state media, highlighting the religious divide. It is still hard to miss the outsider and insider stances of the papers' editorial pages when they opine on Mormon Church–related matters. Notably the *Salt Lake City Weekly* (http://city-weekly.net), a newspaper of more recent and center-left vintage, looks askance at both papers. However, there is no LDS boycott of the *Tribune*. Many Mormons read and value it because of its more independent perspective.

Rates of reader response to YFZ raid stories have tended to be much higher in the *Salt Lake Tribune* than in the *Deseret News*. Readers of the *News* are also somewhat more reserved in their comments and post far fewer of them. This reticence might be owing to a number of factors, including hesitation by predominantly Mormon *News* readers to speak publicly about polygamy. Of course, those who comment on the Web pages of news outlets are not necessarily representative of readerships as a whole. Their views may sometimes mark the extremes, rather than the mean, of broader opinion.

Public Response to the FLDS Raid

Polling in 2008 on the YFZ raid showed that Utah public opinion was mixed during the first few months after the state action in Texas. In April, the month of the raid, a poll commissioned by *Deseret News* and KSL-TV found that only 13 percent believed that the authorities' actions were "probably not justified"; 6 percent thought they were "definitely not justified"; and the majority concurred that "they were justified in removing the children" (Winslow 2008a). A second poll, conducted about two months later, in June, and also commissioned by *Deseret News*/KSL-TV, focused more specifically on the state detention of the children and provoked stronger public opposition. The poll found that 33 percent strongly disagreed "with the decision to take the children and put them in state custody"; 17 percent somewhat disagreed; 22 percent strongly agreed with the action; 20 percent somewhat agreed; and 8 percent had no opinion (Winslow 2008b).[3] The poll numbers reveal that approximately 50 percent of Utahans disagreed with the state's custodial detention of the FLDS children. This figure was more than two and a half times as large as the percentage of people who in the previous poll thought that the initial raid was unjustified (19%). One may infer from these poll data that the public was more disturbed by the state's treatment of the FLDS children following the raid than the actual raid of the YFZ property. It may also reflect, however, shifting public response to the unfavorable news that emerged in the weeks and months following the raid (e.g., hoax phone calls, the state's failure to verify the caller's charges or information, the dissembling by state officials, and the overreach and exaggerated claims by CPS). In either case, the poll numbers do suggest that there was substantial disapproval among Utahans with regard to some of the state's actions surrounding the raid.

The polls provide important aggregate data giving us an insightful snapshot of public opinion. But they do not provide the underlying and nuanced meanings imputed to the Texas state raid, polygamy more generally, and the distinctive culture out of which the FLDS has arisen. To supplement the poll data, we shall look at reader responses to media coverage of the FLDS raid in the two most important Utah newspapers. These data offer a very different perspective on the subject drawing from a self-selected pool of men and women who comment—occasionally or compulsively—in news or online forums. Although their views should be regarded as anecdotal, they yield a fascinating, idiosyncratic, highly pixilated picture that polls or social science surveys are not designed to provide. Even the distortions revealed in polarized responses—and there is substantial bifurcation in the reader comments—point to voices of ordinary people passionately engaged with the issues as they interpret them.

Reader comments in the Salt Lake papers cannot be classified as simply pro-polygamy or anti-polygamy/FLDS. They are a mosaic that defies neat categorization. Patterns do emerge, however. The FLDS and other contemporary polygamist groups pose a dilemma for mainstream Mormons and, to a lesser extent, for Utah non-Mormons living alongside them. Why? Largely because the FLDS claims to be the true heir of Mormonism's founder, Joseph Smith, preserving his central doctrine of Celestial Marriage. There is considerable ambivalence among mainstream Mormons about "the Principle," and the Texas state raid on the FLDS has shone a dazzling light on this family dilemma and the resultant struggle over the meaning of their faith.

Interpreting Polygamy

In a March 2009 interview I conducted with *Salt Lake Tribune* reporter Brooke Adams, who has invested substantial time and effort in covering Mormon polygamy for the paper, she suggested that responders tend to fall into three categories. I found this attempt to categorize responses intriguing and offer this as a typology based on her comments. The first category includes those who regard polygamy as strictly abuse; no concessions are made for the historical and theological roots of polygamy. The second includes those who have a more nuanced evaluation of polygamy, distinguishing between different groups involved in the practice. The third entails those who focus on the state's response to polygamists, arguing that the authorities are heavy-handed and that federal law enforcement tramples on states' rights. My review of hundreds of reader posts on the Web sites of the two newspapers in 2008 and 2009 tend to support Adams's evaluation.

Adams's typology also brings to light parallel patterns I have observed in which readers have responded online to the problem of polygamy by employing particular linguistic motifs or frames. These motifs can be described as follows: (1) using the language of *sacred experience* to explain it, (2) using the language of American *patriotism* to distance themselves from it, and (3) invoking the language of *libertarianism* to question state and federal power. I offer a few examples from reader responses as typical of these motifs. In response to the *Deseret News* article, "13 FLDS Children Still in Court Custody" (January 20, 2009), for example, a reader with the screen name "Joey" replied to an off-putting comment by another reader critical of the FLDS by invoking the sacred experience motif. He writes, "Some people live in a different dimension, a more spiritual one, separate from earthly pursuits. But you would never understand, of course." Most of the twenty other comments in this stream of responses were stridently negative. To illustrate the patriotism motif, one respondent ("Old men") wrote, "These polygamists are lousy Americans and need to be stopped! Save the kids!" This reader's comments reveal a different value index or criteria for judging the marital practices of the FLDS.

Another writer, "Mark," typifies the libertarian motif by expressing an ambivalent angst rooted in the present but with an eye to the past: "I don't like polygamy either, but where does government interference end? Good thing you weren't around when Abraham, or Jacob (Israel) were. Would you have stoned them for polygamy?" Although Mark invokes the biblical patriarchs, the analogy is clearly meant to spotlight the more recent Mormon past.

These comments are examples of three strands of responses that have precedents in LDS history. They are part of the regional narrative. Joey responds to the raid with the language of sacred experience. His reference to "a different dimension" seems to correspond to historian Jan Shipps's (1987) description of early Mormons as living outside mainstream experience while reenacting the Israelites' exodus from bondage, and their conquest and settlement of Canaan. Shipps points out that the Mormons understood themselves as recapitulating biblical history, particularly in their famous trek from Nauvoo, Illinois, to the Great Basin, and their establishment of a renewed society.

Hostile reaction to the FLDS sometimes echo contemporaneous critiques of nineteenth-century LDS polygamy. For example, in a response to the *Tribune* article "Texas FLDS Raid: Defense Attorney Alleges Search Too Broad, Evidence Tainted" (July 13, 2009), the reader "Blackbird" wrote:

> The problem is that parents, religious leaders and an adult male all conspire in the sexual abuse of a child. That is not about marriage. Teaching girls that the only way to be saved is to have sex with married men is a federal crime under the United States Code which states that if someone has sex out of fear (other than fear of physical harm) that is sexual abuse and punishable by 10 years in federal prison. Fear of eternal damnation fits that category.

Note the religious vocabulary of this animadversion. The FLDS would take strong exception to Blackbird's characterization of their marriage system today, as the LDS did in the nineteenth century. However, this epoch ended for mainstream Mormons with the Manifesto of 1890, which suspended the practice of polygamy. For the FLDS, the trek out of time and the conventions of broader American society continues. As the YFZ raid story plays out, pitting the FLDS against the State of Texas, perhaps it is the audience in Utah that is recapitulating an earlier, wrenching confrontation with civil power. The explanations Jan Shipps (1987) offers might provide further insight for legal and social work professionals about polygamists' worldview, and even for the FLDS itself, as the Church faces the threat of its community being dismantled. They did not abandon "the Principle" of plural marriage in 1890 and merge into American life. On the contrary, they continue to move on toward a desideratum of their own.

Whether or not the writer screen-named "Old men" is an LDS member, his comment ("These polygamists are lousy Americans and need to be stopped!") represents another historically rooted adaptation by Mormons. While the FLDS is not accepted as Mormon by the mainline Church and its communal practices differ substantially from those of nineteenth-century Mormonism, "Old men" nonetheless bluntly inverts the powerful patriotic rhetoric that post-polygamy Mormons deployed as they sought acceptance as Americans in the twentieth century. Mormons drew upon their own founding principle of American exceptionalism, increasingly identifying themselves with the values of American civil religion. They worked hard to be good Americans. The paradox of the attempt was that Mormons wanted to be both an accepted people and a "peculiar people," a Church respected by and respectful of other churches, and the only true Church. The latter impulse is reflected in the highly contextualized language used for insider religious rhetoric; the former, with the more generalized, conciliatory language of American pluralism. But "Old men" may be appealing to something more than patriotism; his assertion that the Fundamentalist Latter Day Saints are "lousy Americans" puts them at odds with one of the primary projects of mainstream Mormonism: they have spectacularly failed where LDS members have remarkably succeeded.

Finally, "Mark's" ambiguous comments begin with a repudiation of polygamy but invoke biblical patriarchs to question government interference with that practice. Where "Old men" uses the language of patriotism, Mark employs the vocabulary of libertarianism. His tone suggests continuity with earlier LDS yearnings for political and religious autonomy, a continuing paradox interwoven with the political ethos of the Intermountain West. Perhaps unintentionally, his comments also echo Mormonism's earlier case for polygamy, as summarized by Ephraim Ericksen (1975:75): "Since the God of Israel approved of their lives [figures from the Hebrew Scriptures who practiced polygamy], and since he is the same yesterday, and today, and forever, why, they argue, should he not sanction polygamy among his favored people in the present age?" The sheer volume of reader responses to some news articles about the raid is also telling. For example, a December 27, 2008, Brooke Adams article in the *Tribune*, "Polygamous Sect Blasts Texas Report," garnered 1,158 comments in less than forty-eight hours. The story details the response of the FLDS to a report by the State of Texas ("Eldorado Investigation") in which the state defends its raid on the polygamous compound. As with any discussion board, recurring comments and assertions can dominate the word flow. In effect, these frequent writers create their own blogs, with a large potential audience, on the newspapers' websites.

The passion in many readers' posts is compelling. While some discuss the arcana of Texas tax rates, more are engaged in no-holds-barred shouting matches as they make their points, complete with the sarcasm and name calling that characterize the forums of so many readers. Their words in some cases reflect a regional narrative that is more than a century old. At times it is almost as though posted comments have been dusted off and recycled from the nineteenth-century popular press! Why is this happening? What does it indicate about religious rights, assimilation, and the uncertain line between past and present?

Polygamy and the Perceived Threat of the State

The current crisis facing the FLDS is rooted in the founding stories of its faith, especially the fabled reaffirmation of polygamy by the fugitive LDS president John Taylor in the 1880s, a time of great danger to Mormonism. It helps to explain the ambivalent kinship with the FLDS that a minority of *Tribune* and *News* reader/writers appear to feel, based on their comments. John Taylor was LDS Church President from 1880 to 1887. He was on the run from federal authorities seeking to arrest him for bigamy in 1886, like many other LDS polygamous husbands. He was purportedly visited in a vision at that time by Joseph Smith and Jesus Christ, commanding him to continue the practice of celestial marriage. Furthermore, Mormon fundamentalists believe that Taylor subsequently entrusted the revelation to five men, imploring them not to let plural marriage die out (Arrington 1958).

Taylor's bona fides among Latter-day Saints are powerful: he was with Joseph and Hyrum Smith in the Carthage jail in 1844, surviving when they were assassinated. He was an eyewitness to the defining martyrdom of Mormon history. However, his 1886 revelation, if veritable, was never incorporated into the LDS canon, a process that Taylor himself could have initiated. On the other hand, the chaos of the 1880s and Taylor's death one year later, in 1887, might point to other credible explanations for such an omission. In any case, Mormonism's death-spiral in the 1880s was arrested by the 1890 renunciation of polygamy by Mormon president and prophet Wilford Woodruff.

Biographer Richard Lyman Bushman (2005) claims that Joseph Smith understood plural marriage as a union completely distinct from common bigamy, a necessary component of "exaltation," the eternal progression of human beings toward the divine state. Purer and more self-sacrificing than monogamy, it eschewed romantic love for a shared, holy purpose. When publicly questioned about whether he practiced polygamy, Smith always answered no, because, according to Bushman, he believed that celestial marriage represented a higher, "celestial" order of life than ordinary polygamy. However, when dissidents in the community printed a newspaper in 1844 with details about Smith's plural marriages, his tactical response was to destroy the press, an act that led to his jailing and assassination. For Smith, the cost of celestial marriage was mortally high.

In 1890 the wrenching move away from plural marriage, "the Principle," created a dangerous spiritual interregnum. Shipps (1987) contends that it marked the end of the LDS re-creation of biblical history. Flake (2004) and Quinn (1985), however, both point out that this shift was not sudden or total, and Ericksen (1975, 73) gives an early view of the divisions among Utah Mormons over the repeal of plural marriage. The Manifesto renounced polygamy and ended it among the majority of practitioners, but a smaller number of polygamous marriages were solemnized for a number of years by Church officials, reminiscent of the secret polygamous wedding ceremonies performed by and for Joseph Smith at Nauvoo in the 1840s. The later hidden practice by Church officials was forced into the open and more completely abandoned after the 1904 U.S. Senate trial pursuant to the attempt to seat Reed Smoot, a Mormon apostle, as U.S. senator from Utah. Polygamy had continued on a smaller scale after the Manifesto and subsequent Utah statehood in 1897. However, the Smoot trial, and the deep desire by Church leaders for fuller participation in American political life, produced a second Manifesto in 1904 and a gradual end to secret, but officially sanctioned, polygamy.

The history of polygamy, and its presence in the American West, Mexico, and Canada, is difficult to realistically frame, in part because of sensationalist portrayals of its history. Scholarly treatments exist, however, such as Kathryn Daynes's *More Wives Than One* (2008), a meticulous sociological study of plural marriage in a typical nineteenth-century Utah community. What remains problematic for some outsiders to understand is the persistence of the practice. Today's polygamists belong to many sects and communities, and their leadership, often hereditary, has both originated and operated at the margins of the Mormon commonwealth for generations. A small number of mainstream Mormons continue to join the polygamists, as dramatized in HBO's series *Big Love*.

The promotion of genealogical research by LDS connects the monogamous present to the polygamous past; many Mormons have polygamous pioneer ancestors. As birthright Mormons research their ancestry, they are confronted with the fascinating tableau of a polygamous interlude in their family tree. Although polygamy was practiced for only two to three generations, and only by a minority in the Church (Van Wagoner 1986), it is not difficult to see that the number of Mormons personally affected by polygamy is almost exponentially expanded as one takes into account the many offspring of these unions.

Appreciation for genealogical research could lead to a more nuanced grass-roots understanding of the people who practice plural marriage today in the name of Joseph Smith, and under the direction of the men they believe to be his successor prophets. Genealogical research is more than a hobby for Mormons; it is rooted in double strands of their evolutionary theology. The practice of Baptism for the Dead, which requires the names of ancestors, and the conviction that families are connected across generations in a kind of spiritual DNA spiral, bridging time and eternity, is fundamental to the practice of Mormon ritual and popular piety. This rite, instituted by Smith in 1840, is believed to offer the deceased an opportunity in the afterlife to accept Mormonism. Living proxies are ritually submerged while the name of the dead person is inserted into the baptismal formula. It is believed that the dead may accept or reject the posthumous offer of salvation.

While genealogical research has helped to move the polygamous past out of the shadows and into the mainstream of American cultural references by the twenty-first century, it is less visible at real-world LDS historical sites. For example, tours of the Nauvoo, Illinois, LDS Visitors' Center conclude in a lovely, statue-dotted Monument to Women memorial garden, presided over by a life-sized depiction of Joseph Smith and his wife, Emma Hale Smith, clasping hands. The marriage idealized in these realistic castings is monogamous, not polygamous, although it was at Nauvoo that Smith codified the practice and urged it upon his closest associates. The only intimation of a different framework might be the archetypal statues of women in different life stages that fill the rest of the garden, in orbit around Joseph and Emma.

The Church of Jesus Christ of Latter-day Saints excommunicates practicing polygamists, and it sometimes seems that "plural marriage" is as foreign to modern Mormon self-understanding as it is to the sensibilities of, say, Presbyterians and Catholics. Predictably the conversation in a public but anonymous space in the reader-comment postings in Salt Lake City's two leading newspapers reveals ambivalent attitudes toward polygamy, both by what is written and, as posited above, by what is left unwritten. In posting after posting, regulars with screen names as varied as "Debater" and "Celtic," as well as hundreds of occasional citizen scribes, have their say about polygamy, the FLDS, the mainstream LDS, and the religio-cultural landscape they share. By turns malevolent, sympathetic, satirical, profane (until irate readers consign them to even deeper anonymity by clicking "Hide Comment"), apposite, and prosaic, these writers demonstrate that polygamy, like Banquo's ghost, will not vanish.

Between April 2008 and August 2009 the *Deseret News* published approximately 450 items on the YFZ raid; the *Salt Lake Tribune* published more than 700. In the immediate aftermath, the reactions of Salt Lake newspaper readers tended to reflect either anguish or relief over the YFZ raid. One wrote to the *Tribune*, "My heart is breaking for the children and mothers in San Angelo, Texas. . . . Taking 401 children away from mothers who are not physically abusive to them and placing these children in foster homes, even for a short time, creates profound, long-term emotional damage to the children which will follow them into adulthood and destroy their ability to cope." A far less sympathetic reader posted this comment in response to the early article "Texas Residents Call Raid of FLDS Ranch 'a Good Thing'" on the *Deseret News* website: "Plural Marriage is considered by these Fundamentalist LDS people as their 'Constitutional Right,' but when women and children are abused, and members are not allowed to have outside access to the public or read newspapers, well, then that's an altogether different story; these groups need to be controlled." The chain of chat room–like dialogues in reader comments like these form an unofficial, grass-roots diary of events that reflect the deep divisions over polygamy that are part and parcel of Mormon culture.

News Coverage of Polygamy as a Perceived Threat

Brooke Adams has been covering polygamy for the *Tribune* as part of her assignment since 2003, and almost exclusively since 2006. The trial of FLDS Prophet Warren Jeffs brought her to the assignment full-time. Her blog at "The Polygamy Files" and "The Plural Life" (http://166.70.44.68/blogs/plural-life/) is a remarkable running commentary on the continuing, multifaceted story of the FLDS, YFZ, and other polygamous communities. Adams points to the polarization of reader responses, both to her blog and to news stories in the *Tribune*. As previously mentioned, response is often huge, with as many as five hundred comments on one of her recent postings. What surprises Adams is the lack of understanding among some readers of her role as a reporter; she sometimes feels attacked by all sides who take exception with the reporting of views at variance with their own. She recently received an angry call asking, "Is your blog a pro-polygamy site?" Others objected to her interview with a woman, Betty Jessop, who initially left but then returned to the FLDS. Betty is the daughter of Carolyn Jessop, an outspoken FLDS apostate and author of the book, *Escape* (Jessop and Palmer 2008). Carolyn Jessop has been somewhat of a heroine to anti-polygamists. Readers seemed to fault Adams for conducting the interview itself, not for its contents. It is not uncommon for a cluster of postings to target Adams before moving on to clamor over Texas Judge Barbara Walther.

Polygamy is a preoccupation for her readership. There is some evidence of historical perspective among them, but many come to the subject with a simple fascination for its place in current events. She also notes the ambivalent response to her reporting by those directly affected by polygamy. For example, the "Lost Boys," teenagers expelled from FLDS communities, and who have been the subjects of national media attention, retain strong sympathies for the families that they have left, and do not want to see them ridiculed, harassed or broken up, even while the boys protest their own plight as outcasts.

Adams believes that the polygamists themselves have created problems with the larger public by being silent. The negative drumbeat of news coverage over the last few years has met with no response from the FLDS. The unchallenged mixture of truth and untruth in the reporting about the FLDS was received as factual by outsiders. Adams listed some of the more outrageous media claims, such as the allegation by some apostates that babies' graves at the Hilldale, Utah/Colorado City, Arizona cemetery showed that the FLDS practiced infanticide or that there was an incinerator in the YFZ temple for disposing of bodies. These "atrocity tales" (Bromley, Shupe, and Ventimiglia 1979), though groundless, gained traction because they were allowed to stand unanswered.

For some time Adams had to go to extraordinary lengths as a reporter to make contacts within the polygamous communities. She developed a handful of acquaintances within these groups and found a credible former member who was willing to talk with her. She also read all FLDS-produced materials that she could find, in order to gain an appreciation for their perspective. The high-profile events of the last year have produced some changes: the FLDS now has an official spokesperson, Willie Jessop. But Adams says that access is still a challenge. Part of that barrier involves the reputation of her newspaper among the FLDS. In this community, "what's past is prologue:" Mormon fundamentalists have a negative view of the *Tribune* because of its unsympathetic coverage of the 1953 law enforcement raid on the Short Creek polygamous settlement. "These are people with long memories," says Adams. When she asked why German news media were being given more generous access to Centennial Park, a more open polygamous community, than was she, members told her that foreign correspondents had shown more understanding of the 1953 raid than had the *Tribune*.

Adams also ran into trouble with the FLDS for her March 2009 story on Warren Jeffs, which involved detailed reporting on documents released by the State of Texas but considered to be private religious papers by Church leaders. They believed that the state had published the documents to embarrass them and that Adams had further disseminated them through her coverage. Adams pointed out to her contacts that her interest lay in what Jeffs was communicating to his followers when he was a fugitive, and that this was certainly news. She wonders if her relationship with the FLDS has been seriously damaged.

Why has the FLDS received the attention and treatment that it has? Adams has puzzled over this question. She notes the several similarities between the FLDS and other religious minorities, such as the Amish, with their distinctive dress, closed communities, and maintenance of high boundaries with mainstream culture. She wonders if the pervasive and intrusive media culture we now see might have spawned a different result if the landmark 1972 case on Amish education, *Yoder vs. Wisconsin*, had been tried today. Given the jaundiced view toward closed religious communities evidenced in the YFZ fallout, it is not implausible. She speculates that the extraordinary focus on the FLDS may have to do with their small size and concentration in a few communities. It is easy to see that they are "different." Some other communities that have faced their own religion-based scandals have been less distinctive and separatist, more readily assimilated with the rest of society and hence seen as less threatening.

The polarization of public opinion around polygamy, especially the YFZ raid and its aftermath, has provoked a recent response that Adams thinks is sinister; she blogged about it on March 13, 2009. "Americans Against Abuses of Polygamy," based in Richardson, Texas (http://www.tripleap.org), seeks to target and expose any person who shows what this group believes is sympathy toward polygamy, whether they are public officials, physicians, or private citizens. Adams notes that the group's purported vision is "a free American [*sic*] for the concubines and children currently trapped in the domestic abuse of polygamy." But the sensationalistic rhetoric and aggressive stance of "Americans Against" is more akin to a McCarthy-like campaign to pressure and harass anyone whom they deem pro-polygamy. This policing of the blogosphere by anti-polygamists raises concerns about freedom of speech for readers who post their comments in the *News*, the *Tribune*, or anywhere else.

As the YFZ story developed, it is clear that, at least in Utah, it had "legs." In the *Tribune*, "Texas Judge Closes Last Custody Case in YFZ Raid," published July 23, 2009, garnered 208 reader comments within twenty-four hours. Thirty-one readers posted their thoughts, but a few dominated the dialogue, particularly reader "chloemitchell" whose 53 comments, almost all explicitly anti-FLDS, made up about 25 percent of all comments. For example, she wrote: "Who was responsible for allowing an underage girl to go through 72hrs of labor with a baby, because they were afraid if they took her to the hospital, a MALE on the ranch would be in trouble?" She received seven positive reviews, or "thumbs-up" from other readers. However, "chloemitchell" sometimes veers off-topic, as do other responders, opining more generally about abortion, the recent conviction of evangelist Tony Alamo on sex-abuse charges, and state teen pregnancy rates. In fact, 56 reader comments were off-topic, neutral, or indecipherable. It is in their seemingly aimless ramblings that these Americans sometimes tell us the most about their underlying assumptions. "Chloemitchell's" twist on libertarian rhetoric, railing against the patriarchal FLDS, demands an end to control by illegitimate authorities and champions the autonomy of those whom she believes are their victims. Among remaining reader comments, almost as many—41—were favorable to the FLDS, as were unfavorable (108 negative comments, but with 53 posted by one writer). Some of the more pensive comments came from less frequent contributors, who tended to concentrate their ideas into one posting rather than treat the reader comments as a chat room. For example, "Sympathizer" wrote:

> Well, I remember a strident accusation at the beginning, from well meaning but foggy thinking FLDS supporters, that the state wanted to seize the children and sell them off by placing them for adoption. Guess those folks who were foaming at the mouth were wrong. Intervention can take many forms, and those who imagine that young girls need to be married off at puberty have been put on notice. Unexamined living conditions got examined. People who cherished an imaginary version of 19th century Mormon life got brought into the 21st century. So, there were results.

Notably this post received no reader ratings, perhaps because it was the last one associated with that story or it simply summarized others' comments.

Conclusion

Plural marriage or celestial marriage or simply "the Principle" was the distinguishing cultural institution of the nineteenth-century Mormon sphere of influence in the Intermountain West. It developed in defiance of mainstream American social and religious mores. Its complex history, and the continuing imprint of polygamy on Utah, is part of a backstory of the reaction to the YFZ raid that is sometimes obscured by the headlines. The roots of polygamy—

and the trauma of its uprooting—run very deep in this dry earth, although what remains today is more of an interstice between Mormon treasured self-identification as a "peculiar people" and adaptive pragmatism.

New evidence suggests that Utah has been undergoing an accelerating religio-demographic evolution, making it less faith distinctive. The comprehensive survey conducted by the Pew Forum's Project on Religion and American Public Life estimates the LDS population of Utah at 58 percent, substantially below the previous generally accepted benchmark of 65–70 percent (http://www.religions.pewforum.org). Although Mormonism is still growing in Utah, job-fueled in-migration, a jump in the largely non-Mormon Hispanic population, and declining LDS birthrates are changing the state. On the other hand, the LDS has extended its international reach, with two-thirds of its twelve million members outside the United States by 2008 (http://pewforum.org/docs/?DocID=427).

Increasing religious diversity creates a more pluralistic pool of readers for the state's newspapers. However, it is hard to identify the newcomers among those commenting on the YFZ raid. The recurring rancor toward the LDS, as well as toward the FLDS, expressed by some respondents, might indicate an alignment of some old and new non-LDS residents against all things Mormon. The vicissitudes of the FLDS have focused attention on polygamy's origins and perceived abuses.

Joseph Smith's Thirteen Articles of Faith include an unambiguous proviso for religious freedom for all people: "We claim the privilege of worshiping Almighty God according to the dictates of our own conscience, and allow all men the same privilege, let them worship how, where, or what they may" (Van Wagoner 1986, 535). However, this generous acknowledgment of pluralism must be understood within the schema of Mormonism's history of persecution and the Mormon faith in "Zion (the New Jerusalem)... built upon the American continent" (Van Wagoner 1986, 536). Smith envisioned a refuge from mob reaction unrestrained by established government, which threatened to wipe out the Mormons. The complicated dance of autonomy and dependency between Utah's Mormon leaders and the federal government stumbled through a continuing series of contretemps, the worst springing from LDS fears of persecution and annihilation. Experience had taught them to be wary of Gentiles; at the same time Mormons gloried in opposition as a sign of the genuineness of their faith. Although modern Utahans have at least five generations of experience living in an increasingly pluralistic state, some Latter-day Saints might fear that the loss of their religious majority in their historic stronghold could portend interference with their way of life.

Against this background, with its fascinating interplay between religion and politics, coexistence and competition, an egalitarian pluralistic "here" and a hierarchical Mormon "hereafter," response to the YFZ raid and its aftermath have tapped into a well of historic consciousness, anger, and anxiety. The reader comments posted on the Salt Lake papers' websites are not the musings of policy makers or the captains of Utah commerce. They are voices tinged with history's tailings.

NOTES

The reader comments in this chapter were published by the Deseret News Publishing Company and the MediaNews Group, August–September 2009, and were accessed online at, respectively, http://www.deseretnews.com/home and http://www.sltrib.com.

1. Allen and Alexander (1984) argue, however, that conflicts between LDS and non-LDS Salt Lakers declined considerably after about 1910, when the anti-Mormon American Party dissolved.

2. The *Salt Lake Herald* and *Telegram* are early papers now defunct.

3. The second poll included a sample of 405 Utahans with a margin of error of 5 percent. The article refers to the first poll but does not give the sample size or margin of error.

REFERENCES

Allen, Thomas G., and James B. Alexander. 1984. *Mormons and Gentiles: A History of Salt Lake City.* Boulder, CO: Pruett.

Arrington, Leonard J. 1958. *Great Basin Kingdom.* Cambridge, MA: Harvard University Press.

Bromley, David G., Anson D. Shupe, and G. C. Ventimiglia. 1979. "Atrocity Tales, the Unification Church, and the Social Construction of Evil." *Journal of Communication* (summer): 42–53.

Brooke, John L. 1994. *The Refiner's Fire.* Cambridge: Cambridge University Press.

Bushman, Claudia L. 2006. *Contemporary Mormonism.* Westport, CT: Praeger.

Bushman, Richard Lyman. 2005. *Joseph Smith: Rough Stone Rolling.* New York: Knopf.

Campbell, Eugene E. 1988. *Establishing Zion.* Salt Lake City, UT: Signature Books.

Daynes, Kathryn M. 2008. *More Wives Than One.* Urbana: University of Illinois Press.

Embry, Jessie L. 2008. *Mormon Polygamous Families.* Draper, UT: George Kofford Books.

Ericksen, Ephraim Edward. 1975. *The Psychological and Ethical Aspects of Mormon Group Life.* Bonneville Books Repr. ed., 1922. Salt Lake City: University of Utah Press.

Flake, Kathleen. 2004. *The Politics of American Religious Identity: the Seating of Senator Reed Smoot, Mormon Apostle.* Chapel Hill: University of North Carolina Press.

———. 2009. Interview with *ebrary.com*. Web. August 30. Accessed online at <http://site.ebrary.com.ezproxy.prin.edu:2048///.action>.

Jessop, Carol, with Laura Palmer. 2008. *Escape.* New York: Broadway.

Ludlow, Daniel H. 1992. *Encyclopedia of Mormonism.* Vol. 2. New York: Macmillan.

"Only Sunday News Bucks Record Drop." 2009. *Deseret News*, October 26.

Quinn, D. Michael. 1985. "LDS Church Authority and New Plural Marriages, 1890–1904." Accessed online at http://www.lds-mormon.com/quinn_polygamy.shtml#essay (May 29, 2009).

Shipps, Jan. 1987. *Mormonism: The Story of a New Religious Tradition*. Urbana: University of Illinois Press.

Van Wagoner, Richard S. 1986. *Mormon Polygamy: A History*. Salt Lake City, UT: Signature Books.

Winslow, Ben. 2008a. "Majority of Utahans Say Removal of FLDS Children Was Justified." *Deseret News*, April 10.

———. 2008b. "Utahans Change Mind on Backing FLDS Raid." *Deseret News*, June 25.

5

Deconstructing Official Rationales for the Texas State Raid on the FLDS

STUART A. WRIGHT

The massive state raid on the Fundamentalist Church of Jesus Christ Latter Day Saints (FLDS) near Eldorado, Texas, in 2008 was predicated on hoax phone calls to a domestic violence shelter hotline from an alleged sixteen-year-old girl inside the FLDS community who said she was raped and beaten by her polygamous husband. As we now know, the calls were made by an emotionally unstable, thirty-three-year-old woman in Colorado Springs. Curiously, as we have seen elsewhere in this volume, officials at the Department of Family and Protective Services (DFPS) and state police, before launching this massive enforcement action, made little effort to corroborate the authenticity of the caller who claimed to be Sarah Jessop. That she was believed so readily by authorities that the State of Texas would mobilize and amass extensive resources on such little evidence requires explanation. Here I suggest that child welfare officials, police, and other moral gatekeepers already concerned about the presence in this West Texas community of the LDS splinter group and its polygamous practices were predisposed to believe sensational tropes or narratives about the sect. Evidence suggests that DFPS officials and social workers were in contact with "cult experts," anticult actors, and FLDS apostates, and had adopted an anticult movement framing of the problem. Officials accepted uncritically allegations that played to the worst cult stereotypes and atrocity tales. This, in turn, contributed to the perception of an exaggerated threat by authorities resulting in another ill-advised government siege of a religious community (Bradley 1993; Palmer 1998, 2010, 2011; Richardson 1998; Swantko 2004; Wright 1995a) and the forced custodial detention of the group's children. Previous studies have shown that government raids[1] on sects or new religious movements (NRMs), sometimes labeled "cults," are often linked to the activities of organized opponents, a collaboration of countermovement or oppositional alliances, and networks involving anticult movement (ACM) actors, apostates, the media, and state agents (Bromley 1998a; Hall 1995; Hall and Schuyler 1998; Palmer 1998; Richardson 1998; Wright 1995b, 1998, 2002). The Texas state raid on the FLDS in Eldorado is explored here in terms of this analytical framework. It identifies and describes the social construction of an alleged threat ("cult") and the lineaments of the oppositional network that fueled the formulation of, and rationale behind, the state's ill-advised raid.

"Cults" and the Social Construction of Threat

A social problem is not always obvious or inherently self-evident. Many are ignored or given little official attention, either because the problems are not subject to great public hue and cry or the people who are victims have less power than others and thus are less able to mobilize resources on their own behalf. Social problems have to be recognized and defined as "threats" to cherished values or institutions by groups of people who are effective in bringing the issue to the attention of authorities. In this manner, officials can be pressured to act to resolve the alleged problem. Thus interest groups and social movements play a critical role in shaping legislation and social policy. If authorities do not feel sufficient pressure to address a grievance, it may not receive the attention it deserves. On the other hand, if authorities are confronted with intense or concerted pressure by interest groups or social movement organizations, they are more likely to respond to grievance claims in order to appear responsive to constituents or selected groups even when the problem is not severe or as threatening as claims-makers allege.

Social constructionist theory explains how such problems are selected, defined, and strategically framed for public consumption (Spector and Kitsuse 1987). A constructionist approach does not assume that a social problem can be taken at face value. Rather, it examines the social processes that lead to its definition by a social audience. As such, it explains how and why the official definition of a social problem may not accurately reflect the objective reality behind the situation or event. The trumpeting of a "threat" by selected groups is more likely to reflect their own social interests and symbolic meanings imputed to the alleged problem. Numerous studies have shown that social problems arise in the public arena and gain official recognition through the claims-making of pressure groups to spotlight or herald perceived dangers (Best 1990; Goode and Ben-Yehuda 1994).

Claims-making is more effective if the issues raised reflect preexisting or widespread social fears and apprehensions. Studies of Red scares, witch hunts, cult scares, pogroms, purges, and moral panics show that these kinds of reactionary campaigns are more likely to occur under specified social and political conditions (Bromley 1982; Goode and Ben-Yehuda 1994; Gusfield 1963; Karlsen 1987; Richardson, Bromley, and Best 1991). In a climate of fear, the manufacture of a defined "enemy" is more readily accomplished by a reactionary party or parties. Claims-making is more likely to find resonance with a broad social audience, receptive and willing to support the definition of the problem promoted by the crusading group. Indeed, history is replete with episodes of scapegoating and hysterical claims lodged against new sects (Mormons, Shakers, Jehovah's Witnesses) engendering conflict and giving birth to far-fetched plans for moral rectification (Moore 1986).

Successful efforts by claimants can take on the features and characteristics of a moral crusade or moral panic (Cohen 1972; Goode and Ben-Yehuda 1994; Gusfield 1963; Hall et al. 1978; Jenkins 1992, 1998). Moral crusades are designed to change, preserve, or reconstitute the moral order and are championed by moral entrepreneurs, an increasingly important force in shaping value conflicts (e.g., culture wars) in modern, pluralistic societies. One example of a moral crusade involves the growing concerns over "threatened children" in the last half of the twentieth century, giving rise to what scholars have called "child-saver" movements (Best, 1990; Zelizer, 1985). With declining birth rates, smaller families, and the extension of childhood and adolescence, children have come to acquire more "social value" and thus in need of more protection from psychological or emotional abuse. Child-saving activities pertaining to child abuse, missing children, family violence, teenage sexual activity, school violence and drug control (D.A.R.E) reflect recently evolved societal concerns. Child-saving frames or narratives can be highly effective rhetorical devices to assail "cults" since these groups often have unconventional family and marriage practices. As such, minority faiths are more vulnerable to attacks by opponents when value conflicts arise or competing moral codes collide. New or unconventional religions are poorly positioned to win over public support or find institutional allies.

Moral panics refer to situations in which strong and disproportionate reactions are expressed toward a group that is perceived to be a threat to the social order and becomes the focus of exaggerated attention from media, politicians, interest groups, law enforcement, and others (Cohen 1972; Goode and Ben-Yehuda 1994; Jenkins 1992, 1998). Moral panics do not arise in a social vacuum; they are products of claims-making and allegations by moral entrepreneurs who lobby officials and implore the media to take action. A distinct characteristic of moral panics is the inflation, exaggeration, or embellishment of claims. Studies consistently show that the behavior or beliefs of targeted groups (in our case, new or minority religions) may challenge conventional morality but do not necessarily rise to the level of illegality (Hall et al. 1978; Jenkins 1992, 1998). Therefore the violations have to be attacked rhetorically and symbolically, touted as threatening to moral values. As such, the campaigns tend to engage in orchestrated exercises of "deviance amplification" by which the targeted group is made to seem more threatening than it actually is. Numerous studies have analyzed overreaction to new or minority religions as moral panics (Bromley and Cutchin 1999; Introvigne 2000; Richardson, Bromley, and Best 1991; Richardson and Introvigne 2007; Wright 1995b). This theoretical framework helps to explain how the attribution of a "cult threat," fostered by apostates and anticult movement (ACM) actors, working with sympathetic news media, contributed to a widely held perception that the separatist sects at Waco and Eldorado posed an imminent danger to their members and to the broader society, eventually leading to the government raids. Antagonists and detractors formed an oppositional alliance to pressure government officials and agencies to act against the targeted religious groups, pressing claims, heralding dangers and threats, which news reporters often disseminated uncritically, creating a public perception of a menacing "cult."

"Cults" and Definitional Strategies of Organized Opponents

The use of the term "cult," by itself, conveys a value-loaded set of disparaging stereotypes (Lewis 1986; Richardson 1993; Robbins 1988; Wessinger, forthcoming) facilitating the claims-making efforts of organized opponents (Shupe and Bromley 1994). Much has been written about the subjective intent and unsettling social ramifications of labeling new or unconventional religions "cults" (Bromley 1982; Bromley, Shupe, and Bromiglia 1982; Lewis 1995; Pfiefer 1992; Robbins 1988; Richardson 1993, 1999; Wessinger, forthcoming). The term "cult" has questionable scientific value and has generally been abandoned by scholars because it has ceased to be a neutral or value-free category (Richardson 1993). "Cult" has come to be seen, in contemporary vernacular, as a term of derision or denigration, an epithet not unlike those used as racial or ethnic slurs. Thus to call a religious group a "cult" is to foist upon it a condemnation; the label is a denunciation, not a neutral description.

Not surprisingly the term "cult" has been applied intentionally as a strategy by anticult movement (ACM) organizations and actors since the early years of the movement (Shupe and Bromley 1994; Shupe and Darnell 2006), and its evolved use in the popular culture can probably be attributed in no small part to ACM influence. ACM leaders and their allies have labored to control the naming of minority faiths in the public square, battling with scholars, civil liberties groups, interfaith organizations, and others over the scientific merits and ethical usage of the term "cult," both here and abroad (Gunn 2000; Introvigne 2001; Richardson 1993, 1999; Richardson and Introvigne 2001; Wright 2002). In order for one to fully understand how and why government raids on minority religious communities occur, one must recognize the importance of this struggle over language and the labeling and framing of the targeted groups. State control and repression of "cults" is not likely to provoke public outcry or protest, since the term connotes cultural illegitimacy. Cults have few institutional allies and little public support (Bromley 1998a, 1998b; Bromley and Breschel 1992; Olsen 2006). As such "cults" are "soft targets" for attacks, vulnerable to inflated claims by opponents and deep-seated suspicions harbored by public officials. On the other hand, state repression of "legitimate" religions is much more likely to elicit protests and outrage, with allies decrying infringement of religious freedoms and practice. In effect, the definitional battle over new or minority religions is a struggle to ascribe cultural legitimacy, and the attendant rights and protections that come with it (Bradney 1999; Lewis 1989; Richardson 1991).

Lineaments of an Oppositional Network: Apostates, ACM Actors and DFPS Officials

According to news accounts, Rozita Swinton placed her first call to Flora Jessop, the outspoken FLDS apostate and founder of Help the Child Brides, on March 29, claiming to be an abused young polygamous wife ("Polygamist Sect Kids to Undergo DNA Tests" 2008). This is a critical point because the call occurred just four days before the Texas state raid. Flora Jessop is the principle link to Texas child welfare officials. Swinton also placed calls to the domestic violence shelter hotline in San Angelo on the same day. We now know that Jessop encouraged Swinton to make the call to Texas following their conversation. Jessop also contacted Texas authorities directly the following day, on March 30, and gave them thirty to forty hours of recorded phone calls with Swinton, who was alleging to be the sixteen-year-old victim. Although Jessop later told news reporters that she thought Swinton's story had holes, this contradicts other accounts she gave. Jessop told the *Colorado Springs Gazette* that "she [Swinton] honest-to-god sounded like a sixteen-year-old or younger child in need of help" (Newsome 2008). Jessop admitted to *crying* over the stories that Swinton related and said she was "amazed at how much Swinton knew about the sect" (ibid.). Jessop went on to say that "I work these cases all the time. We have been searching for family members . . . and yet we had no idea where some of the people were that she knew about" (ibid.). Evidently Jessop believed Swinton's claims at the time that she passed the information to Texas authorities. It was only after Swinton's arrest and release from jail that Flora Jessop realized the calls were fraudulent. This may also explain why DFPS officials made no effort to verify or corroborate the authenticity of the caller. Flora Jessop's direct involvement was seen by Texas officials as verification of the caller's credibility. The apostate Jessop validated the caller's accusations, since Jessop worked with former members of FLDS in a professional capacity.

Flora Jessop clearly fits the description of what scholars call a "career apostate" (Bromley 1998b; Brown 1996; Wright 1998). A career apostate is one who carves out a professional career as an "ex," offering counseling or advisory services and laying claim to expertise as a former member. A prominent feature of the career apostate is that the disgruntled ex-member endeavors to broaden personal grievance claims into a public issue. The career apostate typically defines and frames his or her former religious group as a larger societal threat that requires an urgent public response, relying on anecdotal evidence and personal narrative. Unlike most leavers or ex-members who tend to hold favorable, sympathetic, or at least mixed attitudes about their former groups (Barker 1988; Galanter 1989; Goldman 1995; Levine 1984; Lewis 1986; Taslimi, Hood, and Watson 1991; Wright 1984, 1987, 1988, 1998, forthcoming; Wright and Ebaugh 1993), apostates assume adversarial roles, becoming public detractors and broadening the dispute process.

Jessop was born into a polygamous family in Hildale, Arizona, one of twenty-eight children. At sixteen, she fled the FLDS and later became a determined critic of the group. According to the *Los Angeles Times*, Jessop "devotes almost every waking moment to exposing the church as a hotbed of child abuse and helping the community's girls and women escape from the polygamous life she fled" (Heller 2004). Jessop experienced personal challenges after leaving the community. She began experimenting with drugs and almost overdosed on cocaine. She moved in and out of relationships with men, giving birth to a daughter from one of the relationships. She struggled to earn a living, working as a topless dancer at one point. She married, divorced, and remarried. Her passion and life's work, however, begins and ends with contesting the FLDS. In 2001 she founded Help the Child Brides, an informational/educational organization designed to provide assistance to underage FLDS women who are allegedly forced to marry into polygamous relationships. She hosts a website (http://www.helpthechildbrides.com/help. htm) that features the narratives of other women who have left the FLDS, and books and news articles critical of the FLDS and especially of Warren Jeffs, their leader. Jessop is also Executive Director of the Los Angeles-based Child Protection Project, a charitable organization, providing direct financial support for young people who have left polygamy, which has its own website (http://www.childpro.org/). She has also written an incendiary autobiography about her experiences in the FLDS (Jessop and Brown 2009), including a charge that she was raped by her father, as well as a detailed catalogue of her involvement with prosecutors and child protective service workers in Arizona, with the stated intent to expose group leaders to criminal charges and state control.

Flora Jessop's public crusade against the FLDS has at times earned her sharp criticism. The *Phoenix New Times* describes her as a "publicity-hungry fanatic whose demands to have control over someone else's children are becoming eerily similar to the dictatorial attitude of her sworn nemesis, Warren Jeffs" (Heller 2004). She has been called a "vigilante" by Church members and a "rock star" by supporters. Jessop has been known for overstating her claims against the FLDS. On a TV news show in Los Angeles, she told an audience that the FLDS was "not a religion" but a form of "terrorism" (Heller 2008). Arizona Attorney General Terry Goddard has questioned her methods, complaining that she has "gotten nastier and nastier," and suggested at times that she has "fanned fears" without reason. Goddard told the *Los Angeles Times* that Jessop's methods have "undermined the state," and he accused her of being "misguided and devious" (Heller 2004). Arizona state representative Linda Binder, one of the most vocal critics of the FLDS in the legislature, told a news reporter that the problem with Jessop's approach is that she "wants to go in there guns ablazing, get everybody out" (Heller 2004). Both critics and supporters describe her as passionate but obsessed.

Jessop describes her own claims-making efforts to gain the attention of authorities and the media in her autobiography. As early as March 2004, following the FLDS purchase of the land for the Yearning for Zion (YFZ) Ranch, Jessop traveled to Texas to "warn" authorities of the dangers of the "cult."

By March 2004 Warren Jeffs had started putting up buildings on his Texas property near the town of Eldorado. And it was in March that I was on ABC's *Primetime* after journalist John Quinones went with me to Colorado City. A lot of people saw that show—including people in Eldorado,

Texas, who were beginning to get worried about what these people from Utah had in mind. I was no longer fearful of the media. I'd learned that they could help me get my message out there. Right away, I started contacting people in Texas, including newspaper editors and other journalists. I made a trip out to Eldorado to warn people about what was coming. The local papers started interviewing me for a series of stories they were writing on the FLDS compound. . . .

In April, I held a news conference in Eldorado. It was attended by government and law enforcement officials from Texas and Arizona—including Mohave County, Arizona, supervisor Buster Johnson, whose district included Colorado City. And it was covered not only by media in the Southwest but also by the *New York Times* and ABC's *Primetime*.

I told them my story. I told them about sexual abuse, forced marriages, child abuse, tax evasion, welfare fraud, and child labor. I told them exactly who had purchased the land that Warren was now calling YFZ, LLC, a limited liability corporation. YFZ stood for Yearn [*sic*] for Zion. The FLDS members believed that Zion would be their place of refuge when the sins of the wicked destroyed the world. The name chilled me to the bone. I wondered what Warren might be planning. (Jessop and Brown 2009, 450–51)

Jessop's cultivation of media contacts in press conferences, prime-time news shows, and through her child-saver organizations provided significant public venues to broadcast and disseminate the victimization narrative and build unfavorable, even hostile, public opinion toward the FLDS and the Eldorado community. By her own account, she started contacting newspaper editors and journalists in Texas and issuing press releases. Indeed, the *San Angelo Standard-Times* published new stories on the FLDS in March 2005, quoting Jessop extensively (Anthony 2005; Phinney 2005). Jessop appears to be the primary source for the news stories, and Jessop's own biographical account is reproduced for the readers. In this manner, the local news stories featuring Jessop and incorporating her inflated claims about the group ("I told them about sexual abuse, forced marriages, child abuse, tax evasion, welfare fraud, and child labor") became part of a larger public perception and narrative. This larger public narrative facilitated an inhospitable political climate for the YFZ and mounting public pressure for authorities to take action.

In her highly visible role as a career apostate and passionate opponent of FLDS, Jessop was a conspicuous mark for the emotionally disturbed Swinton. Jessop, the crusader and child saver, was apparently predisposed to believe the caller's claims and pleas for help ("She honest-to-god sounded like a sixteen-year-old or younger child in need of help"). More important, Jessop was well connected to the network of child and adult protection agencies and appropriate state enforcement personnel in Arizona, Utah, and Texas. Details of her extensive involvement with county and state government officials in three states, including the Utah Attorney General's office, are well documented in her book. Needless to say, she had achieved a degree of credibility and respect among child protection workers and state agencies across the country. Many were already familiar with her Child Protection Project, so when she contacted state authorities in Texas with the abuse charges, she was taken seriously. According to her autobiographical account, she had contacts with Texas officials four years prior to the raid, and apparently cultivated and maintained these contacts in the years, months, and days leading up to the raid.

Independent of these connections to law enforcement and child protection workers and networks, there is also evidence linking Flora Jessop to anticult movement (ACM) organizations and actors, providing a fuller and more complete picture of the emergent oppositional network in this case. Ties to anticult organizations and actors can be found on the Child Protection Project website. Under the "Resources and Links" page, there is a listing of organizations identified as resources to contact. The listings include five ACM links: (1) Apologetics Index: Apologetics Research Resources on Religious Cults, Sects, World Religions, and Related Issues (an evangelical Christian countercult organization); (2) International Cultic Studies Association (formerly the American Family Foundation which publishes the ACM-based *Cultic Studies Review*; (3) Steven Hassan's Freedom of Mind Center; (4) Meadow Haven (a cult rehabilitation center billed as "a resource for cult survivors to transition into society"); and (5) Religion News Blog, operated by the Apologetics Index group mentioned above. The explanation for these listings on the website is described, in part, as follows: "Often we combine resources with other organizations while working on certain projects *in which we all share a common goal*" (emphasis mine). The common goal, it appears, refers to "rescuing" members of religious groups deemed "destructive cults" or "terrorists," to use Jessop's terminology, and would seem to require some institutional cooperation, if not coordination and collaboration.

On one of Flora Jessop's websites, Help the Child Brides, one can find a link to Rick Ross's Institute for the Study of Destructive Cults, Controversial Groups, and Movements. Rick Ross had carved out a professional career as a deprogrammer in the ACM network until he was successfully sued by one of his victims following a failed deprogramming in Washington state in

1995 (see Shupe and Darnell 2006). The jury in the U.S. District Court of Washington found in favor of the plaintiff, Jason Scott, a young Pentecostal convert who was forcibly abducted and restrained, carried across state lines, and held in a remote cabin for several days before he escaped. Mr. Scott was awarded $2.5 million in damages from Ross. Subsequently Ross abandoned his career as a deprogrammer and began promoting himself primarily as a "cult expert," founding the virtual Institute for the Study of Destructive Cults. Ross's website features an archive of news articles highlighting alleged abuses of cults, as well as interviews with him and other ACM leaders. But the fundamentalist polygamist sect is one of the most prominently featured; one can find over 800 news articles on the FLDS alone.

Ross is interviewed and cited in the same *San Angelo Standard-Times* article featuring Flora Jessop in March 2005. He is referred to as a "New Jersey expert on fringe religious groups who has studied the FLDS for 20 years" (Anthony 2005, 2). The reporter evidently made no attempt to corroborate Ross's claims. Ross possesses no educational credentials to make him an expert on fringe groups; he is a self-proclaimed anticult activist, and his "study" of the group likely amounts to collecting damaging information. In the news story Ross invokes a typical ACM framing to describe the group: "There is [an] eerie quality [about them]; what some would call brainwashing" (Anthony 2005, 2). Following the brainwashing claim, Ross inflates the threat even further, offering the reporter a comparison between the FLDS and Jonestown, and likening FLDS leader Warren Jeffs to Jim Jones:

> "What he [Jeffs] seems to be doing is cocooning," Ross said, comparing the situation to that of Jim Jones, the San Francisco preacher who in the 1980s [*sic*] fled with his cult to Nicaragua [*sic*] as legal scrutiny increased. Jones and his followers later committed mass suicide when legal pressures continued. (Anthony 2005, 4)

Curiously the threat attribution supplied here by Ross escalates from brainwashing and "cocooning" to "mass suicide" without any evidence to support the outlandish claim. Moreover, the reporter—who factually misstates both the time in which the People's Temple "fled" (it was in the 1970s) and the country where they established their community (it was Guyana)—makes no effort to question Ross about the strained comparison. Thus the reader is left with a perilous and unsubstantiated statement about the FLDS made by a so-called cult expert who is, in fact, part of the oppositional coalition.

One of the other links found on Jessop's Child Protection Project website is Steve Hassan's Freedom of Mind Center. Hassan is a former member of Reverend Sun Myung Moon's Unification Church and an outspoken career apostate dating back to the 1970s. He converted as a student while at Queen's College in New York at the age of nineteen. He left the movement after twenty-seven months when he was successfully deprogrammed by two other former members of the Unification Church. Hassan returned to school and earned a master's degree in counseling at Cambridge College. He became a Licensed Mental Health Counselor in the state of Massachusetts and later wrote two books on "exit counseling." The first book, *Combating Cult Mind Control* (1988), became a widely used manual for cult counseling. He has been a key figure in the evolution of the cult exit counseling/rehabilitation industry over the last twenty years.

Thus the websites for the two organizations for which Jessop is deeply involved—the Child Protection Project and Help the Child Brides—provide cyberlinks to anticult movement (ACM) organizations, career apostates, key anticult figures, and an array of anticult services, resources, materials, and information carefully framing the conflicts surrounding new or unconventional religions in terms of abuse stereotypes.

Given Jessop's connections and activism in Texas, it is not surprising in the aftermath of the raid that Texas DFPS officials evidenced the adoption of an anticult framing of the FLDS incident, inflating or exaggerating the child abuse claims. This is supported by accounts of independent child protection workers who were brought in to counsel the children in state custody in the weeks following the raid. Linda Werlein, Chief Executive Officer of the Hill Country Community Mental Health and Mental Retardation (MHMR) Center in Kerrville, Texas, was asked by the state to bring approximately a dozen social workers to San Angelo to assist the DFPS after the raid. Ms. Werlein was disturbed by what she witnessed and later told the *Las Vegas Review Journal* that "much of what she was told by [DFPS] officials turned out to be wrong" (Smith 2008). She stated in an affidavit that family and child protection officials misrepresented evidence of child abuse. "My staff and I soon learned," she wrote, "that each and everything that we were told was either inaccurate or untrue" (Smith 2008). Wanda Brown, the Hill Country Community MHMR's director of nursing, said in an affidavit, "These women and children show absolutely no signs of abuse. The only signs of abuse I saw took place in the pavilion where these women and children were being held like prisoners of war" (Smith 2008). Ms. Brown condemned the manner in which the state officials were treating the FLDS women and children, even using the term "abuse" to describe this treatment.

I reached Linda Werlein in Kerrville a few months after the raid and was able to interview her. She repeated her previous allegations and expressed great concern that DFPS workers were making unfounded abuse claims about the mothers and the children.

> In our work, we know the difference between nurturing mothers and non-nurturing mothers. We get children in our clinic who have been abused and we know what that child looks like. Now I know that's not scientific; I know it's anecdotal. But we did not see children who were being abused. (Interview with Linda Werlein, 2008)

Ms. Werlein and her staff determined that the DFPS claims were baseless and then began asking for the sources of evidence of child abuse. Upon questioning officials about the charges, she said state child-protection workers became defensive and labeled her and her staff as "sympathizers." She and her staff were even "kicked out" of the pavilion at one point because officials deemed them too sympathetic toward the FLDS mothers. "Well, we were just out-and-out told that we were to do their [the DFPS's] bidding," she said. "It was made really clear to us that if we were too sympathetic we would be kicked out, and at one point we were." They were later asked to return but were clearly chastened by those in charge.

In a more revealing part of the interview Ms. Werlein said that the state's investigation was being guided by outside "cult experts" for whom she attributed much of the misinformation and confusion. She keenly observed that the so-called experts had no expertise on the FLDS per se, but on "cults" as a generic category.

> I was interested in asking people about their sources. Where are you getting this information? Like they had information that they [the FLDS] had tunnels underneath the houses. Now, I know Eldorado as one of the towns in the nineteen counties we serve and I said, "Have you ever been there?" to this one lady. And she said, "No, why?" I said, good luck on finding a tunnel, it's solid rock out there. I know they searched for tunnels and there were none.
>
> I was told it was an investigation, and the "experts"—and I never knew who they were—they said they understood and studied a lot about this group. And it turned out actually they were experts on "cults" generally,

and not on this FLDS group. . . . When I would ask specific questions, they would just quote the "experts" and then say, "You don't understand." (Interview with Linda Werlein, 2008)

Ms. Werlein said that she did not know the identity of the "cult experts," and officials did not use their names. However, she clearly describes the situation at the detention site in San Angelo as one in which DFPS workers were deferring to "cult experts," adopting their framing of the incident, and even quoting them when challenged about their decisions. Ms. Werlein's description of the relationship between the "cult experts" and state social workers at the pavilion supports the thesis advanced here that an oppositional alliance had formed involving collaboration and coordination between the parties. Werlein's own expertise and experience as a CEO and a director of an MHMR Center was summarily dismissed, as was her staff's, because it challenged the hegemonic anticult frame of the oppositional coalition. "You don't understand," she was told. We have experts who know about these groups and they can detect abuse that you and other trained professionals cannot see. When Werlein and her staff refused to accept this dubious explanation, they were labeled "sympathizers" in McCarthy-like fashion and evicted from the facility.

Court documents have not been terribly helpful in determining the identification of the "cult experts." News coverage cites the involvement of one anticult activist, Janja Lalich, who is listed on the Cultic Research website (CultResearch.org) as the "founder and director of the Center for Research on Influence and Control." She is a faculty member at California State, Chico, and is featured on the university's website as a "cult expert" (http://www.csuchico.edu/faculty-staff/index.shtml). Lalich coauthored a book, with the matriarch of the anticult movement Margaret Singer, that some critics call the ACM manifesto, *Cults in Our Midst: The Hidden Menace in Our Everyday Lives* (Singer and Lalich 1995). According to a report by the *Salt Lake City Tribune*, Lalich "went to Texas last summer to help caseworkers" with the FLDS children (Adams 2009). On her blog for the newspaper, Brooke Adams provides more details about Lalich's involvement, noting that the cult information specialist "participated in a two-day training seminar for shelter providers and CPS [Child Protection Services] workers involved in the YFZ Ranch case" (Adams 2008). Lalich's role in advising and assisting child protection workers in the FLDS case in Texas is significant for several reasons. First, Lalich brought a decidedly anticult framing to the site, stating in one media interview that the FLDS was "abusing hundreds and hundreds of women and children" (Bryner 2008). Second, according to news reports (Adams 2008), Lalich came to this conclusion apparently by interviewing disgruntled ex-members of the FLDS—Carolyn Jessop, in particular. The Lalich-Jessop connection is significant because it supports an ACM-apostate link that is direct and collaborative. Not surprisingly, in the Adams news article (2008), we find Lalich's comments coupled with Jessop's. Jessop tells the reporter, "Once you go into the compound, you don't ever leave it." Jessop's remarks are framed by Lalich who went on to make oversimplified generalizations about "cults" and explain that "fear" is the motive for loyalty to the group. The news story featuring interviews with Lalich and Carolyn Jessop was also posted on Flora Jessop's Help the Child Brides website, indicating substantive ACM network ties.

One health professional with connections to the ACM who was identified in the court documents was Bruce Perry. Perry is a psychiatrist and senior fellow at the Child Trauma Academy in Houston. Notably Perry was used as a consultant in the disastrous federal siege on the Branch Davidian community in 1993. He led a child trauma team into Waco to evaluate the Davidian children. Some of Perry's evaluations of the Branch Davidian children were criticized for a blaming-the-victim approach and for not recognizing the state's exacerbation of the trauma experienced by the children (Coleman 1994; Ellison and Bartkowski 1995). Perry's ties to the ACM are not insignificant. Among other activities, he has been a featured speaker at several anticult conferences, is listed in the International Cultic Studies Association (ICSA) directory and profiles section, and has recently coauthored an article in the International Cultic Studies e-newsletter on the Branch Davidian incident (Perry and Szalavitz 2007). According to CBS News coverage of the custody hearings of FLDS children, Perry was identified as one of the state's "experts" and described as "an authority of children in cults" ("Polygamist Sect Kids to Undergo DNA Tests" 2008).

Curiously, in their article cited above, Perry and his coauthor (writing before the FLDS raid) generally assailed the DFPS and the state for mismanaging children taken into custody after enforcement actions (a judgment conspicuously omitted in Perry's congressional testimony at the Waco hearings). "Government agencies—especially the chronically underfunded and overburdened Child Protective Services systems," they wrote, "rarely have concrete plans to deal with sudden influxes of large groups of children" (Perry and Szalavitz 2007, 3). They went on to say that Texas authorities wanted to separate the Branch Davidian children from their siblings and peers after the initial raid, a tactic which they found deeply flawed.

It was only dumb luck that kept the Davidian children together after the first raid. Originally, Texas CPS had planned to place them in individual foster homes, but could not find enough homes fast enough to take all of them. Keeping them together turned out to be one of the most therapeutic decisions made in their case. After what [the children] had just experienced, ripping them from their peers and/or siblings would only have increased their distress. (Perry and Szalavitz 2007, 3)

It is instructive to note that DFPS and other state officials repeated the same pattern of mismanagement in the FLDS case, separating children from their mothers and, in some cases, placing children in foster homes as far away as three hundred miles from Eldorado.

Perry, of course, has received his own share of criticism. In one legal case in which Perry was involved, he was criticized for submitting a psychiatric evaluation of children in a new religious movement (The Family International) to a court in Melbourne, Australia, without ever having seen or examined a single child in the group. The Department of Health and Community Services (DHCS) conducted predawn raids on The Family in 1992 and took sixty-two children into state custody (see Palmer, this volume). Perry was asked to provide assessments of the children but relied instead on secondhand materials, some of which were provided by an anticult organization (Perry 1994, 2). Without having performed any evaluations of the children in question, Perry concluded that the religious group exhibited "1) the clear presence of destructive practices as they relate to the development of primary parent/child attachments which are required for the development of healthy, flexible emotional functioning and 2) the clear presence of destructive practices as they relate to the development of independent cognition" (ibid., 2). In a disturbing line of reasoning, Perry asserted that "these children are likely to have been 'damaged' in a fashion that is not easily observed by untrained eyes," analogous to "undetected cancer, slowly silently growing inside a child only to be detected many years later; the emotional, cognitive and social problems within these children will grow silently—undetected without special evaluation" (ibid., 3).

Another psychiatrist in the Australian case, Lee Coleman, submitted an affidavit to the court refuting Perry's evaluation and taking him to task for unethical conduct. Coleman criticized Perry's "outrageous methodology" which relied on the claim that the psychiatrist had studied another group whose practices were "similar" yet offered no evidence in support of the claim (Coleman 1994, 2). Coleman accused Perry of violating even minimal standards of professional conduct by manufacturing psychiatric evaluations of individuals from afar. Coleman observed in the affidavit that the court-ordered evaluation of children by state investigators and child-protection authorities found no evidence of abuse. Coleman rejected Perry's claim that the children had been psychologically damaged in a fashion not easily detected by other professionals.

> This means, of course, that the psychiatric, social work, and legal professionals (including the judges) of Australia have all been duped, and only someone "trained" in a manner Dr. Perry or one of his like-minded colleagues would approve will be able to "detect" the undetected cancer of a childhood in the Family. The use of the "silently growing" cancer analogy reminds me of the Nazi's description of Jews as a creeping vermin about to engulf the world. This is religious bigotry, pure and simple, thinly masquerading as "science" (Coleman 1994, 3)

Coleman proceeded to question Perry's impartiality in the case, linking him to the ACM and criticizing him for his reliance on anticult framing in lieu of direct clinical evaluation.

> Throughout his report Perry speaks of "cults" and thereby demonstrates his willingness to use a term which has no legitimate place in an evaluation impacting the best interests of a child. It has no accepted place in the social work or psychiatric literature and can only intrude religious bias into a matter related to the welfare of children. In addition, scholars of new religious movements have long ago recognized that the anticult literature Dr. Perry relies is renowned for its ability to make accusations based on small, one-sided samples, primarily those ex-members who choose to associate themselves with the anticult movement. The vast majority of ex-members who decide to leave a group someone else calls a "cult" but do not then join the anticult movement are not consulted. When legitimate researchers have sampled a more representative selection of ex-members, the extreme statements of the anticult movement have never been corroborated (Coleman 1994, 3).

In light of Perry's faulty methodology and the lack of physical evidence of child abuse, the assessments Perry provided to the court were discredited. Subsequently the New South Wales Supreme Court ruled the actions of the state illegal and said that the children were entitled to seek damages from the government (Nicholas 1999; Richardson 1999).

Perry's role in the FLDS case is noteworthy because his links to the anticult movement have already been established in the Branch Davidian and The

Family International cases wherein he offered a predictable ACM framing of the problem. This same anticult frame, alleging widespread "cult" child abuse, was reproduced conveniently for the District Court in San Angelo following the state raid on the FLDS. One must ask whether the DFPS decision to bring Perry into this case was to manufacture the evaluation they wanted. Indeed, more than a decade ago, Dr. Coleman astutely observed that Perry's "outrageous methodology" would always make the child abuse claim a foregone conclusion in *any* case: "There is no community, and no family, which, if Dr. Perry's recommendations were adopted, would be safe from State interference. If no evidence of danger is found, this only shows how dangerous the situation really is, because the parents and the community are so devilishly clever that the 'ordinary' experts have been fooled" (Coleman 1994, 4).

The selection of Perry by state officials to evaluate the FLDS children is revealing. It is safe to assume that these officials knew, or should have known, that Perry would provide the court with a predictable evaluation of psychological damage to the children, even if other "ordinary experts" could not detect harm, and that the solicited evaluation would be favorable to a program of state intervention and control.

It is instructive to note that the responses of mental health experts *not* associated with the ACM in two NRM cases involving alleged child abuse (The Family and FLDS) are strikingly similar in suggesting that the more serious potential abuse to children might have been committed not by the religious group in question but by the state. Consider the following comments by, respectively, Lee Coleman in the Australian case and Linda Werlein in the Eldorado case:

> Dr. Perry writes that "it is important that investigators insure that religion is not used to legitimize unacceptable childrearing practices." In my study of the documents from the child protection investigations of these children, I see no evidence of any practices otherwise dangerous to children being "legitimized." This would hardly be likely since the investigators were not part of the Family. I offer to Dr. Perry and all those tempted to be persuaded by his specious arguments, the following: It is important that investigators insure that *psychiatry* is not used to legitimize unacceptable interference in the lives of children, based not on legitimate evidence of child endangerment, but religious bigotry. (Coleman 1994, 6)

> We are an agency that answers to child protection services and adult protection services to ensure that we are not violating our clients rights—the

people who receive our services, in any way. And that includes everything from the tone of voice we use to how limiting we are in their activities. I watched them [the DFPS] violate all the rules. I watched them talking harshly. Women were asking to see their lawyers and not being allowed to talk to their lawyers and this bothered me. . . . They only got us in to comfort a child when the mother was pulled away or when the child was pulled away to distract the mother. . . . My concern was the psychological damage we were doing to these children. That was astounding to me. (Interview with Linda Werlein, 2008)

Explaining the Recurrent Pattern of State Raids on Minority Religions

The state raid and custodial detention of FLDS children appears to reproduce a pattern that NRM scholars have seen repeatedly over the last twenty to thirty years. The disfavored minority religion is branded a "cult" and labeled as "subversive," requiring special social control agencies to meet the supposed "danger" or threat posed to its members and to the greater public. Apostates and anticultists collaborate to build a case against the targeted cult and implore social workers and state agents to act against the group to protect children from alleged abuse or prevent a host of putative atrocities (mass suicide, sexual abuse, forced labor, killings, beatings). Because minority faiths, seen as odd, strange, or deviant, often exist in a high level of tension with the host society, they are more vulnerable to these kinds of antisubversion campaigns and moral crusades. Thus the disfavored religious group "is likely to be confronted with unilateral, pre-emptive, coercive control measures" by a coalition of state and cultural opponents (Bromley 1998b, 24).

Apostates play a key role in the oppositional coalition by strategically lodging grievances and attempting to broaden personal disputes. Through appeals to sympathetic but ambitious news reporters they forge alliances and use print and electronic media to disseminate "victim" and "captivity" narratives (Wright 1998, 100) to a wider public. These narratives (with the help of anticult framing) cast members as victims of "brainwashing" or manipulative "mind-control" techniques, unable to exercise independent decision making or cognition. As such, believers are depicted by opponents as captives in need of "rescue" through coercive intervention by state control agencies. Apostates have some credibility and broad appeal in the eyes of the public because they can claim to have been insiders at one time. They can lay claim to describing their own experiences and observations, which appear to be objective and sincere. As research has shown, however, apostate narratives are hardly objective; they "consist of highly selective, idealized accounts of the lives of the people who write them" (Johnson 1998, 118). All biographies are edited narratives of achievement, or what Adams (1990) calls "private mythologies." Apostate accounts raise even more issues than do ordinary biographies regarding objectivity and impartiality. Apostates, by definition, refer to ex-members who have taken an adversarial posture. Indeed, Lewis Coser writes that the apostate is one "who, even in his new state of belief, is spiritually living not primarily in the content of that faith . . . *but only in the struggle against the old faith and for the sake of its negation*" (emphasis mine; quoted in Johnson 1998, 119).

Anticult organizations and actors are typically at the leading edge of the oppositional coalition and critical to understanding both how public perceptions of exaggerated threat about new or minority religions have developed and how these perceptions translate into government raids. Because they tout themselves as "cult experts," anticult activists are often invited to appear on television or be interviewed by print journalists, ostensibly as independent third parties, to confirm and support the narratives, when they are in fact part of the oppositional coalition. In turn, these claims-making activities by opponents are aimed at increasing public pressure on authorities to take punitive measures against the "cult." NRMs are susceptible to pressures because they face obstacles of widespread and socially embedded cult stereotypes as well as a dearth of institutional allies to come to their defense. Research suggests that a large portion of the U.S. population harbors deep suspicions about new or minority religions (Bromley and Breshel 1992; Olsen 2006). "The result," according to Bromley (1998, 24), "is a dispute broadening process that incorporates a range of organizational attributes and practices as external control organizations define their missions in terms of repressing such groups, operate with numerous allies, and face few restraints."

Hall and Schuyler (1998, 142) have aptly described the configuration of antagonists as one that seeks "to control 'cults' through loosely institutionalized, emergent, oppositional alliances." These alliances are typically crystallized by

> (1) cultural opponents of deviant groups, especially apostates and distraught relatives of members, . . . (2) news reporters who frame cult stories in terms of moral deviance; and (3) modern governments that have incorporated the "religious" interest in enforcing cultural legitimacy into a state interest in monopolizing political legitimacy.

The "culture work" or "frame alignment" (Snow et al. 1986; Snow and Benford 1992; McAdam, Tarrow, and Tilly 2001) carried out by counter-movement activists to define the minority religion as a "subversive" organization draws in state actors who are invested in reinforcing the established social order. Hall and Schuyler (1998) argue that, in modern states where the institutional power of churches tends to wane, states increasingly act as their surrogates in enforcing the boundaries of cultural legitimacy. As such, oppositional coalitions are formed between cult opponents and state agents with this common interest in mind. State agents join the antisubversion campaign claiming state interest in quelling a subversive organization and employing an anticult framing of the problem to justify their actions.

New or minority religions tend to have little institutional support and are confronted usually with a broad alliance of antagonists and foes. Fortunately, however, in democratic countries with strong civil and human rights traditions, key organizations may serve as "intermediate" groups (scholars, civil liberties organizations, interfaith or ecumenical organizations) that can curb, temper, or correct the inflated and embellished claims of anticult actors and oppositional coalitions (see Wright 2002). Scholars who have conducted firsthand research on the religious groups in question, for example, can provide empirical studies that contradict the overstated claims of oppositional coalitions. Civil liberties organizations can remind authorities of constitutional guarantees of religious freedom and provide examples of case law and even prior incidents of violations that were taken up by the courts. Interfaith or ecumenical organizations and leaders can puncture inflated claims by exposing the religious bigotry often underlying attacks on new or minority religions. When intermediate groups are included in the loop of consideration of claims by opponents and allowed to have a voice in the decision-making process of authorities, different outcomes can be expected (Wright 2002) and raids are much less likely to occur. Indeed, in reducing the risk of state raids (and the potential for subsequent violence), intermediate groups serve two functions. First, when intermediate groups counteract the control of information by oppositional alliances, this will likely have the effect of *preempting* unwarranted, aggressive state actions. Second, to the degree that new or minority religions enjoy institutional allies in disputes and conflicts (i.e., intermediate groups), they will likely exhibit more confidence in the ability of governments to settle them peacefully, even after an aggressive state action has taken place. If and when intermediate groups or their representatives are brought into the dispute-settlement process, new or unconventional religions will be more likely to hold out hope for a peaceful resolution (Wright 2002, 118).

At the same time, evidence in some state raids, such as the federal raid on the Branch Davidians outside Waco, suggests that ACM actors and apostates deliberately advised and persuaded federal authorities (the ATF) to *avoid* contacting or listening to groups or people who would offer contravening evidence, alleging that such groups were secretly conspiring to help the NRM (Wright 1995b, 86). The circumvention of intermediate groups, or any group for that matter, providing countervailing evidence to exaggerated ACM claims will almost assuredly result in a grossly distorted, one-sided narrative. Government agencies must not be complicit in the antisubversion campaigns of reactionary groups with political motives, and it must certainly consider all sources of evidence before taking dangerous, high-risk enforcement actions such as raids against religious communities.

Conclusion

This chapter began by asking why authorities in Texas were so swift to accept the abuse claims of a single caller to a domestic shelter hotline in San Angelo, apparently making no attempt to corroborate the authenticity of the complainant or the details of her story, mobilizing extensive resources and joint-agency personnel to mount a massive raid on the FLDS in Eldorado in 2008. That state officials would act in this irresponsible and puzzling manner with so little evidence requires explanation. The chapter concludes that child welfare officials, state police, and other moral gatekeepers already concerned about the perceived threat posed by the new FLDS community in West Texas and its polygamous practices were more inclined to believe sensational claims about the sect. In most instances, claims against "cults" are easily marshaled and tend to proliferate rapidly. Evidence reveals that DFPS officials and other child protection workers in Texas were in contact with "cult experts," anticult movement actors, and FLDS apostates, and had adopted an anticult framing of the problem. State authorities came to accept uncritically allegations targeting the FLDS that played to the worst cult stereotypes and atrocity tales. This, in turn, contributed to the perception of an exaggerated threat by authorities resulting in an ill-advised government siege on a stigmatized minority religious community.

This chapter delineates how the imminent "threat" of the FLDS was constructed, identifies components of the oppositional alliance, and explains how and why the imprudent government raid on the FLDS materialized. The lineaments of this oppositional network formed in ways that reflect other incidents in which new or minority religions have been targeted in raids, suggesting a recurrent pattern. This recurrent pattern is briefly outlined in the chapter and serves as a model to evaluate and conduct comparative analyses of other state raids on NRMs. I contend that in the FLDS case ACM actors, apostates, child protection workers, and other cultural opponents of the fundamentalist Mormons seized upon a political opportunity to advance an agenda (i.e., expose the danger of cults) by offering up a dubious 911 call as proof of cult child abuse. An oppositional coalition was mobilized for action, based on faulty and unreliable evidence, but firmly rooted in the cultural belief that abuse is pervasive in "cults." So the caller's allegations were not questioned, nor did authorities make adequate efforts to substantiate them; they did not need substantiation. The allegations neatly conformed to preconceived ideas about "cults" and conveniently confirmed what opponents already knew to be true. Moreover, anticult and apostate claims as to the highly organized criminal enterprise allegedly undertaken by the FLDS (Jessop and Brown 2009), or even the "terrorist" label applied to this polygamist community (Heller 2004), significantly elevated the threat level and gave credence to an extreme enforcement action such as a government raid. In the end, a less dangerous and less elaborate method of enforcement was not taken by Texas officials against the group because the inflated claims of organized opponents were believed.

NOTES

1. I am defining "raid" as "a sudden incursion or surprise attack by a small force of law enforcement agents."

REFERENCES

Adams, Brooke. 2008. Are 'Polygamy" and "Cult" Synonymous? Accessed online at http://blogs.sltrib.com/plurallife/archives/2008_06_01_archive.htm.
———. 2009. "Listening to the Lord: Jeffs Exerted 42-7 control over FLDS Faithful." *Salt Lake City Tribune*, March 5.
Adams, Timothy. 1990. *Telling Lies in Modern American Autobiography*. Chapel Hill: University of North Carolina Press.
Anthony, Paul. A. 2005. "Shrouded in Secrecy: Former Members of Eldorado Sect Speak of Abusive, Closed Society, Fanaticism," *San Angelo Standard-Times*, March 27. Accessed online at http://nl.newsbank.com/nl-search/we/Archives?
Barker, Eileen. 1988. "Defection from the Unification Church: Some Statistics and Distinctions," pp. 166–84 in David G. Bromley (ed.), *Falling from the Faith*. Newbury Park, CA: Sage.
Best, Joel. 1990. *Threatened Children*. Chicago: University of Chicago Press.
Bradley, Martha Sonntag. 1993. *Kidnapped from That Land: The Government Raids on the Short Creek Polygamists*. Salt Lake City: University of Utah.

Bradney, Anthony. 1999. "Children of a Newer God: The English Courts, Custody Disputes, and NRMs," pp. 210–26 in Susan J. Palmer and Charlotte Hardmann (eds.), *Children in New Religions*. New Brunswick, NJ: Rutgers University Press.

Bromley, David G. 1982. *Strange Gods: The Great American Cult Scare*. Boston: Beacon.

——. 1998a. *The Politics of Religious Apostasy*. Westport, CT: Praeger.

——. 1998b. "The Social Construction of Contested Exit Roles: Defectors, Whistle-blowers, and Apostates," pp. 19–48 in David G. Bromley (ed.), *The Politics of Religious Apostasy*. Westport, CT: Praeger.

Bromley, David G. and Edward Breschel. 1992. "General Populations and Institutional Elite Support for Social Control of New Religious Movements: Evidence from National Survey Data." *Behavioral Sciences and the Law* 10 (1): 39–52.

Bromley, David G., and Diana Gay Cutchin. 1999. "The Social Construction of Subversive Evil: The Contemporary Anti-Cult and Anti-Satanism Movements," pp. 195–220 in Jo Freeman (ed.), *Waves of Protest*. Lanham, MD: Rowman and Littlefield.

Bromley, David G., Anson D. Shupe, and G. C. Ventimiglia. 1979. "Atrocity Tales, the Unification Church, and the Social Construction of Evil." *Journal of Communication* (summer): 42–53.

Brown, J. David. 1996. "The Professional Ex-: An Alternative for Exiting the Deviant Career," pp. 439–47 in Earl Rubington and Martin Weinburg (eds.), *Deviance: The Interactionist Perspective*. Boston: Allyn & Bacon.

Bryner, Jeanna. 2008. "Texas Group: Religious Sect or Cult?" MSNBC.com, April 9. Accessed online at www.msnbc.com/id/24032149/print/1/dsiplamode/1098.

Cohen, Stanley. 1972. *Folk Devils and Moral Panics*. New York: St. Martin's.

Coleman, Lee. 1994. "Declaration of Lee Coleman, M.D.," December 13. Submitted to the New South Wales Supreme Court. Document on file with author.

Ellison, Christopher G., and John P. Bartkowski. 1995. "'Babies Were Being Beaten': Exploring Child Abuse Allegations at Ranch Apocalypse," pp. 111–52 in Stuart A. Wright (ed.), *Armageddon in Waco*. Chicago: University of Chicago Press.

Galanter, Marc. 1989. *Cults, Faith, Healing, and Coercion*. New York: Oxford University Press.

Goldman, Miriam. 1995. "Continuity in Collapse: Departures from Shiloh." *Journal for the Scientific Study of Religion* 34 (3): 342–53.

Goode, Erich, and Nachman Ben-Yehuda. 1994. *Moral Panics: The Construction of Deviance*. Cambridge, MA: Blackwell.

Gunn, Jeremy. 2000. "Discrimination on the Basis of Religion and Belief in Western Europe." Testimony before the House International Relations Committee, U.S. House of Representatives, June 14.

Gusfield, Joseph R. 1963. *Symbolic Crusade: Status Politics and the American Temperance Movement*. Urbana: University of Illinois Press.

Hall, John R. 1995. "Public Narratives and the Apocalyptic Sect: From Jonestown to Mt. Carmel, pp. 205–35 in Stuart A. Wright (ed.), *Armageddon in Waco*. Chicago: University of Chicago Press.

Hall, John R., and Philip Schuyler. 1998. "Apostasy, Apocalypse, and Religious Violence: An Explanatory Comparison of Peoples Temple, the Branch Davidians, and the Solar Temple," pp. 141–70 in David G. Bromley (ed.), *The Politics of Religious Apostasy*. Westport, CT: Praeger.

Hall, Stuart, Chris Critcher, Tony Jefferson, John Clarke, and Brian Roberts. 1978. *Policing the Crisis: Mugging, the State, and Law and Order*. London: Macmillan.

Hassan, Steven. 1988. *Combating Cult Mind Control*. Rochester, VT: Park Street.

Heller, Matthew. 2004. "Flora's War: Flora Jessop Knows What It's Like to Flee an Insular and Polygamous World." *Los Angeles Times Magazine*, August 1.

Interview with Linda Werlien. 2008. Transcript on file with author.

Introvigne, Massimo. 2000. "Moral Panics and Anti-Cult Terrorism in Western Europe." *Terrorism and Political Violence* 12:47–59.

———. 2001. "Blacklisting or Greenlisting? A European Perspective on the New Cult Wars." *Nova Religio* 2:16–23.

Jenkins, Phillip. 1992. *Intimate Enemies: Moral Panics in Contemporary Great Britain*. New York: Aldine de Gruyter.

———. 1998. *Moral Panics: Changing Concepts of the Child Molester in Modern America*. New Haven, CT: Yale University Press.

Jessop, Carol, with Laura Palmer. 2008. *Escape*. New York: Broadway Books.

Jessop, Flora, and Paul T. Brown. 2009. *Church of Lies*. New York: Jossey-Bass.

Johnson, Daniel Carson. 1998. "Apostates Who Never Were: The Social Construction of *Absque Facto* Narratives," pp. 115–38 in David G. Bromley (ed.), *The Politics of Religious Apostasy*. Westport, CT: Praeger.

Karlsen, Carol. 1987. *The Devil in the Shape of a Woman*. New York: Norton.

Levine, Saul. 1984. *Radical Departures*. New York: Harcourt, Brace Jovanovich.

Lewis, James R. 1986. "Reconstructing the 'Cult' Experience." *Sociological Analysis* 40:197–207.

———. 1989. "Apostates and the Legitimation of Repression: Some Historical and Empirical Perspectives on the Cult Controversy." *Sociological Analysis* 49:386–96.

McAdam, Doug, Sidney Tarrow, and Charles Tilly. 2001. *Dynamics of Contention*. Cambridge: Cambridge University Press.

Moore, Laurence R. 1986. *Religious Outsiders and the Making of America*. New York: Oxford University Press.

Newsome, Brian. 2008. "Springs Woman Suspected of Hoax Call Says Father Abused Her." *Colorado Springs Gazette*, April 21. Accessed online at http:www.gazette.com.

Nicholas, Grace. 1999. "Seizure of Sect Children Ruled Unlawful." *Sydney Morning Herald*, April 1.

Olsen, Paul J. 2006. "The Public Perception of 'Cults' and New Religious Movements," *Journal for the Scientific Study of Religion* 45 (1): 97–106.

Original Petition for Protection of Children in an Emergency and for Conservatorship in Suit Affecting the Parent-Child Relationship, In the Interest of 330 Children from the YFZ Ranch. 2008. District Court of Schleicher County, Texas, 51st Judicial District, Cause 2902, April 7.

Palmer, Susan J. 1998. "Apostates and Their Role in the Construction of Grievance Claims against the Northeast Kingdom/Messianic Communities," pp. 191–208 in David G. Bromley (ed.), *The Politics of Religious Apostasy*. Westport, CT: Praeger.

———. 2010. *The Nuwaubian Nation: Black Spirituality and State Control*. Surrey, UK: Ashgate.

———. 2011. *The New Heretics of France*. New York: Oxford University Press.

Perry, Bruce. 1994. "Destructive Childrearing Practices by the Children of God." Report to the Health and Community Services, Melbourne, Australia, March 28. Document on file with author.

Perry, Bruce, and Maia Szalavitz. 2007. "Stairway to Heaven: Treating Children in the Crosshairs of Trauma." *International Cultic Studies Association E-Newsletter* 6 (3). Accessed online at http:www.icsahome.com/infoserve_articles/perry_szalavitz_trauma_en0603.htm.

Pfiefer, Jeffrey E. 1992. "The Psychological Framing of Cults: Schematic Representations and Cult Evaluations." *Journal of Applied Psychology* 22:531–44.

Phinney, Matt. 2005. "Religious Sect Out in Eldorado Causing Unrest in the Community," *San Angelo Standard-Times,* March 27. Accessed online at http://nl.newsbank.com/nl-search/we/Archives?

"Phone Number Could Tie Colorado Woman to Calls Sparking Raid of Polygamist Sect." 2008. Fox News, April 23. Accessed online at http://www.FoxNews.com.

"Polygamist Sect Kids to Undergo DNA Tests." 2008. CBS News, April 18. Accessed online at http://cbsnews.com/stories/2008/04/18/national/.

Richardson, James T. 1991. "Cult/Brainwashing Cases and the Freedom of Religion." *Journal of Church and State* 33:55–74.

———. 1993. "Definitions of Cult: From Sociological-Technical to Popular Negative." *Review of Religious Research* 34 (4): 348–56.

———. 1998. "Apostates, Whistleblowers, Law, and Social Control," pp. 171–90 in David G. Bromley (ed.), *The Politics of Religious Apostasy*. Westport, CT: Praeger.

———. 1999. "Social Control of New Religions: From Brainwashing Claims to Child Sex Abuse Accusations," pp. 172–86 in Susan J. Palmer (ed.), *Children in New Religions*. New Brunswick, NJ: Rutgers University Press.

Richardson, James T., David G. Bromley, and Joel Best. 1991. *The Satanism Scare*. New York: Aldine de Gruyter.

Richardson, James T., and Massimo Introvigne, 2001. "'Brainwashing' Theories in European Parliamentary and Administrative Reports on 'Cults' and 'Sects.'" *Journal for the Scientific Study of Religion* 40:143–68.

———. 2007. "New Religious Movements, Countermovements, Moral Panics, and the Media," pp. 91–111 in David Bromley (ed.), *Teaching New Religious Movements*. Oxford: Oxford University Press.

Rizzo, Russ, and Pamela Manson. 2008. "Texas FLDS Case: Was Massive Raid Based on Bogus Call from Colorado Woman?" *Salt Lake Tribune*, April 4. Accessed online at http://sltrib.com.

Robbins, Thomas. 1988. *Cults, Converts, and Charisma*. Newbury Park, CA: Sage.

Shupe, Anson D., and David G. Bromley. 1994. *Anti-Cult Movements in Cross-Cultural Perspective*. New York: Garland.

Shupe, Anson D., and Susan Darnell. 2006. *Agents of Discord: Deprogrammers, Pseudo-Science, and the American Anticult Movement*. New Brunswick, NJ: Transaction.

Smith, John L. 2008. "Affidavits Paint a Disturbing Picture of Texas Child Protective Services." *Las Vegas Review Journal*, June 3. Accessed online at http://www.reviewjournal.com.

Snow, David A., and Robert D. Benford. 1992. "Master Frames and Cycles of Protest," pp. 133–55 in Aldon D. Morris and Carol McClurg Mueller (eds.), *Frontiers in Social Movement Theory*. New Haven, CT: Yale University Press.

Snow, David A., E. Burke Rochford, Steven Worden, and Robert D. Benford. 1986. "Frame Alignment Processes, Micromobilization, and Movement Participation," *American Sociological Review* 51:468–81.

Spector, Malcolm, and John Kitsuse. 1987. *Constructing Social Problems*. New York: Aldine de Gruyter.

Swantko, Jean. 2004. "The Twelve Tribe Messianic Communities, the Anti-cult Movement, and Government Response," pp. 179–200 in James T. Richardson (ed.), *Regulating Religion*. New York: Kluwer.

Taslimi, Cheryl, Ralph Hood, and P. J. Watson. 1991. "Assessment of Former Members of Shiloh." *Journal for the Scientific Study of Religion* 30: 306–11.

Wessinger, Catherine. Forthcoming. "'Cults' in America: Discourse and Outcomes," in Stephen Stein (ed.), *History of Religions in America*. New York: Cambridge University Press.

Wright, Stuart A. 1984. "Post-Involvement Attitudes of Voluntary Defectors from New Religious Movements." *Journal for the Scientific Study of Religion* 23 (2):172–82.

———. 1987. *Leaving Cults: The Dynamics of Defection*. Washington, DC: Society for the Scientific Study of Religion.

———. 1988. "Leaving New Religious Movements: Issues, Theory, and Research," pp. 143–65 in David G. Bromley (ed.), *Falling from the Faith*. Newbury Park, CA: Sage.

———. 1995a. *Armageddon in Waco: Critical Perspectives on the Branch Davidian Conflict*. Chicago: University of Chicago Press.

———. 1995b. "Construction and Escalation of a 'Cult' Threat: Dissecting Moral Panic and Official Reaction to the Branch Davidians," pp. 75–94 in Stuart A. Wright (ed.), *Armageddon in Waco*. Chicago: University of Chicago Press.

———. 1998. "Exploring Factors That Shape the Apostate Role," pp. 95–114 in David G. Bromley (ed.), *The Politics of Religious Apostasy*. Westport, CT: Praeger.

———. 2002. "Public Agency Involvement in Government-Religious Movement Confrontations," pp. 102–22 in David G. Bromley and J. Gordon Melton (eds.), *Cults, Religion, and Violence*. New York: Cambridge University Press.

———. (Forthcoming). "Disengagement and Apostasy in New Religious Movements," in Lewis Rambo and Charles Farhadian (eds.), *The Oxford Handbook on Religious Conversion*. New York: Oxford University Press.

Wright, Stuart A., and Helen Rose Ebaugh. 1993. "Leaving New Religions," pp. 117–38 in David G. Bromley and Jeffrey K. Hadden (eds.), *The Handbook on Cults and Sects in America*. Vol. 3, pt. B. Westport, CT: JAI.

Zelizer, Viviana A. 1985. *Pricing the Priceless Child: The Changing Social Value of Children*. New York: Basic Books.

6

Texas Redux

A Comparative Analysis of the FLDS and
Branch Davidian Raids

STUART A. WRIGHT AND
JENNIFER LARA FAGEN

In the initial days after the Texas state raid, in 2008, on the Fundamentalist Church of Jesus Christ of Latter Day Saints (FLDS) in Eldorado, some observers invoked a comparison with the disastrous federal raid on the Branch Davidians outside Waco fifteen years earlier. Although the raids had some ostensible similarities, the differences were obvious, primarily the absence of a shootout, standoff, or any violent confrontation between sect and state in the FLDS raid. The comparison with the 1993 Waco raid quickly faded as news stories focused on the fate of more than four hundred FLDS children taken into custody by the Texas Department of Family and Protective Services (DFPS). A few weeks after the raid, the Texas Appeals Court overturned the District Court's decision to allow mass custodial detention of the children (see Shreinert and Richardson, this volume, for a critical analysis). The Texas Supreme Court upheld the Appellate Court's decision forcing the state to release the children back into the custody of the FLDS parents. The Court's ruling declaring the actions of the state illegal further strained any comparison to the Waco raid, given the very different outcomes of the two incidents. In effect, the FLDS had achieved a partial victory in the courts, whereas the Branch Davidian community was utterly destroyed by the federal siege, leaving eighty-two sect members dead in its wake (Wright 1995a). A closer examination of the events surrounding the Eldorado raid, however, reveal some alarming and substantial similarities with the Waco raid that invite a more intensive comparison.

Herein we offer a focused and in-depth comparative analysis of the two raids. There are striking parallels in terms of process and structure that have not been acknowledged or fully understood. The two raids share important commonalities and features, particularly the development and mobilization of organized opponents of the religious groups in question, and the formation of alliances with state actors to launch unilateral enforcement operations. Indeed, the same social and organizational dynamics can be found in the planning and execution of the two raids, and even some of the same people. Though news media and critics have offered superficial comparisons, we contend that the similarities are robust and reveal disturbing patterns of state and countermovement actions against minority religions.

A Comparative Analysis of the Raids

The lineaments of the oppositional coalition of apostates, ACM organizations and actors, media, and government officials have been described separately in the Waco case (Wright 1995b) and in the Eldorado case (Wright, this volume). Here we conduct a comparative analysis by highlighting the similarities between the two raid incidents. Before proceeding, a brief overview of the federal raid on the Branch Davidians is in order.

The 1993 raid against the Branch Davidians, carried out by the U.S. Bureau of Alcohol, Tobacco, Firearms and Explosives (ATF), was the result of an investigation of firearms violations against the sect and, more specifically, against its leader, David Koresh, who was the only person named in the arrest warrant. In June 1992 a package delivered by the United Parcel Service (UPS) to the Davidians's property outside Waco broke open and revealed empty pineapple grenade shells.[1] The UPS driver reported the discovery to the county sheriff Jack Harwell, who passed on the information to the ATF. The ATF initiated an investigation a few weeks later. A key issue on which the case turned was whether some of the Davidians were converting legal semiautomatic weapons into illegal automatic weapons in a machine shop. The Davidians were purchasing semiautomatic weapons wholesale and selling them retail at gun shows. The ATF accused the Davidians of "stockpiling weapons" in preparation for a possible conflict with the U.S. government. Because ATF officials obtained their intelligence on the sect almost exclusively from apostates and ACM actors, they garnered an exaggerated and overly sinister image of the group. Later research suggests that ATF investigators believed that the Davidians were tied to the violent Posse Comitatus and Christian Identity movements (Wright 2005), but the Davidians had no such ties. On February 28, 1993, the ATF launched a paramilitary raid on the Mt. Carmel residence of the Davidians. Eighty paramilitary-trained Special Response Team (SRT) agents hidden in the back of two cattle trailers pulled onto the property and executed what was thought to be a surprise attack. But the ATF's own informant inside Mt. Carmel learned just minutes before that Koresh and the Davidians were aware of the raid. The informant, Robert Rodriguez, contacted the SRT leaders and told them to call off the raid, but the commanders decided to go forward anyway. Two SRT members assigned to the "dog team" fired the first shots, killing the Davidians's dogs and sparking a shootout that lasted several hours. As a result, four ATF agents and six Davidians were mortally wounded. The FBI's counterterrorism unit, the Hostage Rescue Team (HRT), was called in the next day to take over the operation. This ordeal began a fifty-one-day standoff in which more than eight hundred federal, state, and military personnel were at one time on site outside Waco. Although twenty-eight Branch Davidians voluntarily exited the Mt. Carmel residence during crisis negotiations, communication eventually broke down and federal officials used the impasse to justify a violent assault. On the fifty-first day of the standoff, the HRT launched a CS gas attack using M728 Combat Engineering Vehicles to breach the building and force sect members out. Six hours into the siege the building exploded into a fiery inferno killing seventy-six men, women, and children.[2] It was the deadliest federal law enforcement disaster in U.S. history.

In the following section we discuss the parallels in the two cases outlined in Table 6.1. The structural features of the comparative analysis include ACM activists, apostates, media, state agents, and claims. By grounding the analysis in common structural features we hope to show just how similar these events were. Here we explore how these same features played a role in the development, execution, and post-raid management of the enforcement operations in both instances, yielding similar and predictable patterns.

ACM Activists

Anticult movement activists played a key role in both government raids. Rick Ross a former deprogrammer, prominent ACM activist, and self-described "cult expert," was a key figure in the Waco Branch Davidian tragedy and, as we shall see shortly, was also involved in the run-up to the Eldorado raid. Ross deprogrammed Branch Davidian David Block in the summer of 1992 at the home of Priscilla Coates, the national spokesperson for the ACM's Cult Awareness Network. Ross obtained information from Block about stored weapons on the Branch Davidian property and relayed this information to federal authorities. According to the Department of Treasury report in the aftermath of the raid, much of the ATF information about the sect's weapons "was based almost exclusively on the statement of one former cult member,

David Block" (U.S. Department of Treasury 1993:143). As the ATF's affidavit for the search and arrest warrant made clear, the charges against David Koresh related specifically to illegal weapons and contraband. The information supplied by Block through Ross, however, turned out to be incorrect. In a review of the ATF's actions, the Department of Treasury report criticized the agency's "failure to consider how Block's relations with Koresh . . . might have affected the reliability of his statements" (ibid.). According to Nancy Ammerman, who was asked by the Department of Justice to review the actions of federal law enforcement at Waco, Ross supplied the ATF with "all the information he had regarding the Branch Davidian cult" (Ammerman 1995, 286). She also states that the ATF "interviewed the persons [Ross] directed them to and evidently used information from those interviews in planning the February 28 raid" (ibid., 289).

This is further corroborated in Branch Davidian apostate Marc Breault's autobiographical account, *Inside the Cult*, leading up to the ATF raid. Breault initially learned about Ross from *Waco Tribune-Herald* reporter Mark England. Breault described his efforts to contact Ross and referred to the deprogrammer as someone who "has detailed information on cult awareness groups and cultbusters" (Breault and King 1993, 137). According to Breault, Ross knew that "something was about to happen real soon" on February 16, just two weeks before the ATF raid. Ross's advance knowledge of the ATF raid suggests that he had more than a peripheral role as an adviser.

Ammerman (1995) provides more information about Ross regarding the negotiations that took place during the fifty-one-day standoff. The FBI's crisis negotiators were working with the HRT and attempting to persuade the Davidians to surrender. She observes that while religious scholars and others were ignored, the negotiators "were still listening to Rick Ross."[3] She states:

> The FBI interview transcripts document that Ross was, in fact, closely involved with the ATF and the FBI. He talked with the FBI both in early March and in late March. He apparently had the most extensive access to both agencies of any person on the "cult expert" list and was listened to more attentively. (1995:289)

Ammerman goes on to describe Ross's possible influence on the FBI's decision-making on the ground:

> In late March, Ross recommended that agents attempt to humiliate Koresh, hoping to drive a wedge between him and his followers. While Ross's sug-

TABLE 6.1
A Comparison of Targeted Religious Communities

	Raided Groups	
Structural Features	*Branch Davidians*	*FLDS*
ACM Activists	Rick Ross	Rick Ross
	Bruce Perry	Bruce Perry
	Priscilla Coates	Janja Lalich
	Murray Miron	Andrea Moore-Emmett
Apostates	Marc Breault	Flora Jessop
	David Block	Carolyn Jessop
	David and Debbie Bunds	Becky Musser
	Robin Bunds	Ross Chatwin
Media	England and McCormick,	Anthony, San Angelo
	Waco Tribune Herald	*Standard-Times*
	Martin King, *A Current Affair*	*Eldorado Success*
State Agents	CPS	CPS/DFPS
	ATF	Texas Rangers
	FBI	State police
Claims	Child abuse	Child abuse
	Polygamy	Polygamy
	Underage marriage	Underage marriage
	Child rape	Child rape
	Slavery/servitude	Slavery/servitude
	"Cult"	"Cult"
	Stockpiling weapons	Stockpiling weapons
	"Brainwashing"	"Brainwashing"
	Terrorism	Terrorism
	Mass suicide/"another Jonestown"	Mass suicide/another Jonestown/another Waco

gestions may not have been followed to the letter, FBI agents apparently believed that their attempts to embarrass Koresh (talking about inconsistencies, lack of education, failures as prophet, and the like) would produce the kind of internal dissension Ross predicted. Because Ross had been successful in using such tactics on isolated and beleaguered members during deprogramming, he must have assumed that they would work en masse. Any student of group psychology could have dispelled that misapprehension. But the FBI was evidently listening more closely to these deprogramming-related strategies than to the counsel of scholars who might have explained the dynamics of a group under siege. (1995, 289)

Ross had a more indirect role in the raid at Eldorado. It appears that FLDS apostate Flora Jessop recommended Ross as a "cult expert" to the media and possibly government authorities in Texas. Jessop posts a link on her Help the Child Brides website to Ross's website, the Institute for the Study of Destructive Cults (as well as five other ACM organizations). In the first of a series of articles appearing in the *San Angelo Standard-Times* in March 2005, Ross is cited extensively alongside Jessop as an authority on the FLDS. Jessop and Ross feed off each other in the news story as a kind of dynamic duo to promote the anticult narrative. Ross is described in the report as a "New Jersey expert on fringe religious groups who has studied the FLDS for 20 years" (Anthony 2005, 2). The news reporter lends uncritical validation to Ross's feigned expertise, and then proceeds to report the inflated claims of the former deprogrammer comparing the FLDS to Jonestown and the FLDS leader Jeffs to Jim Jones. Jonestown, named after its leader Jim Jones, was the site of the People's Temple community in Guyana in which more than nine hundred people committed mass suicide in 1979.[4] The outlandish inference that the FLDS could be the next Jonestown, a group harboring thoughts of mass suicide, is made without any evidence but obviously intended to invite fear and spread public alarm.

John R. Hall (1995), in his excellent work on the Branch Davidian conflict, observes that this same "intrinsic narrative" was invoked at Waco by anticult actors, apostates, media, and federal agents. Intrinsic narratives refer to the "diverse stories that various social actors tell within emergent situations to which they are mutually oriented, but in different ways (1995, 206). This approach can "help show how cultural meanings become nuanced, shaded, interpreted, challenged, and otherwise reworked by participants, and how such meaning-shifts affect the course of unfolding events" (206). Koresh's opponents continually invoked the claim that the Branch Davidians were "another Jonestown" in a manner that actually shaped the course of events and influenced the way federal agents conducted the standoff and siege. Hall notes that the mass suicide discourse became a self-fulfilling prophecy carried out by federal agents acting, in part, on unreliable information and advice from Ross and other oppositional claimants. Ross's recommendation to federal agents during the standoff that they "drive a wedge between Koresh and his followers" (U.S. Department of Justice 1993, 129) in an attempt to humiliate him backfired. The psychological warfare or "stress escalation" strategy employed by the FBI's HRT only solidified the Davidians' resolve (Wright 1999, 46–47) and confirmed their worst fears: that this hostile government operation was a sign of the Endtime and that the Davidians might have to be martyred for their faith (Wessinger 2009).

That Ross would summon the same intrinsic narrative ("another Jonestown") at Eldorado that contributed to the deadly tragedy at Waco is deeply disturbing but not surprising. As in the Waco case, the objective was not to provide authorities with an accurate description of the FLDS but rather to inflate the putative threat posed by the group in order to press for coercive state action. To bolster the otherwise baseless mass suicide narrative, Ross infers that the FLDS members might kill themselves because they had been "brainwashed" by the cult leader. "There is [an] eerie quality" about them, Ross warned in the 2005 news interview, "what some would call brainwashing. Much of their value judgments and critical thinking is handed over to the leader" (Anthony 2005, 2).

ACM activist Andrea Moore-Emmett warned listeners of the *Paula Zahn Now* show on CNN as early as 2006 that the FLDS "expect to have a shootout, a bloodbath," invoking the Waco standoff. She further asserted that FLDS leader Jeffs was "armed" and "would like to be a martyr" (CNN.com Transcripts 2006). Moore-Emmett is a journalist based in Salt Lake City, the author of *God's Brothel* (2004), an adviser to the adversarial organization, Tapestry Against Polygamy, and a regular speaker at the annual meetings of the International Cultic Studies Association.

It is not known if the state authorities in Texas anticipated encountering a group capable of mass suicide or a shootout. But if they didn't, it was not because Jessop, Ross, Moore-Emmett, and others failed to try to make this argument. In an interview with a British newspaper in 2004, Jessop reinforced the mass suicide narrative: "They [FLDS members] are prepared to die for their leader, and that's exactly what is going to happen if American citizens choose not to show concern. These people are no different than suicide bombers in Iraq" ("We Fear Another Waco" 2004). When the state raid did not provoke a violent response, the mass suicide narrative subsided. But this did not prevent ACM actors from continuing to attack on other fronts. After the raid Ross was quoted in one news report as saying, "The level of harm done by polygamist groups is horrific . . . Out of all the groups called cults in North America that I've dealt with, some of the most horrific complaints of sexual and physical abuse have come from these polygamist groups" (Cross 2008).

Another ACM figure who appears in both the Waco and Eldorado cases is Bruce Perry. Perry's role in the Branch Davidian incident and one involving The Family International in Australia has already been described by Wright in chapter 5 of this volume. Perry assumed a similar role in the FLDS case. He was asked by DFPS, according to one news report, "to advise nearly 300 caseworkers in West Texas about what they're up against with the 416 children taken from a fundamentalist sect" (Langford 2008). The news report highlighted the comparison to Perry's work with the Branch Davidian children, suggesting that both groups of sect children were "deceptive." "When it came to responding to a question," Perry asserted, "the answers were purposely deceptive." "Sect children act cooperative but know how to dodge questions." Perry was also hired by DFPS officials to testify in support of state custody court hearings. Perry told the court that the sect's sheltered environment made members more "immature" than children in the outside world. He repeated the claim that the group was abusive and said that the children are "trained to be obedient and compliant" in an "authoritarian" culture (Sandberg and Langford 2008).

In the FLDS case, as in the prior cases, Perry offers as evidence of abuse the fact that the sect's children were nonresponsive, evasive, highly controlled, hypervigilant, and suspicious of caseworkers who questioned them. Apparently it did not occur to Perry that the same reactions would be expected of children removed by force from their family and community and placed in state custody. Another psychiatrist, Dr. Lee Coleman, who challenged Perry's boilerplate analysis of sect children years earlier, proved to be prescient in the FLDS case as well: "Dr. Perry may love 'Big Brother,' but that doesn't mean the children did. The children would certainly be aware of the fact their new caretakers were hostile to their parents and their community. Does Dr. Perry expect the children to smile and say "thank you?" (Coleman 1994, 5).

One other ACM activist deserves mentioning here. Janja Lalich is listed on the Cultic Research website (n.d.) as the "founder and director of the Center for Research on Influence and Control." Evidently she was recruited to assist caseworkers in the FLDS case (Adams 2009). Among other activities, Lalich "participated in a two-day training seminar for shelter providers and CPS workers involved in the YFZ [Yearning for Zion] Ranch case" (Adams 2008b). Lalich, a professor of sociology at California State University, Chico, has become an increasingly important figure in the ACM. Before advising and assisting child protection workers in San Angelo, Lalich was apparently convinced from interaction with apostates that the FLDS was "abusing hundreds and hundreds of women and children" (Bryner 2008; Adams 2008b). According to the ACM's online Apologetics Index (n.d.), Lalich's work has focused primarily on "abusive cults" and "post-cult counseling and therapy" in order to "encourage and assist those former cultists struggling to readjust to the 'real world.'" In the days following the state raid, Lalich echoed the comments of other ACM activists (Cross 2008; McLaughlin 2008), telling one news reporter that the group was definitely a "cult" ("lets say what it is") that treated women as "baby factories" (Bryner 2008). Lalich's comment was followed by Carolyn Jessop who warned, "Once you go into the compound, you don't ever leave it" (Bryner 2008). Lalich was also interviewed for the popular weekly magazine *People* and stated that the group bore "many of the earmarks" of a cult; the "followers' lives are strictly controlled," she said, "as is information from the outside society" ("Life in the Cult" 2008).

Apostates

The narratives of chief apostates Marc Breault (Branch Davidians) and Flora Jessop (FLDS) reveal similarities in the ways these claims-makers acted in concert with other oppositional allies to engage in deviance amplification. Since Breault and Jessop were the principal provocateurs who organized other apostates, the following section focuses more on these two key figures. But we also briefly discuss some other important figures as they help to elucidate a common theme, namely, that some apostates have left "cults" under less than favorable conditions and have become involved in dispute broadening processes (Bromley 1998).

The allegations of child abuse in the Branch Davidian case were spearheaded by a group of apostates led by Marc Breault (Ellison and Bartkowski 1995; England and McCormick 1993; Wright 1995b). Breault and others pressured authorities in Texas to take action against Koresh and the Davidians. Breault contacted the FBI and ATF, hired a private investigator to collect damaging information on the sect, approached authorities in LaVerne, California, alleging statutory rape of young female adherents, and collaborated with *Waco Tribune-Herald* reporters on a scandalous seven-part news series on Koresh ("The Sinful Messiah"), among other things. He also contacted one sect member's estranged husband (David Jewell) alleging sexual abuse of his daughter by Koresh, and Breault served as a witness in the custody battle over the young girl (Wright 1995b, 84).

Largely as a result of this "cultbusting" activity (Breault and King 1993, 218), Breault was contacted by ATF special investigator Davy Aguilera in December 1992, approximately ten weeks before the raid, to obtain information about the Davidians (Breault and King 1993, 294). Breault became a primary source for the ATF and other federal and state agencies. Indeed, Breault boasts in his book that he received "almost daily phone calls . . . [from] senior officials of the United States Government, which included the BATF [Bureau of Alcohol, Tobacco, and Firearms], the FBI, Congress, the State Department and the Texas Rangers" (1993, 295).

Like Flora Jessop, Marc Breault provides extensive documentation of his anticult activity in his sensationalized autobiographical account (Breault and King 1993). Breault told ATF officials that David Koresh would not respond to a summons, would not permit a search of the Mt. Carmel property for illegal weapons, and that Koresh might kill others, order a mass suicide, or start a holy war if approached by law enforcement. By all available evidence from local law enforcement and authorities in Waco, Breault's claims were unfounded. McClennan County sheriff's department had good relations with the Davidians and visited Mt. Carmel on numerous occasions over the years without incident (Wright 1995b, 86). The former district attorney in Waco, Vic Feazell, who had some previous interaction with the Davidians, told reporters after the raid that "if they'd [the ATF] called and talked to them, the Davidians would've given them what they wanted" (Bragg 1993, 7A). Yet Breault's grossly inflated claims were received as factual evidence by ATF and even repeated later to media and congressional oversight committees as justification for the raid plan (Wright 1995b, 1999, 2005).

Other Davidian apostates played important roles as well. Debbie and David Bunds were expelled from Mt. Carmel in June 1990 for violating dietary restrictions. Soon after the expulsion, Breault contacted David Bunds and apparently "converted" him to the opposition. David Bunds subsequently persuaded his sister, Robyn Bunds, to leave the Davidians and encouraged her to contact Breault. Robyn Bunds had a son by Koresh and was one of his "spiritual wives." She later lodged a child abuse complaint against Koresh in LaVerne, California, in a custody battle for the child. The claims of child abuse made against Koresh appear to begin at this juncture. Eventually a group of former members solidified and leveled complaints against Koresh to authorities in California, Texas and Australia (Wright 1995b, 84–85).

By her own admission, Flora Jessop has been called "an apostate, vigilante, and crazy bitch" (Jessop and Brown 2009, 1). Jessop played an integral part in the FLDS raid in Eldorado, Texas. As a high-profile critic and anti-FLDS apostate, Jessop was the obvious choice to be contacted by the alleged sixteen-year-old "girl" (thirty-three-year-old Rozita Swinton). That Jessop took Swinton's word without question is not at all surprising, since the accusations of polygamy, underage marriage, and child rape were entirely consistent with Jessop's long-standing claims against the FLDS. Jessop's involvement in organizations such as the Child Protection Project and Help the Child Brides evidently provided her access to child protection officials as an "expert" on the subject of the FLDS. By all accounts, Jessop is the most important and vocal apostate in the moral campaign against the FLDS.

Jessop's relentless crusade seems not to have been assuaged by factual contradictions or inconvenient questions of legality. Even after authorities determined that the telephone call was a hoax, Jessop continued to legitimize her actions and those of the state. The following exchange between Jessop and Greta Van Susteren in an interview on Fox News (2009) illustrates this point.

> JESSOP: I'm still having a hard time wrapping my mind around the fact that it was a 33-year-old woman that was making these calls to me…They [Texas child protective authorities] still did the right thing, because what they found once they entered that compound was absolutely valid. The men inside the FLDS are predators.
>
> VAN SUSTEREN: Okay, so here's what I don't get. If it didn't add up to you . . . do you have any theory why it didn't add up to the Texas authorities before they went to a judge and got a warrant and went in? If you were suspicious, as a non-law enforcement [officer], why didn't they have some suspicion that this was a hoax?
>
> JESSOP: . . . I would like to point out that the system worked in this case. When—as hotlines get calls from children purporting to be abused, just as I do, it's not my responsibility and my job to decide whether those calls are legitimate.
>
> VAN SUSTEREN: No, it's the state's.
>
> JESSOP: The system absolutely worked . . . It's very unusual that a hoax is carried out to this proportion . . . in a little bit of a way, I wanted to give her [Swinton] a big hug because she's protected hundreds of children from the abuses, the widespread systematic abuses they were suffering in this group.

For Jessop, the moral logic of the campaign against the FLDS trumps all other legal and ethical issues. Jessop readily dismisses both her complicity in perpetrating the hoax calls and the state's failure to corroborate the credibility of the caller. Indeed, she praises the criminal actions of the emotionally disturbed Swinton because it essentially produced the outcome Jessop sought. Similarly, the "system worked," she claimed, despite the deficiencies in the cause of action and the courts' reversal of the detention of the FLDS children by the state.

It is revealing that criticism of Jessop is not limited to adversaries. Even some fellow critics of the FLDS view Jessop as an opportunist and "media hound." Vicky Prunty, of the Salt Lake City–based Tapestry against Polygamy, has criticized Jessop for "using FLDS girls as photo ops and for transporting them to a location more than four hundred miles from their homes." Another apostate, Bob Curran of the Help the Child Brides Center in St. George, Utah, which Jessop helped found, said about previous activities that he was fearful that "Flora Jessop's actions could result in kidnapping charges and place Help the Child Brides in further jeopardy" ("Blasphemous Backlash" 2004). Others have expressed concern that some of Jessop's allegations, such as the claim that the FLDS has a secret baby graveyard with two hundred buried bodies on its property, are baseless and wildly outrageous. This has not stopped Jessop from the frequent use of hyperbole, such as calling the FLDS "worse than terrorists" and comparing them to "Al Qaeda" (Heller 2004).

But Jessop has also cultivated a valuable social network of apostates, anticult actors, state officials, and media contacts in her campaign against the FLDS. Her websites for Help the Child Brides and the Child Protection Project reveal extensive links to other allied anticult actors and organizations. Jessop provides detailed descriptions of her crusade and the coalition of opponents she has built in her autobiography (Jessop and Brown 2009), lest her critics underestimate her. Her ties to state and local law enforcement in Arizona and Texas are identified, as is her connection to the Office of the State Attorney General in Utah.

Legal documents shed light on some of Jessop's zeal and fanaticism involving the FLDS. A motion filed by the attorneys of Warren Jeffs in the Superior Court of the State of Arizona illustrate Jessop's obsession with the media and her apparent need to prioritize media coverage over the welfare of FLDS children. Attorneys took issue with Jessop's opportunistic use of a deposition as a "publicity stunt," bringing her own filming crew to the deposition.

Ms. Jessop is clearly a material witness for the purpose of Rule 15.3 because, among other reasons, she was in constant contact with the woman believed to have made the hoax phone call to authorities in Texas, leading to the raid of the FLDS property in Texas that is the subject of the defendant's motion to suppress. Ms. Jessop's interview is necessary to explore the degree of her involvement and knowledge of the hoax . . . In a case where this Court has already prohibited cameras from the courtroom in order to mitigate against unwarranted pretrial publicity, Ms. Jessop's publicity stunt is clearly an unacceptable condition to her Rule 15 interview.

The *Phoenix New Times* . . . has stated that Ms. Jessop's "tactics which center on manipulating the press and government officials with half-truths have become increasingly reckless" ["Too Little too Late" 2004]. The article notes that "Jessop used [purported victims of the FLDS] as props in a media campaign that included prominent photographs of the teens and Jessop in newspapers, magazines and television" [ibid.]. The article quotes Arizona Attorney General Terry Goddard as stating that Ms. Jessop's conduct "has destroyed her credibility." The article also describes Ms. Jessop as "misguided," "devious," and "unethical." . . . Apparently, it is Ms. Jessop's desire to turn her Rule 15 interview into "the Jerry Springer Show." The only possible result of Ms. Jessop's latest publicity stunt is to generate adverse publicity to prejudice the defendant in the local media, and possibly on the national level. ("Motion for the Deposition of Flora Jessop" 2008, 2–4).

Rule 15 of the Arizona Rules of Criminal Procedure authorizes the court to order the deposition of a material witness who refuses to cooperate in granting an interview. Jessop, forced to comply with the court's Rule 15 and the defense attorneys' request, "arrived at the interview with her own television reporter and television cameraman and insisted that her interview be covered and filmed by media personnel of her own choosing" ("Motion for the Deposition of Flora Jessop" 2008, 2). Defense attorneys objected to the choreographed media spectacle, requesting the court to constrain Ms. Jessop's antics. Jessop's contempt for the appropriate legal protocols shocked attorneys and observers. In spite of Jessop's history of outrageous statements, questionable actions, and opportunistic machinations, however, she has developed considerable understanding of how to use the media for her own purposes, as she chronicles in her book (Jessop and Brown 2009). She has been remarkably effective in framing a narrative of victimization and disseminating her story for public consumption that defines the FLDS in largely unfavorable and predatory terms.

Other important FLDS apostates include Carolyn Jessop, Rebecca Musser, and Ross Chatwin. Carolyn Jessop has been a high-profile figure in the media coverage surrounding the raid. Her autobiographical account of life in the FLDS, aptly titled *Escape* (Jessop and Palmer 2008), provided her with credibility about the group for news reporters. She has been a persistent and outspoken critic of the FLDS for years. She also took an active role in the attempted rehabilitation of the YFZ children while they were in state custody and assisted caseworkers in San Angelo in the aftermath of the raid (Adams 2008b; Jessop and Palmer 2008, 419). In the weeks following the raid, she frequently appeared on television giving interviews and retelling her story about the "escape."

Rebecca Musser is the older sister of Elissa Wall, another apostate and outspoken critic who wrote the book, *Stolen Innocence* (2008). Musser was married to Rulon Jeffs in her late teens and evidently was pressured to marry Warren Jeffs after Rulon's death. She refused the marriage and eventually left the group. Musser formed a close relationship with Shleicher County Sheriff David Doran in the months leading up to the raid and was accused of helping law enforcement obtain a search warrant to raid the YFZ Ranch. Doran denied the charge, saying only that he "networked with Becky, she is not my confidential informant" (Perkins 2008). Doran went on to tell reporters that "Becky helped us with questions concerning this group that would assist law enforcement" and that "she assisted child protection services with their investigations" (Perkins, 2008). Musser also became an expert witness for the state in the prosecution of FLDS defendants charged with sexual assault. One defense attorney for the FLDS described her as "a very effective witness."[5]

Ross Chatwin is a disgruntled apostate who was expelled from the FLDS and became embroiled in a property battle with the group over the ownership of his home.[6] A few years prior to the YFZ raid, Ross Chatwin was described by one news media source as the "most visible rebel" contesting the FLDS, denouncing Warren Jeffs and likening him to Adolf Hitler ("We Fear Another Waco" 2004). Chatwin also accused the FLDS leader of brainwashing, rape, murder through a "blood atonement" doctrine, stockpiling weapons in a tightly guarded cave, and using twenty-four-hour video surveillance to control members, among other things. Chatwin became a popular figure sought out by the media after the Texas raid, granting interviews, expressing grievances, and pressing claims against the FLDS (Hunsicker 2008; Winslow 2008).

Media

Media sources played a critical role in promoting the claims of apostates and opponents of the two religious groups. In the Branch Davidian case, chief apostate Marc Breault formed a partnership with an Australian TV reporter for *A Current Affair*, Martin King, to target David Koresh through a carefully calculated media exposé. Breault would later declare in his autobiographical account that the objective of this "secret agenda" was to "expose him [Koresh] as a sex-crazed despot" (Breault and King 1993, 256). Relying on Breault as a confidant and adviser, King conducted and filmed interviews with nine Davidian apostates in December 1991 and later with Koresh in January 1992. The interviews were subsequently edited and shown on Australian television in a program that ran for four nights, from April 15 to April 18, 1992, casting the Davidians as a "dangerous cult" and lodging a litany of claims against Koresh, including child abuse, sexual abuse, and brainwashing. Simultaneously the *Herald Sun*, an Australian newspaper, covered the story in print. Breault then sent copies of the news coverage and the filmed show to allied opponents and authorities in the United States.

Not coincidentally, the *Waco Tribune-Herald* began its investigation of the Davidians the following month, in May 1992. The connection between Breault and *Waco Tribune-Herald* reporter Mark England is chronicled in Breault's book. The seven-part series *The Sinful Messiah*, published by the Waco paper only days before the federal raid, depicted Koresh as a crazed cult leader who brainwashed his followers. The reporting relied heavily on Breault's own framing of events, exhibiting a striking similarity to the lurid paperback. The report cited Breault as a source and quoted him numerous times throughout the series. The day after the raid, England and fellow reporter Darlene McCormick ran an article titled "Experts: Branch Davidians Dangerous, Destructive Cult," which relied exclusively on Ross and other key ACM figures to frame the group in the most threatening terms (McCormick and England 1993). The allegations instigated by Ross, Breault, and allied opponents were treated uncritically as fact by Waco journalists, and then became sources for state agents in public claims against the group, particularly after the raid on Mt. Carmel (Richardson 1995; Shupe and Hadden 1995; Wright 1995b).

In a similar fashion the *San Angelo Standard-Times* gave Flora Jessop considerable coverage and voice in her campaign against the FLDS as early as 2005. Jessop explicitly acknowledges this successful foray in her book, stating that "the local papers started interviewing me for a series of stories they were writing on the FLDS compound" (Jessop and Brown 2009, 450). She recounts how she held press conferences, contacted news editors and other reporters, regaling them with stories "about sexual abuse, forced marriages, child abuse, tax evasion, welfare fraud and child labor" (Jessop and Brown 2009, 451). Indeed, the San Angelo paper published a series of news stories in 2005 quoting Jessop extensively (Anthony 2005; Phinney 2005). Jessop also put reporters in contact with a key anticultist, Rick Ross, who was also interviewed and quoted in the news series, alleging brainwashing and potential mass suicide at the YFZ Ranch (Anthony 2005).

Jessop's inflated perception of threat became part of the larger public narrative, engendering a hostile climate for the FLDS and increasing pressure on authorities to take action. Jessop continued to be a primary news source for the local paper in the years leading up to the raid and, after the siege, she was a popular source for national and international media. Usually reliable media sources such as CNN, ABC's *Primetime*, the *Boston Globe,* and others gave Jessop major media exposure as she repeated the exaggerated claims against the FLDS. As a result, news stories comparing FLDS to the Taliban, al-Qaeda, domestic terrorists, the Peoples Temple, and other threatening and sinister groups were widely disseminated.

State Agents

In the Branch Davidian case, Texas Child Protective Services was contacted by an anonymous person—likely Marc Breault—in 1992 reporting child abuse at Mt. Carmel. In response to the tip, CPS caseworkers made three separate visits to Mt. Carmel, interviewing adults and children, including Koresh and his legal wife, Rachel. The children denied being abused or having any knowledge of others experiencing abuse. The adults adamantly denied using severe or abusive physical punishment in disciplining children, and the CPS caseworkers could find no evidence of abuse. Physical examinations of twelve of the children did not turn up any meaningful signs of abuse or injury. Because of a lack of evidence to support the child abuse allegations, CPS officials terminated the investigation after two months. Some of the CPS caseworkers—an investigator named Joyce Sparks, in particular—disagreed with the decision to drop the case. Sparks believed that the case deserved further monitoring. After the disastrous federal siege, Sparks denounced her supervisors at CPS for not being more aggressive in the investigation.

Although the CPS did not have nearly the same influence in the Branch Davidian raid as in the FLDS raid fifteen years later, it is worth noting that the ATF affidavit accompanying the search and arrest warrant for Koresh was filled with references to child abuse (Ellison and Bartkowski 1995). Despite the fact that the ATF has no legal jurisdiction over child abuse, the charge was evidently inserted into the affidavit by federal officials to inflame allegations and augment the case against Koresh.[7] The affidavit cites information supplied by Joyce Sparks of CPS who told ATF investigator Davy Aguilera that an unidentified underage female claimed that Koresh molested her (U.S. District Court 1993). Before, during, and after the disastrous siege, apostates, ACM activists, and government officials persistently pressed these allegations of child abuse, inciting public acrimony. FBI officials even referred to Koresh as a "child molester" and a "pervert" in press conferences during the fifty-one-day standoff ("FBI Heaps Ridicule on Koresh" 1993, 1A).

The parallel between the anonymous phone call to CPS claiming child abuse at Mt. Carmel and the hoax calls by the emotionally disturbed Rozita Swinton feigning to be an abused underage girl inside the YFZ Ranch is significant. Child abuse laws in the United States invert the presumption of innocence in the interests of the child. Because children must be protected, the mere allegation sets into motion state-sponsored investigative activity. New or minority religious communities are particularly vulnerable to these kinds of claims by apostates or opponents (Palmer 1998, 1999; Richardson 1999; Schreinert and Richardson, this volume). In the FLDS case, the child abuse claim is the critical trigger that mobilized authorities to amass the coordinated raid (simultaneously called an "investigation") on the community. As described here and elsewhere in this volume, state child protection officials were in contact with key FLDS apostates in advance of the raid. And as Richardson and Schreinert reveal in their chapter in this volume, the state machinery was fully prepared to take unilateral, preemptive action against the FLDS almost immediately after the complaint was lodged.

The collaboration between state actors, ACM activists, and apostates in the FLDS raid mirrors the conditions leading up to the government raid on the Branch Davidians in crucial ways. Both raids were undertaken by state control agents based on skewed information provided by antagonists and opponents of the targeted groups. In both cases, government officials failed to consider the reliability and lack of impartiality of the information, accepting uncritically the framing of the putative threat by disgruntled apostates whose claims have been shown to be wildly exaggerated. Thus state officials garnered an inflated perception of threat posed by the groups and became complicit in the deviance amplification process that culminated in dubiously legal and, in the case of the Branch Davidians, deadly and catastrophic police actions.

One can hardly understate the extent to which law enforcement agencies in both of these cases became instruments of partisan interest groups. Countermovement activists effectively mobilized state entities on their behalf to carry out coordinated tactical operations. The oppositional campaigns instigated by apostates and anticultists could only be achieved by forging alliances with state actors and co-opting the official apparatus of the state. The grossly disproportionate state responses to what were relatively minor offenses (alleged sexual assault, firearms violations) hardly required massive, paramilitary raids involving an extensive show of martial force. But these extreme enforcement operations reveal the degree to which state agents adopted the inflated claims of opponents. State agents were prepared to meet much more dangerous threats based on the exaggerated narratives of their sources. At Eldorado, officials were told that the FLDS were worse than terrorists, likened to the Taliban and al-Qaeda, heavily armed, stockpiling weapons in caves and underground tunnels (Jessop and Brown 2009; "We Fear Another Waco" 2004; Werlein 2008). State officials were also told that they might expect "a violent reaction" from the FLDS when CPS attempted to take the children into state custody only days after the initial raid. A spokesperson for Texas governor Rick Perry's office told the *Dallas Morning News* that "experts feared that emotional outbursts [from FLDS] could turn violent" when they attempted to separate the children from their mothers (Hoppe 2008). None of these claims or fears turned out to be accurate.

At Waco the excessively aggressive actions by a Special Response Team raid force clad in camouflage, bullet-proof vests, and Kevlar helmets and armed with MP-5 submachine guns, semi-automatic 9MM pistols, sniper rifles, and stun grenades provoked a shootout that congressional investigations later found could have been avoided had law enforcement adopted a different tactic. A report by the House Committee on Government Reform and Oversight castigated the ATF raid plan calling it "significantly flawed" and "poorly conceived" for "utliz(ing) a high risk tactical approach *when other tactics could have been used successfully*" ("Investigation into the Activities of Federal Law Enforcement Agencies Toward the Branch Davidians" 1996, 3; emphasis ours). The report condemned the "ATF's propensity to engage in aggressive law enforcement" (p. 15) and concluded that the predisposition to use military tactics was a fatal flaw. "The ATF deliberately chose not to arrest Koresh outside the Davidian residence," the investigation found, "and instead determined to use a dynamic entry approach" (p. 17). In effect, the overreaching actions of federal law enforcement sparked the violent confrontation, making the inflated and distorted perception of threat, garnered from opponents, a self-fulfilling prophecy. The report also faulted the federal agency for using unreliable sources in developing the raid plan.

Claims

Space does not permit a detailed inventory of opponents' claims. Many of these claims have already been discussed in this chapter. But for comparative purposes, it is important to highlight the similarities in order to press the argument that this kind of claims-making activity adopts a common template. As shown in Table 6.1, the allegations of organized opponents in both cases are remarkably similar, even though the two religious communities are quite different in terms of historical origins, doctrines and faith traditions. These differences, however, tend to be ignored or intentionally diminished by countermovement activists. Opponents typically adopt a strategy of "definitional reductionism" when making claims against targeted groups, labeling them as "cults" in an effort to eradicate important distinctions and project a false and overly simplistic uniformity.

Setting aside the obvious child sexual abuse claims which dominate these two cases and have been sufficiently covered up to this point, we turn our attention to a few of the other key claims. These claims echo historical charges made against marginal religious movements in the past—for example, the Shakers, the Oneida Community, the Doukhobors, and the Mormons (Miller 1983; Moore 1986; Palmer, this volume), as well as contemporary groups.

Physical Abuse/Servitude

In both the Waco and Eldorado cases, countermovement activists and allies lodged claims of physical abuse of children. According to Flora Jessop, the physical abuse of children has been and continues to be pervasive in the FLDS community. She contends that parents are taught that God finds crying babies "offensive" so that FLDS parents are ordered to silence their children from infancy by slapping them or holding their faces under running water (Jessop and Brown 2009). Apostate Carolyn Jessop echoed this claim, telling reporters after the Texas raid that her former husband used a form of "water torture" on children: "He would spank the baby until it was screaming out of control and then he would hold the baby face up under a tap of running water so it couldn't breathe. He would do this repeatedly. . . .

This method he called 'breaking them'" (Celizic 2008). Young girls, Flora Jessop further asserts, are prepared for a future of "servitude" by spending days completing household chores lest they face severe repercussions from FLDS men. The girls are barred from obtaining an education in order to keep them subservient (Jessop and Brown 2009). Anticultist and former deprogrammer Rick Ross told a Phoenix news station that "this group [FLDS] has a long history of very seriously damaging children through sexual abuse, neglect and physical abuse" (Cross 2008). Bruce Perry was quoted in the *Houston Chronicle* as saying, "This is one of the most challenging situations you face in a child protective situation where you have children who are socialized into an abusive lifestyle, yet they feel it is normative" (Langford 2008). ACM activist Janja Lalich informed MSNBC that "a lot of these groups operate on fear. You're afraid of whatever punishment you might get from the group" (Bryner 2008). In the aftermath of the raid some of the seized children were attended to by volunteers from a local Baptist Church in San Angelo. One of the volunteers, Helen Pfluger, told CNN that there were troubling "signs of indoctrination": "The children shunned processed food, white bread and sodas, and essentially subsisted on yogurt, fruit and lots of almonds" (McLaughlin 2008). ACM activist Andrea Moore-Emmett (2008), writing for *Ms.* magazine, told readers that the FLDS case revealed how religion was used as "a cloak for abusive and criminal behavior."

At Waco physical abuse allegations were also lodged against Koresh and the Davidians by apostates and opponents. The claims appeared in the seven-part series published by the *Waco Tribune-Herald* which relied heavily on apostates and key ACM actors. In one reported incident former Davidians alleged that Koresh became irritated with the cries of his son, Cyrus, and spanked the child severely for several minutes on three consecutive visits to the child's bedroom. In another incident Koresh was said to have beaten the eight-month-old daughter of another member for approximately forty minutes until the little girl's bottom bled. In a third incident a man involved in a custody battle visited Mt. Carmel and claimed to have witnessed the beating of a young boy with a stick. According to this account, the beating lasted fifteen minutes (see Ellison and Bartkowski 1995, 120–21). Finally, the FBI's justification for forcing an end to the fifty-one-day standoff with the Davidians was predicated on the charge that Koresh was beating children inside Mt. Carmel. In the immediate aftermath of the deadly conflagration, Attorney General Janet Reno told reporters, "We had specific information that babies were being beaten. I specifically asked [the FBI], 'you mean babies?' Yes, he's slapping babies around" (Verhovek 1993).

It was later learned that this charge was baseless. FBI Director William Sessions countered the attorney general's claim and told reporters that the FBI had no such information about ongoing child abuse inside Mt. Carmel (Labaton 1993). A careful investigation of the other child abuse allegations also found the evidence to be weak and ambiguous, casting serious doubt on the charges (Ellison and Bartkowski 1995).

Brainwashing/Mind Control

In both the Branch Davidian and FLDS cases, opponents accused the groups of brainwashing their members. Although it has been shown that the brainwashing argument does not meet acceptable standards for scientific evidence in a court of law (Anthony 1990; Anthony and Robbins 1992; Ginsberg and Richardson 1998), opponents have persisted in touting the charge. In the Branch Davidian case, chief apostate Marc Breault accused David Koresh of "brainwashing" and "mind control," charges that appeared in the *Waco Tribune-Herald* series before and during the standoff (McCormick and England 1993). Breault also described his efforts to expose the Davidian leader in his tabloid-style autobiography, referring to Koresh as a "cruel, maniacal, child-molesting, pistol-packing religious zealot who brainwashed his devotees" (Breault and King 1993, 256). The charge of brainwashing also appeared in the Australian TV exposé that reporter Martin King filmed at the behest of Breault in 1992. The claims of brainwashing leveled by Breault and other apostates were abetted by ACM activists such as Rick Ross, who routinely promoted the notion that brainwashing/mind control was a core principle of cult ideology (Collins and Frantz 1994).

Years before the raid on the YFZ Ranch in 2008, apostates and ACM activists were proclaiming that FLDS members were brainwashed. In 2004 Apostate Ross Chatwin described the religious regimen of the FLDS as "one of the most effective brainwashing schemes since Hitler" ("We Fear Another Waco" 2004). In 2005 Rick Ross invoked the "brainwashing" claim and compared Warren Jeffs to Jim Jones, the leader of the Peoples Temple who orchestrated a mass suicide in 1979 (Anthony 2005). In 2006 Apostate Laurie Allen told *Deseret News* that the FLDS was not about religion but about "the denigrating of women and mind control" (Winslow 2006). Allen produced a documentary film, *Banking on Heaven*, that was panned by *Variety* magazine as "amateurish and more agitprop than balanced reportage" (Winslow 2006). Arch-apostate Flora Jessop repeated the "brainwashing" charge multiple times in her book (Jessop and Brown 2009) and in interviews (St.

Germain 2001). Former deprogrammer and ACM activist Joe Szimhart told ABC News, "I have no doubt that they've [FLDS members] been brainwashed" (Friedman 2008). Apostate Carolyn Jessop, only a few days after the YFZ raid, told MSNBC that the FLDS practiced "mind control" on its members: "With this level of mind control, its something you're born into and it's generational. The babies born into this don't stand a chance" (Celizic 2008). Larry Beall, a Utah psychologist and the state's "cult expert" in the criminal trial of the first FLDS defendant, Merrill Jessop, told *Time Magazine* a few weeks after the raid that "the FLDS is a cult involved in plain ole brainwashing since birth" (Hylton 2008).

Mass Suicide/Collective Violence

In both the Branch Davidian and FLDS cases, the groups were accused by opponents and their allies of preparing for mass suicide. John R. Hall's insightful work on the Branch Davidians describes how opponents "reinvoked and reworked narratives about mass suicide" in ways that "cast Mt. Carmel as another Jonestown" (1995, 206). Indeed, chief apostate Marc Breault declared in his book that Koresh was "planning a mass suicide somewhere around April 18 [1992]. . . . I believe that over 200 persons will be massacred next month. . . . Every day brings us closer to another Jonestown" (Breault and King 1993, 290–91). Breault made this same claim to other apostates, to family and kin of Davidians, to at least one congressman, Fred Upton of Michigan, to Australian media, and to U.S. law enforcement officials (Hall 1995, 218–19). In April 1992 the U.S. Consulate in Australia sent a cable to Washington, warning that, according to his sources, the Branch Davidians were gathering at Mt. Carmel "where they expected to die as part of a mass suicide" (Hall 1995, 219). The trope of mass suicide emerged again in the *Waco Tribune-Herald* series and was invoked by federal officials as a concern during the fifty-one-day standoff (Wright 1999).

In the FLDS case, apostates and ACM activists invoked the doomsday warnings of mass suicide and collective violence on numerous occasions. In 2004 Flora Jessop told a British news reporter that FLDS members "are prepared to die for their leader" ("We Fear Another Waco" 2004). Jessop also alleged that the FLDS had a "fall-out shelter" packed with emergency supplies and stockpiles of weapons. Apostate Ross Chatwin, in 2006, said of the YFZ: "It's ready to blow. It's going to turn into another Waco" (Walters 2006). Apostate Carolyn Jessop told another news source that she and her sister had a grim joke when they were growing up: "Don't drink the punch," a reference to the mass suicide at Jonestown (Jessop 2008). Apostate Elaine Jeffs was quoted in Laurie Allen's film as saying, "What I'm afraid of is another Jonestown or another Waco" (Winslow 2006). A few days after the raid, Texas officials told the *Fort Worth Star-Telegram* that FLDS members resisted efforts by investigators to enter the temple, "raising fears of a Branch Davidian-style standoff" (Hanna 2008). In searching the YFZ Ranch following the raid, authorities also claimed to find a "cyanide poisoning document," though no explanation was offered for the outlandish claim and the news report went on to suggest that the claim was baseless: "Nothing in the eighty-page list of items seized indicated that members of the sect planned to use cyanide," it said (Blaney and Roberts 2008).

Conclusion

Our comparative analysis of the two raids at Waco and Eldorado reveal striking parallels in terms of process and structure. We show that the two raids share important commonalities and features, particularly the development and mobilization of organized opponents of the religious groups in question, and the formation of alliances with state actors to launch unilateral, preemptive raids. By pressing a "cult" stereotype based more on popular imagination and prejudices, lodging exaggerated charges and claims, opponents were able to gain *political* ground for their moral campaigns by appealing to issues such as child protection that served the mutual interests of state actors. Elected officials and other state actors saw little risk, and perhaps even acquired political capital, in pursuing "child-saving" activities by targeting disfavored minority religions that tend to have little institutional support. In this context, the failure of officials to carefully consider mitigating or contradictory evidence of child abuse—or allegations of brainwashing, terrorism, mass suicide, and so on—is more readily explained. State actors became complicit in the moral campaigns of countermovement activists under the guise of public interest and framed social control efforts as combating perilous threats to the social order. Embellishments of these putative threats by opponents were allowed to go unchecked by officials because they were not weighed with sufficient rigor against counterfactual evidence or competing explanations. The exclusive reliance on oppositional organizations and actors for information about the targeted groups produced wildly inflated perceptions of threat by authorities leading to poor decisions and actions that proved to be over-reaching and, in the case of the Branch Davidians, lethal.

1. The Davidians apparently used the empty grenade shells to attach to wood plaques and sell at gun shows.

2. Seventy-six sect members died on April 19 as a result of the FBI assault; six others died as a result of the initial ATF raid on February 28; thus a total of eighty-two sect members were killed. This figure includes two children in utero who died with their mothers.

3. Ammerman does note that at least three other mental health professionals were consulted as well: Bruce Perry, Park Dietz, and Murray Miron. Perry and Miron both had strong ACM ties. Thus the advice from Ross may have echoed the advice of these other anticult "experts" who were part of the oppositional alliance. It was Murray Miron who told the FBI on April 15, four days before the deadly fire, that Koresh was "a determined and hardened adversary who has no intention of delivering himself" (U.S. Department of Justice 1993, 175). The FBI must have accepted Miron's opinion, since they began planning to force the Davidians out by launching the CS gas attack a few days later on March 17, despite the advice of two other experts, James Tabor and Phil Arnold, to wait. Tabor and Arnold were convinced that Koresh would come out after he finished writing his theological position on the "Seven Seals" (Tabor 1995). Their advice was ignored.

4. Some of these suicides were likely homicides, particularly the children who died as they were forced to drink the Kool-Aid.

5. Communication with attorney Don Payne after the trial of the first FLDS defendant. Musser's testimony had a significant impact on the jury according to Payne. The first two FLDS defendants to go on trial were both convicted, partly because of Musser's testimony.

6. Chatwin was born into the FLDS where he spent thirty-five years of his life. Having dropped out of school in the eighth grade, he operated a car-repair business in the community ("Blasphemous Backlash" 2004). Despite the fact that FLDS men are permitted to have multiple wives only with the consent of their prophet, Warren Jeffs, Chatwin pressured Jennifer Johnson, a minor (and her underage sister), to join his family, which consisted of his wife, Lori, and their six children. In response, Johnson's father obtained a protective order against Chatwin as well as an injunction against harassment (when Jennifer turned eighteen she filed an injunction in her own name). Chatwin's behavior resulted in his excommunication from the FLDS. As recorded in court documents, Jeffs claimed that Chatwin was "stalking young girls to become [his] wives against their wishes and the wishes of their father" (*United Effort Plan Trust vs. Ross Chatwin* 2004). On Tuesday, March 2, 2004, Chatwin was issued an eviction notice by the FLDS Trust as his house was on church property ("Dissident Polygamist Goes on Trial in Lawsuit," Kingman Daily Miner, March 3, 2004). Rod Parker, the lawyer representing the FLDS Board of Trustees, also claimed that Chatwin was operating an illegal business since he did not have an automobile dealer's license, that at one time he had approximately one hundred wrecked cars on his property, and that his home was "unkempt" and "unfinished" (*United Effort Plan Trust vs. Ross Chatwin* 2004). The court found that Mr. Chatwin was entitled to compensation for his property (restitution for improvements) after which the United Effort Plan could claim possession.

7. This observation was made by retired ATF Deputy Director Robert Sanders during testimony in the congressional hearings on Waco in 1995 and is recorded in the Emmy Award–winning documentary film *Waco: The Rules of Engagement*.

REFERENCES

Adams, Brooke. 2008a. Are "Polygamy" and "Cult" Synonymous? Accessed online at http://blogs.sltrib.com/plurallife/archives/2008_06_01_archive.htm.
———. 2008b. "People Who Have Left Sect Go to Texas to Help." *Salt Lake City Tribune,* April 7, 4A.
———. 2009. "Listening to the Lord: Jeffs Exerted 24-7 Control over FLDS Faithful." *Salt Lake City Tribune,* March 5.
Ammerman, Nancy T. 1995. "Waco, Federal Law Enforcement and Scholars of Religion," pp. 282–98 in Stuart A. Wright (ed.), *Armageddon in Waco.* Chicago: University of Chicago Press.
Anthony, Dick (1990). "Religious Movements and Brainwashing Litigation," pp. 295–344 in Thomas Robbins and Dick Anthony (eds.), *In Gods We Trust.* New Brunswick, NJ: Transaction.
Anthony, Dick, and Thomas Robbins. 1992. "Law, Social Science, and the 'Brainwashing' Exception to the First Amendment." *Behavioral Sciences and the Law* 10:5–30.
Anthony, Paul. A. 2005. "Shrouded in Secrecy: Former Members of Eldorado Sect Speak of Abusive, Closed Society, Fanaticism," *San Angelo Standard-Times,* March 27. Accessed online at http://nl.newsbank.com/nl-search/we/Archives?
Apologetics Index. N.d. Accessed online at http://www.apologeticsindex.com (May 5, 2009).
Best, Joel. 1990. *Threatened Children.* Chicago: University of Chicago Press.
Blaney, Betsy, and Michelle Roberts. 2008. "Cyanide Document Found at Texas Compound." Associated Press, April 12.
"Blasphemous Backlash." 2004. *Phoenix New Times,* January 29.
Bradney, Anthony. 1999. "Children of a Newer God: The English Courts, Custody Disputes, and NRMs," pp. 210–26 in Susan J. Palmer and Charlotte Hardmann (eds.), *Children in New Religions.* New Brunswick, NJ: Rutgers University Press.
Bragg, Roy. 1993. "Ex-Prosecutor Laments Agents' Storm Trooper Tactics." *Houston Chronicle,* March 2, p.7A.
Breault, Marc, and Martin King. 1993. *Inside the Cult.* New York: Signet.
Bromley, David G. 1998. *The Politics of Religious Apostasy.* Westport, CT: Praeger.
Bryner, Jeanna. 2008. "Texas Group: Religious Sect or Cult? MSNBC.com, April 9. Accessed online at www.msnbc.com/id/24032149/print/1/dsiplaymode/1098/.
Celizic, Mike. 2008. "Woman Describes 'Escape' from Polygamy." MSNBC.com, April 8. Accessed online at www.msnbc.com/id/24009286/print/1/displaymode/1098/.
CNN.com Transcripts. 2006. *Paula Zahn Now,* May 10. Accessed online at http://transcripts.cnn.com/TRANSCRIPTS/0605/10/pzn.01.html.
Cohen, Stanley. 1972. *Folk Devils and Moral Panics.* New York: St. Martin's.
Coleman, Lee. 1994. "Declaration of Lee Coleman, M.D.," December 13. Submitted to the New South Wales Supreme Court. Document on file with author.
Collins, Catherine, and Douglas Frantz. 1994. "Tales from the Cult." *Modern Maturity,* June. Accessed online at www.rickross.com/reference/waco/waco293.html.
Cross, Jim. 2008. "Expert: FLDS Polygamist Group Is a Classic Cult." KTAR Radio, Phoenix, April 11. Accessed online at www.rickross.com/reference/polygamy/polygamy826.html.

Cultic Research. N.d. Accessed online at http://www.CultResearch.org.

"Dissident Polygamist Goes on Trial in Lawsuit." 2004. *Kingman Daily Miner*, March 3.

Ellison, Christopher G., and John P. Bartkowski, 1995. "'Babies Were Being Beaten': Exploring Child Abuse at Ranch Apocalypse," pp. 111–49 in Stuart A. Wright (ed.), *Armageddon in Waco*. Chicago: University of Chicago Press.

England, Mark, and Darlene McCormick. 1993. "The Sinful Messiah." *Waco Tribune-Herald*, February 27–March 5.

"FBI Heaps Ridicule on Koresh." 1993. *Houston Chronicle*, April 17, 1A.

Fox News. 2009. Transcript of Greta van Sustern interview with Flora Jessop, April 21. Accessed online at http://www.foxnews.com.

Foster, Lawrence. 1984. *Religion and Sexuality: The Shakers, the Mormons, and the Oneida Community*. Urbana: University of Illinois Press.

Friedman, Emily. 2008. "Sect Members: Brainwashed or Believers?" ABC News, April 16. Accessed online at www.rickross.com/reference/polygamy/polygamy832.html.

Ginsburg, Gerald, and James Richardson, 1998. "'Brainwashing' Testimony in Light of *Daubert*," pp. 265–88 in Helen Reece (ed.), *Law and Science*. Oxford: Oxford University Press.

Goode, Erich, and Nachman Ben-Yehuda. 1994. *Moral Panics: The Construction of Deviance*. Cambridge, MA: Blackwell.

Hall, John R. 1995. "Public Narratives and the Apocalyptic Sect: From Jonestown to Mt. Carmel," pp. 205–235 in Stuart A. Wright (ed.), *Armageddon in Waco*. Chicago: University of Chicago Press.

Hanna, Bill. 2008. "Temple Used for Sex with Young Girls, Officials Say." *Forth Worth Star-Telegram*, April 9. Accessed online at http://www.rickross.com/reference/polygamy/polygamy810.html.

Heller, Matthew. 2004. "Flora's War: Flora Jessop Knows What It's Like to Flee an Insular and Polygamous World." *Los Angeles Times Magazine*, August 1.

Hoppe, Christy. 2008. "Texas Had Secret Plan to Separate Polygamist Mothers, Children." *Dallas Morning News*, June 4, 1A.

Hunsicker, Brent. 2008. "Who Is Willie Jessop?" ABC4News.com, June 6.

Hylton, Hilary. 2008. "The Future of the Polygamist Kids." *Time*, April 15. Accessed online at http://www.time.com/time/printout/0,8816,1730471,00.html.

"Investigation into the Activities of Federal Law Enforcement Agencies toward the Branch Davidians." 1996. Thirteenth Report by the Committee on Government Reform and Oversight Prepared in Conjunction with the Committee on the Judiciary, August 2. Washington, DC: U.S. Government Printing Office.

Jessop, Carolyn. 2008. "One Woman's Harrowing Tale of Escaping the Texas Polygamist Sect." *Daily Mail*, April 21. Accessed online at http://www.dailymail.co.uk/femail/article-559132.

Jessop, Carolyn, with Laura Palmer. 2008. *Escape*. New York: Broadway Books.

Jessop, Flora, and Paul T. Brown. 2009. *Church of Lies*. New York: Jossey-Bass.

Karlsen, Carol. 1987. *The Devil in the Shape of a Woman*. New York: Norton.

Labaton, Stephen. 1993. "Confusion Abounds in the Capital on Rationale for Assault on Cult." *New York Times*, April 20.

Langford, Terri. 2008. "Sect Youths Conditioned to Deceive Outsiders." *Houston Chronicle*, April 10, 1A.

Lewis, James R. 1989. "Apostates and the Legitimation of Repression: Some Historical and Empirical Perspectives on the Cult Controversy." *Sociological Analysis* 49:386–96.

———. 1995. "Self-Fulfilling Stereotypes, the Anticult Movement, and the Waco Confrontation," pp. 95–110 in Stuart A. Wright (ed.), *Armageddon in Waco*. Chicago: University of Chicago Press.

"Life in the Cult." 2008. *People*, April 8.

McCormick, Darlene, and Mark England. 1993. "Experts: Branch Davidians Dangerous, Destructive Cult." *Waco Tribune-Herald*, March 1, 1.

McLaughlin, Eliot C. 2008. "Ex-sect Members Escape Polygamy but Not Pain." CNN News, April 17. Accessed online at http://www.cnn.com/2008/CRIME/04/16/polygamy.escapes/index.html.

Miller, Donald. 1983. "Deprogramming in Historical Perspective," pp. 15–28 in David G. Bromley and James T. Richardson (eds.), *The Brainwashing/Deprogramming Controversy*. Lewiston, NY: Edwin Mellen.

Moore, Laurence R. 1986. *Religious Outsiders and the Making of America*. New York: Oxford University Press.

"Motion for the Deposition of Flora Jessop." 2008. State of Arizona v. Warren Steed Jeffs, No. CR-2007-953, November 28.

Perkins, Nancy. 2008. "Texas Officials Deny Ex-FLDS Members Involved in Search Warrant." *Deseret News*, April 19. Accessed online at http://findarticles.com/p/articles/mi_qn4188/is_20080419/ai_n25352.

Perry, Bruce. 1994. "Destructive Childrearing Practices by the Children of God." Report to the Health and Community Services, Melbourne, Australia, March 28. Document on file with author.

Pfiefer, Jeffrey E. 1992. "The Psychological Framing of Cults: Schematic Representations and Cult Evaluations." *Journal of Applied Psychology* 22:531–44.

Phinney, Matt. 2005. "Religious Sect out of Eldorado Causing Unrest in the Community." *San Angelo Standard-Times,* March 27. Accessed online at http://nl.newsbank.com/nl-search/we/Archives?

Richardson, James T. 1995. "Manufacturing Consent about Koresh: A Structural Analysis of the Role of the Media in the Waco Tragedy," pp. 153–76 in Stuart A. Wright (ed.), *Armageddon in Waco*. Chicago: University of Chicago Press.

———. 1999. "Social Control of New Religions: From Brainwashing Claims to Child Sex Abuse Accusations," pp. 172–86 in Susan J. Palmer (ed.), *Children in New Religions*. New Brunswick, NJ: Rutgers University Press.

Robbins, Thomas. 1988. *Cults, Converts, and Charisma*. Newbury Park, CA: Sage.

Sandberg, Lisa, and Terri Langford. 2008. "Sect Members Less Mature Than Outsiders, Psychiatrist Testifies." *Houston Chronicle*, April 18, 3A.

Shupe, Anson D., and Susan Darnell. 2006. *Agents of Discord: Deprogrammers, Pseudo-Science, and the American Anticult Movement*. New Brunswick, NJ: Transaction.

Shupe, Anson D., and Jeffrey K. Hadden, 1995. "Cops, News Copy, and Public Opinion," pp. 177–204 in Stuart A. Wright (ed.), *Armageddon in Waco*. Chicago: University of Chicago Press.

St. Germain, Patrice. 2001. "Flora Jessop Escaped a Polygamy Life 15 Years Ago—Seeks to Help Her Sister." *The Spectrum* (St. George, Utah), June 17. Accessed online at hhtp:helpthechidbrides.com/stories/rubyjess617.htm.

Tabor, James D. 1995. "Religious Discourse and Failed Negotiations: The Dynamics of Biblical Apocalypticism in Waco," pp. 263–81 in Stuart A. Wright (ed.), *Armageddon in Waco*. Chicago: University of Chicago Press.

United Effort Plan Trust vs. Ross Chatwin. 2004. Superior Court, State of Arizona, Mohave County, No. CV2004-83, May 20.

U.S. Department of Justice. 1993. *Report to the Deputy Attorney General on the Events at Waco, Texas: February 28 to April 19, 1993.* Redacted version, October 8. Washington, DC: U.S. Government Printing Office.

U.S. District Court. 1993. "Application and Affidavit for Search Warrant." W93-15M. Western District of Texas. Filed February 26.

Verhovek, Sam Howe. 1993. "In Shadow of Texas Siege, Uncertainty for Innocents." *New York Times*, March 8.

Walters, Joanna. 2006. "Fears of New Waco as FBI Hunt for Svengali Leader of Polygamy Cult." *London Observer*, August 24. Accessed online at http://www.childbrides.org/abuses_Afternet_behind_the_cloak_of_poly-gamy.html.

"We Fear Another Waco." 2004. *The Independent,* February 19.

Werlein, Linda. 2008. Interview with Linda Werlein, on file with Stuart A. Wright.

Wessinger, Catherine. 2009. "Deaths in the Fire at the Branch Davidians' Mount Carmel: Who Bears Responsibility?" *Nova Religio* 13 (2): 25–60.

Winslow, Ben. 2006. "New Film by Ex-Wife Takes Aim at FLDS." *Deseret News*, August 27. Accessed online at http://www.deseretnews.com/.

———. 2008. Hildale and Colorado City Worry over Texas Raid." *Deseret News*, April 5. Accessed online at http://www.deseretnews.com/.

Wright, Stuart A. 1995a. *Armageddon in Waco: Critical Perspectives on the Branch Davidian Conflict.* Chicago: University of Chicago Press.

———. 1995b. "Construction and Escalation of a 'Cult' Threat: Dissecting Moral Panic and Official Reaction to the Branch Davidians," pp. 75–94 in Stuart A. Wright (ed.), *Armageddon in Waco.* Chicago: University of Chicago Press.

———. 1999. "Anatomy of a Government Massacre: Abuses of Hostage-Barricade Protocols during the Waco Standoff." *Terrorism and Political Violence* 11 (2): 39–68.

———. 2002. "Public Agency Involvement in Movement-State Confrontations," pp. 102–22 in David G. Bromley and J. Gordon Melton (eds.), *Cults, Religion, and Violence.* New York: Cambridge University Press.

———. 2005. "Explaining Militarization at Waco: Construction and Convergence of a Warfare Narrative," pp. 75–97 in James R. Lewis (ed.), *Controversial New Religions.* New York: Oxford University Press.

7

Large-Scale FLDS Raids

The Dangers and Appeal of Crime Control Theater

CAMILLE B. LALASZ AND
CARLENE A. GONZALEZ

The Fundamentalist Church of Jesus Christ of Latter Day Saints (FLDS) has been portrayed by the media, politicians, and law enforcement officials as a sect that engages in and encourages illegal and immoral behavior. The negative portrayal of this religious group has resulted in two arguably ill-conceived and dangerous large-scale raids on FLDS communities; in 1953 a settlement in Short Creek, Arizona, was raided to save women from the alleged oppression of polygamous marriages, and in 2008 a settlement near Eldorado, Texas, was raided to rescue one alleged victim of sexual and physical abuse. These very public raids and the drastic acts that followed (e.g., taking custody of all FLDS children) propagated an initial illusion of crime control but were ineffective in controlling the targeted crimes and thus can be characterized as "crime control theater" (CCT) (Griffin and Miller 2008). We use the case study method, with evidence from the media and previous studies, to demonstrate how the raids on these communities may be understood in terms of CCT and the dangers of relying on such CCT actions.

Background on the FLDS and Large-Scale Raids

Polygamy, or plural marriage, was observed by several cultural groups in the United States from the 1600s to the mid-1800s (Francoeur 1995), but it was not viewed as a social and cultural morality problem that deserved legislative action until Brigham Young, the leader of the Church of Jesus Christ of Latter-day Saints (LDS), officially incorporated the practice into the doctrine of Mormonism in 1852 (Peterson 1992). A short time later the U.S. government began passing acts (e.g., Morrill Anti-Bigamy Act of 1862, Poland Act of 1874, Edmunds Act of 1882) and prosecuting individuals engaged in plural marriages in an attempt to eliminate the practice (Smith 2010). After more than one thousand successful polygamy or unlawful cohabitation prosecutions against LDS members, Church leader Wilford Woodruff reluctantly decreed that the Church no longer endorsed the practice. Refusing to abandon what they considered to be a major tenet of the Mormon religion and fearing mass persecution, small groups of "fundamentalists" broke away from the Church and settled their own communities in isolated areas across the western United States, Mexico, and British Columbia (Anderson 1992). One such group, the FLDS, created a colony in the 1930s in the border town of Short Creek, now called Colorado City, Arizona, and Hildale, Utah (Bradley 1993; Castle 2005; Weis 2006).

The 1953 Raid on Short Creek

The isolation of Short Creek provided refuge for the FLDS community for a brief period; residents were left virtually undisturbed and allowed to continue engaging in plural marriages (Erwin 2009). Increasing media coverage and growing public concern over the perceived immoral activities occurring within the community, however, convinced officials of the need to take action to protect the FLDS women from an enslaved life within a polygamous marriage. At dawn on July 26, 1953, law enforcement officers, under the command of Arizona governor John Howard Pyle, launched a full assault on the community at Short Creek and placed the entire population (i.e., 36 men, 86 women, and 263 children) under military control (Castle 2005). A week later, state welfare workers took custody of 153 Arizonan children and bused them, along with their mothers, to the cities of Phoenix and Mesa, where they were kept isolated from one another, as well as from their fathers or husbands. The state retained custody of these children for up to two years before allowing them to return home to their polygamous lifestyle (Bradley 1993; Maloney 1974; Smith 2010).

The officials responsible for initiating the Short Creek raid proclaimed that their actions were appropriate and that the raids were a "success" (Castle 2005). The general public, however, did not share their sentiments. Instead, they were outraged by national news footage that showed gut-wrenching images of children being separated from their parents (Sigman 2006). The media portrayal of the Short Creek raid also led many to view the raid as an inhumane public policy solution and an ineffective way to eliminate polygamy. Thus what had begun as a moral crusade to save women from a polygamous lifestyle became a public relations nightmare (Hylton 2008a). Furthermore, public opinion on plural marriage was evolving; polygamy ceased to be viewed as a serious threat to the dominant American culture, and the public no longer wanted the government to disrupt the lives of ostensibly good religious people to enforce anti-polygamy laws (Weis 2006). As a result, the FLDS community avoided further government intervention for more than fifty years.

The 2008 Raid on the Yearning for Zion Ranch

In 2003 the FLDS Church purchased property for the Yearning for Zion (YFZ) Ranch outside Eldorado, Texas, under the guise of a corporate hunting retreat. It soon became clear, however, that the ranch was more of a self-contained community than a vacation property, complete with a cement plant, gleaming white temple, and ten-foot-high walls topped with spikes and flanked by watchtowers, for several hundred FLDS members (Johnson 2008; Lewan 2008). After four years of surveillance by county officials, pressure by anti-FLDS activists, unfavorable media coverage, and growing concern regarding the alleged illegal behaviors that might be occurring within the ranch, law enforcement officials received the "confirmation" they had been waiting for.

On March 29, 2008, authorities received phone calls from a young woman claiming to be Sarah Jessop, a sixteen-year-old member of the FLDS community who confided that she had been assaulted by her husband and was pregnant with her second child (West 2008). Although this report was later determined to be a hoax, it was initially taken seriously, and law enforcement and officials from the Department of Family and Protective Services (DFPS) swiftly coordinated efforts to raid the YFZ Ranch (Johnson 2008). Though unable to find the alleged victim, officials spent the next few days searching the ranch and interviewing adults and children. During this time, DFPS observed what appeared to be underage females who were either pregnant or had already given birth, and determined that the children living on the property either had been or were in immediate danger of being abused ("219 Children, Women Taken from the Sect's Ranch" 2008; McFadden 2008, as cited by Smith 2010). As a result, 468 children residing at YFZ were forcefully removed from their community and placed under the custody of the State of Texas.[1] As with the Short Creek raid, the children's mothers willingly chose to leave the ranch to remain with their children. After months of complaints by FLDS members regarding improper conduct by DFPS, overcrowded and chaotic conditions in the detention facility, and violations of civil liberties, a Texas appeals court ruled that there was insufficient evidence to justify keeping the children in state custody. Although the raid failed to locate and rescue the alleged victim, officials did eventually file charges relating to underage marriage against eleven men. To date, three of these men have been convicted and are currently serving time in jail; appeals are ongoing, however (Adams 2010; McKinley 2009).

Once again, officials were cited in the press as being "pleased" with the raids and with the actions of law enforcement officers. Initially the public appeared to share this favorable attitude toward the raid. Support declined, however, after extensive media coverage presented the pubic with disturbing images of the raids (e.g., crying and confused looking women and children surrounded by gun-toting law enforcement officials [Johnson 2008]). In addition to generating public sympathy toward the FLDS community, media coverage also led many to question the effectiveness and legality of the raid after the state's inability to care for the removed FLDS members was highlighted.

Both the aforementioned raids on FLDS communities resulted from reports of illegal behavior. The magnitude of the raids, however, and their aftermath appear to be grossly disproportionate to any real threat posed by the Mormon polygamists in 1953 and of the reported prevalence of physical and sexual abuse in 2008. Furthermore, although these reactionary responses initially appeared successful in controlling the targeted crimes, further inspection reveals that they were not. This pattern of overreactions to seemingly minor or limited illegal behaviors in a manner that only results in a semblance of mitigating the criminal behavior fits the definition offered above of "crime control theater."

FLDS Raids as Crime Control Theater

As we have seen, the term "crime control theater" is used to describe very public responses to reported crimes that demonstrate an illusion of crime control but are inefficient and possibly ineffective in actually controlling the targeted crimes (Griffin and Miller 2008). Responses of this nature are dangerous because they are often perceived to be legitimate and even gallant, but have the unintended consequences of intensifying the problem or leading to additional negative outcomes (Hammond, Miller, and Griffin 2010). In order for a legal or social response to be conceptualized as CCT, the action must be characterized by four criteria: (1) reactionary social response to moral panic, (2) unquestioned acceptance and promotion of the response, (3) acceptance of the response based on appeals to mythic narratives, and (4) empirical failure of the response.

Reactionary Responses to Moral Panic

The first criterion for a legal response to be characterized as CCT is that the action must be a reactionary social response to moral panic. A moral panic is said to occur when an individual or group is identified by agents of social control (e.g., politicians, law enforcement officials, religious leaders, the media) as a threat to society's interests and values because the individual or group acts in a socially undesirable manner (Cohen 1972; Zgoba 2004). This portrayal is sensationalized and results in a prevalent perception that the threat posed by the individual or group is more widespread and serious than it actually is (Goode and Ben-Yehuda 1994). Unfortunately, as a result of these moral panics, public responses that are ill-conceived and potentially destructive are often undertaken (Griffin and Miller 2008).

Five elements have been identified that must exist before an individual or group can accurately be described as targets of moral panic: (1) *concern*, or a heightened level of apprehension regarding the group, (2) *consensus*, or public agreement that the group poses a danger to societal interests and values, (3) *hostility*, or an elevated level of antagonism that is directed toward the group, (4) *disproportionality*, or a perception that the danger posed by the group is greater than it really is, and (5) *volatility*, or propensity for the level of panic to fluctuate over time (Goode and Ben-Yehuda 1994). Thus, to demonstrate that the FLDS raids were reactionary responses to moral panics, we must first establish that these five characteristics were present prior to the raids.

The 1953 Short Creek Raid

The FLDS sect has never been fully accepted by American mainstream society or even the mainstream Mormon Church. The degree to which this group has been vilified and antagonized, however, has varied over the years (Weis 2006). As we saw earlier, the community at Short Creek was virtually ignored for nearly twenty years until agents of social control (i.e., media, politicians, law enforcement officials) identified the community as a threat to societal values. During this time the media portrayed polygamy as an immoral act that severely endangered the well-being of Short Creek women and children, as well as the moral foundations of the dominant American culture. Media reports also focused on the fact that membership in the larger FLDS Church, as well as the immediate Short Creek community, were growing (Weis 2006). These reports led to an increase in the level of *concern* that both government officials and the general public expressed toward the FLDS community at Short Creek (Bradley 1993; Evans, this volume; Weis 2006): the first condition for the development of a moral panic.

Over time politicians and government officials began to express alarm over the critical and ever growing threat posed by the community at Short Creek. As an apparent result of the consistent messages being sent by multiple agents of social control, there appeared to develop a *consensus* in the media and among elected officials and the general public that the FLDS community at Short Creek posed a growing peril to American society and its values (Bradley 1993; Weis 2006). It is likely, however, that this widespread fear was *disproportionate* to any real threat posed by the FLDS, since it is improbable that a small isolated group of individuals engaging in what they believed to be religiously sanctioned actions would be capable of corrupting the dominant American culture.

As a result of the exaggerated level of panic toward this group, officials and the general public began to openly express *hostility* toward the FLDS community at Short Creek (Sigman 2006). For instance, officials faced public pressure to curtail the illegal and immoral activities assumed to be taking place within Short Creek (Bradley 1993; Sigman 2006). In response, politicians and law enforcement officials vowed to dedicate their time and energy to eradicating the practice of polygamy and, with it, its potential danger to society (Weis 2006; White and White 2005). Arizona governor Pyle exemplified this position when he declared that the FLDS community at Short Creek was a "community dedicated to the production of white slaves" (cited in Castle 2005, 34) and that it was his duty to eliminate the "foul conspiracy" (cited in Hylton 2008a) to engage in polygamy within the FLDS community.

However, after the raid the media released sympathy-inducing media images of crying children being ripped from the arms of their parents (Sigman 2006). These images appeared to change the public's perception of the FLDS community from crazy fundamentalists that enslaved women and threatened American culture to essentially good religious people who loved their families. As a result, the level of alarm directed toward the FLDS community at Short Creek appeared to subside, exhibiting the *volatility* characteristic of moral panic. Based on this discussion, the five elements of moral panic were clearly present in the Short Creek raid. Media, government officials, and the general public began to become increasingly concerned that this group posed a grave threat to society, and, as public pressure mounted, the state reacted with hostility toward the targeted community. But after the raid the moral panic that characterized the polygamous group suddenly dissipated and remained low for at least the next twenty years.

The 2008 YFZ Ranch Raid

The FLDS communities and their widespread practice of plural marriage were largely ignored by the media, and thus by the majority of the American public, until 1977, when a fundamentalist prophet murdered a rival fundamentalist sect leader and reignited media coverage of the ongoing practice of polygamy in FLDS communities (Weis 2006). This re-characterization of FLDS communities as threats to society resulted in another shift in public opinion. Negative media coverage of the FLDS communities increased again in 1996, when opponents of gay marriage argued that its legalization would lead to the legalization of polygamy (Weis 2006). Consequently critics and other agents of social control once again defined polygamy as a problem of cultural morality. Some isolated events since the public debate over gay marriage (e.g., the kidnapping of Elizabeth Smart) have continued to result in negative media attention toward the FLDS communities and possibly exaggerated fear that these groups present a threat to the American way of life.

When the local paper in San Angelo, Texas, discovered and subsequently announced that the newly purchased land outside Eldorado was being established as an FLDS community rather than a hunting retreat, residents, politicians, and law enforcement officials expressed concern about the threat this group might pose to their community and state (Hylton 2008c; Johnson 2008; Lewan 2008; Richardson and Schreinert, this volume; Wright, this volume). Once again, the media acted as a key agent of social control, as newspapers in Arizona, Utah, and Texas produced nearly weekly articles on the dangers of the FLDS sect and their prophet, Warren Jeffs (Lewan 2008). The combination of this sensationalized portrayal of the FLDS members and very limited personal contact with the group resulted in nearby residents wondering if the FLDS would produce an incident similar to the Branch Davidian tragedy (Wright 1995). Residents also worried that FLDS members might kidnap and corrupt their children or somehow take legal control of Eldorado (e.g., by voting as a bloc for individuals sympathetic to their lifestyle; see Lewan 2008). Because the FLDS members continued to keep to themselves, these fears, combined with rumors about the illegal activities taking place behind the compound walls, promoted and abetted by anti-FLDS activists, led the general public, politicians, and law enforcement officers to adopt a socially constructed and exaggerated level of fear toward the FLDS community at the YFZ Ranch.

Over time this fear led to increased feelings of apprehension and hostility toward the sect and the desire to eliminate its presence (Hylton 2008d). For instance, in response to the fear that FLDS leaders were ordaining underage marriages, lawmakers raised the legal age of consent to marry in Texas from fourteen to sixteen (Hylton 2008d; Johnson 2008; Richardson and Schreinert, this volume). In 2005, when the FLDS leader Warren Jeffs prophesized Armageddon, anti-FLDS activists taunted sect members by marching in front of the compound gates in grim reaper costumes (Lewan 2008). Further, politicians and law enforcement officials, fearful of the "awful stuff going on in there" (Texas State Representative Harvey Hilderbran, as cited in Johnson 2008, 1), warned owners of neighboring ranches to be on the lookout for girls fleeing the ranch and were prepared to take action in the event that a complaint would eventually be filed (Lewan 2008). A sequence of hoax calls from an alleged underage victim of abuse was the opportunity law enforcement officials were waiting for to justify intervention.

Based on this series of events, clearly the key elements of a moral panic were present in the development of the 2008 raid on the YFZ Ranch. The level of *concern* toward the FLDS community steadily grew after the establishment of the new YFZ Ranch in Eldorado. From 2004 to 2007 Texas officials and the local public *consensually* began to become increasingly concerned that the FLDS community posed a serious threat to society (Richardson and Schreinert, this volume; Wright, this volume). The perceived level of danger posed by this group, however, was grossly *disproportionate* to its actual threat level. Nonetheless, *hostility* toward the group grew, and, as a result, CPS and law enforcement officials responded to reports by a single individual of physical and sexual abuse with a massive state raid.

Unquestioned Acceptance and Promotion of the Legal Responses

The second criterion for a social response to be considered CCT is unquestioned and extensive political and public support (Hammond et al. 2010). Previous CCT analyses have demonstrated that politicians and the public quickly accepted laws that were initiated in response to social issues but failed to adequately control crime (e.g., AMBER Alert) (Hammond et al., 2010; Griffin and Miller 2008). Furthermore, politicians resolutely promoted the virtues of these laws (Griffin and Miller 2008).

Political Acceptance and Support

Both the Short Creek and YFZ Ranch raids received unquestioned support from politicians and law enforcement officials both before and after they were carried out. For instance, before the raids, officials promoted the need to take swift and decisive action to protect their communities and the greater culture from the supposed threat posed by the FLDS communities (Castle 2005; Johnson 2008). The decisions to initially accept and enact the large-scale raids may be understood by examining what information individuals use to make different decisions. The Cognitive-Experiential Self-Theory (CEST) of personality suggests that individuals process information either through rational or experiential systems (Epstein 1990, 1994; Epstein et al. 1992; Epstein et al. 1996). Rational systems are logic-based, whereas experiential systems are affect-based. CEST implies that individuals experiencing or learning about an emotional event are likely to respond to the event with affect-based judgments. Thus an individual who is deciding on a course of action in an experiential manner will be unable to recognize the tangible threats of the proposed legal action. In relation to the FLDS raids, it appears that politicians and law enforcement officials may not have been able to appropriately weigh the pros and cons of their reactionary behaviors as they were focused on the emotional aspect of the alleged event (i.e., rescuing women and children whom they believed to be susceptible to their fellow FLDS members).

After the raids state officials continued to justify their decisions to raid these FLDS communities. Specifically they praised the actions of the law enforcement officials who carried out their orders, promoted the virtues of the raid plans, and adamantly maintained that the legal responses were appropriate in the face of growing questions and concerns (Castle 2005; Johnson 2008). That politicians and law enforcement officials doggedly maintained their level of support and acceptance for these raids may be explained further by Festinger's (1957) theory of cognitive dissonance. This theory proposes that individuals have difficulty maintaining cognitions that contradict one another and therefore may acquire a new belief or modify their original belief in order to reduce the uncomfortable feelings that accompany dissonance. For instance, individuals who have actively promoted or engaged in an action may experience dissonance after learning of the negative consequences of their action. This dissonance may arise from the conflict between the presented negative information and either the originally held cognition that the action was appropriate or an individual's self-concept that he or she is a good person who only promotes or engages in honorable actions. In either case, the dissonance can be reduced most effectively by leaving the existing cognition intact and acquiring a new belief that the recently presented information is inaccurate. Thus it is not surprising that politicians and law enforcement officials involved in the FLDS raids would continue to promote the virtues of the raids and refuse to concede to accusations that the raids were an inappropriate way of dealing with the alleged crimes taking place in the FLDS communities. After all, accepting that their actions were improper would force them to change their own self-image or the initial belief that the alleged crimes warranted the raids, or both.

Public Acceptance and Support

Unlike political support for the raids on FLDS communities, the level of public support for the raids does not appear to remain consistent before and after the legal responses. Instead, public support appears to ebb and flow over time in correspondence with the fluctuating levels of moral panic directed toward this group. Public opinion polls regarding the level of support for raids as legal actions designed to curtail the suspected illegal activities taking place within the FLDS communities were not taken prior to either raid. Evidence seems to suggest, however, that the majority of those residing adjacent to these communities would have supported the raids, as many of them believed that FLDS members were committing crimes against innocent women and children (Hylton 2008c; Johnson 2008; Weis 2006). This hypothesis is based on numerous reports that the public encouraged officials to take action to curtail the illegal and immoral activities (e.g., polygamy, child abuse, and incest) suspected of taking place within these communities and had supported previous actions that were designed to do so (e.g., prosecutions and the modification of laws). It is also known that Americans, in general, detest abuse toward women and children, and thus support legal and social actions that will protect innocent victims (Cragun and Nielsen, in press; Darley and Pittman 2003). Based on this information and the media's documentation of support for the raids immediately after they were conducted, we argue that the majority of the general public would have supported the idea of raiding these communities to save innocent women and children from illegal and immoral activities.

This level of support for the raids, however, appears to have declined after more information about their aftermath became available to the general public. After the Short Creek raid, for instance, media coverage that focused on the mistreatment of the FLDS community resulted in much of the public expressing outrage at these actions and adopting the viewpoint that the raid was both inhumane and ineffective as a response to polygamy (Bradley 1993; Evans, this volume; Weis 2006). A similar pattern emerged after the raid on the YFZ Ranch; criticism grew after media news coverage rapidly shifted from presenting the raid as justified by the need to save children to a raid that targeted a religious group and resulted in civil and custody right violations (Cragun and Nielsen, in press). This shift in media framing and the efforts of the FLDS itself to elicit sympathy by presenting its own perspective of the raid were successful in diminishing the public's level of support for the raids (Winslow 2008).

Based on the aforementioned discussion, it appears that the idea of rushing in to save women and children from illegal and immoral activities through large-scale raids is initially appealing to, and unquestionably supported by, both law enforcement officials and the general public. However, once media sources probed deeper into the state's actions, published sympathetic images of FLDS members, and discussed the empirical failure of these raids, the public began to waiver in its support for the raids. This demonstration of a vacillating level of support for the FLDS raids differs from previous instances of CCT which focused on laws that receive unquestioned political *and* public support over long periods of time (Griffin and Miller 2008; Hammond et al. 2010). We believe that the continued level of unquestioned support by the public need not be a criterion of laws or actions that fail to demonstrate more than an illusion of crime control and that this criterion of CCT may depend on the amount of information the public receives about the legal response or the law. Thus the finding that both raids lost public support quickly does not indicate that they cannot be characterized as CCT. Rather, it simply means that the raids maintain a characteristic that is somewhat different from other CCT laws that have been previously identified.

Acceptance of the Responses Based on an Appeal to Mythic Narratives

The third criterion of CCT is acceptance of a response based on an appeal to mythic narratives (Hammond et al. 2010). Past applications of CCT to legal responses (e.g., AMBER Alert and Safe Haven Laws) have explained the unquestioned acceptance of these social responses by focusing on the mythic nature of the victims of these crimes, namely, young children (Griffin and Miller 2008; Hammond et al. 2010). The mythic narrative appeals to expectations that all members of the public, but particularly young children, will be protected from social threats by laws and the officials who uphold them. The most important component of the mythic narrative is that the proposed solution must be executed immediately and successfully by "brave" protectors or guardians of the community.

In the case of the Short Creek raid, the polygamists' wives were presented as the unquestioned victims. This was made clear to the public when Governor Pyle referred to the polygamous FLDS wives as "white slaves" who were in need of rescuing (Johnson 2008). Likewise, the mythic victims who appeared to justify the raid on the YFZ Ranch were the vast number of young women and children who were believed to be victims of various physical and sexual abuses (Cragun and Nielsen, in press). One might argue that the women and children in the two FLDS communities were viewed as innocent victims in need of "rescuing" by the vast majority of individuals who were aware of the situation. This desire to protect those who are incapable of protecting themselves led politicians and law enforcement officials to adopt and promote the virtues of the raids. Because of the rapid execution of the raids, it is uncertain whether community members would have overwhelmingly accepted these mythic narratives *prior* to law enforcement decisions to launch the raids; it is clear, however, that mythic narratives were utilized to tug at the heartstrings of the public *after* the raids were conducted. Although mythic narratives such as these can be emotionally appealing, they have considerable drawbacks as solutions to social ills.

Empirical Failure of the Responses

The last and arguably most important characteristic of CCT is that, despite being "intuitively logical, viscerally appealing, and emotionally soothing," the social response enacted simply does not, and most likely will not, work as expected (Hammond et al. 2010, 8). There are a number of reasons why large-scale raids are generally ineffective methods for the investigation or prosecution of illegal behavior of this nature within FLDS communities.

First, finding physical evidence that can prove an individual has engaged in illegal behavior of this nature (e.g., polygamy and sexual abuse) can be very difficult. When engaging in celestial marriages, for example, FLDS males only obtain marriage licenses for their first wives; subsequent marriages are conducted secretly, and additional wives present themselves to outsiders as single women (Berkowitz 2006–2007). Similarly, finding physical proof of abuse of an adult during a search of a FLDS community is unlikely. Therefore raiding and searching entire communities to save women from lives of polygamy or abuse is impractical, as it is extremely difficult to find evidence that their husbands are breaking anti-polygamy or other statutes.

Second, relying on obtaining cooperation from the victims under the circumstances that exist during and after a large-scale raid is impractical. During the raids, for instance, victims may be uncooperative because they are overwhelmed by the chaos of the raid, as well as intimidated by the presence of guns, armored vehicles, and search dogs. After the raids victims may be unaccommodating, as they have been separated from one another and sequestered in unfamiliar surroundings. Victims' lack of cooperation was evidenced following the Short Creek raid, as officials reported that it was virtually impossible to obtain witness testimony from FLDS members about the polygamous relationships of fellow members (Berkowitz 2006–2007). Likewise, the authorities did not receive a single report of personally experienced abuse or firsthand accounts of any illegal behavior performed within the YFZ Ranch after the raid (Hylton 2008b). To the contrary, officials reported that they had a difficult time obtaining cooperation with even minor issues such as recording names and family relationships.

This documented lack of legal cooperation by women and children FLDS members following large-scale raids can be explained by four factors. First, the FLDS doctrine emphasizes the importance of obedience and loyalty to one's family, especially one's father, and one's Church (Berkowitz 2006–2007). Second, FLDS individuals do not view polygamy as wrong and may not view underage celestial marriages as sexual abuse. Thus they are unlikely to view themselves as "victims" in need of saving from outside officials or be thankful for the opportunity to leave their families and communities. Third, the FLDS teaches members that outsiders are untrustworthy sinners who should be feared and that individuals who abandon the Church, or even seek protection from outside officials, will not only be permanently separated from their families but will also suffer eternal damnation (Hylton 2008b). Thus it may be the case that a crime would have to be perceived as particularly heinous before an FLDS member would defy his or her culture and risk eternal damnation to cooperate with authorities during or after a raid. Fourth, the atmosphere surrounding a large-scale raid may frighten and confuse FLDS members. Even if a member felt victimized and wanted to seek outside assistance, the chaos of the raid may decrease the likelihood that he or she would do so. Based on these factors, it is not surprising that officials have encountered difficulties obtaining firsthand accounts of any illegal activities within the FLDS community following large-scale raids. Nor is it hard to imagine that this trend would continue in the event of any future raids.

A third reason why large-scale raids are ineffective legal responses is that, because of the aforementioned difficulties in finding physical evidence and obtaining cooperation from victims and witnesses, raid officials are likely to be forced to rely on obtaining other sources of evidence (e.g., DNA tests) to prove that illegal behavior of this nature is occurring within FLDS communities. Although this type of evidence may be useful, it is often difficult and expensive to administer such tests to the large number of suspected victims within these communities (e.g., more than four hundred women and children were taken into state custody following the YFZ Ranch raid). Furthermore, evidence of this nature would not be helpful in proving certain types of crimes such as polygamy. That said, it is important to note that DNA evidence was obtained following the 2008 raid and that it was used as the primary source of evidence in the 2009 sexual assault case against Raymond M. Jessop (McKinley 2009). To date, however, this is the only sexual assault conviction against a polygamist sect member that has been made using DNA evidence (Adams 2010). Though few would discredit the importance of prosecuting FLDS members who have broken sexual assault laws, this fact may lead some to argue that the state costs associated with removing and housing all the suspected victims (and their mothers), as well as conducting medical tests of this kind, is not the most efficient way to prosecute a handful of husbands. In fact, some may argue that engaging in another legal response or, at the very least, just taking custody of those who were in danger of imminently being forced into celestial marriages may have been more prudent (Smith 2010).

Finally, in addition to failing to prosecute but only a few individuals for the suspected illegal behavior that motivated the raids, large-scale raids are also likely to be ineffective legal responses as they are unlikely to result in a reduction of future illegal actions. For instance, the Utahans in Short Creek were not convicted of any crime or forced to stop engaging in polygamy after the raid (Evans, this volume; Weis, 2006). Likewise, after being convicted on conspiracy to commit polygamy charges and given probation, the Arizonans from Short Creek were also allowed to return home and resume their polygamous lifestyles. Thus the raid failed to accomplish Governor Pyle's objective of eradicating the "foul conspiracy" of polygamy. On the contrary, polygamy not only continued in Short Creek, but the FLDS also continued to grow in numbers and spread into other newly established communities after the raid (White and White 2005). It remains to be seen if the 2008 raid and its handful of subsequent prosecutions will succeed in changing FLDS religious ideology and long-established beliefs regarding polygamy and celestial marriages. Based on historic trends and the reported increase in distrust of outsiders (Hylton 2008a), it seems unlikely (especially where polygamy is concerned). Although there is little empirical evidence of unequivocal failure, it appears that raids of this nature have been ineffective in prosecuting past or present illegal actions. It is unlikely, therefore, that future illegal behavior within FLDS communities will be prevented (see Evans, this volume).

In sum, the 1953 and 2008 FLDS raids appear to fit the criteria of CCT. The raids are reactionary responses to social issues that give the appearance, but not the actual effect, of crime control. Both raids were precipitated by moral panics, were sensationalized by their appeals to mythic narratives, and were demonstrable failures at stopping the crimes that they initially targeted. In addition, both FLDS raids received extensive political support both before and after the legal actions and were likely supported by the public before the raids occurred. Characterizing a social response as CCT does not ensure that the response will be dangerous. However, previous scholars have identified a number of problems with illusionary legal responses (Griffin and Miller 2008; Hammond et al. 2010) and, unfortunately, a number of these dangers appear evident in the FLDS raids.

The Dangers of Crime Control Theater

Several problems are associated with legal responses that masquerade as effective public policy but are ineffective in actually controlling the targeted crimes (Griffin and Miller 2008; Hammond et al. 2010). These include false claims of success, unintended deleterious effects, and stunted public discourse.

False Claims of Success

After both raids, law enforcement officials immediately claimed that the actions taken were successful (Castle 2005; Johnson 2008). These claims, however, were misleading and inaccurate. As discussed previously, the raids were unsuccessful in investigating and prosecuting the specific individuals who were believed to be engaging in the illegal behavior. Furthermore, only a very small percentage of individuals within these FLDS communities have been charged with a crime as a result of the raids, and only a handful of the charges that have been filed or prosecuted are for crimes that mirror the seriousness of the "threat" on which the raids were originally based. Additionally, the 1953 raid was unsuccessful in stopping the illegal activity from occurring again. This will likely be the case with the 2008 raid as well. False claims of success by authority figures are dangerous, as they contribute to the illusion that the perceived problem has been effectively addressed and may even act to promote the use of raids as a successful method for halting illegal behavior in other isolated communities in the future.

Unintended Deleterious Effects

Not only have the FLDS raids failed to curtail illegal activity from occurring, but these raids also have the unintended negative consequence of causing emotional and psychological harm to FLDS members. The government intrusion into their communities during the raids themselves caused some members to feel that the security and sanctity of their homes had been violated. For those women and children removed from their homes, the result of the raids likely caused even more serious damage. Removing individuals, especially young children, from their families and culture for extended periods (up to two years in the case of the Short Creek raid) can have detrimental effects on attachment bonds and psychological well-being. Similarly physical separation from spouses can put a serious strain on the health of marital relationships.

Inefficient raids are also capable of causing future deleterious effects for FLDS members and the U.S. government. It has been widely reported that FLDS members became increasingly distrustful of the U.S. government and law enforcement officials after the raids took place (e.g., Hylton 2008a, 2008b). This increase in distrust is likely the result of a perception that the raids lacked procedural justice (i.e., the decision to raid the FLDS communities was not just, and the FLDS members were not treated justly during and after the raids [Tyler 2006; Tyler and Lind 1992]). Individuals who perceive procedural justice to be unfair are more likely to view the authorities that instigate the action as illegitimate and therefore are less likely to accept their decisions, obey social rules, and recognize the legitimacy of their rules and formal institutions (Cole 1999; Tyler and Lind 1992). Thus the raids may have actually had the unintentional consequence of decreasing the likelihood that FLDS members will cooperate with officials in the future and increasing the likelihood that FLDS members will continue to break U.S. laws.

Stunted Public Discourse

Although public opinion toward FLDS raids is currently unfavorable, no one would question the need to protect innocent women and children from illegal behavior in the future. If the wax and wane cycle of moral panic surrounding FLDS communities continues, it is likely that, with time, officials and the general public will forget about the images that resulted from the 2008 raid and a similar event will occur in the future. Because of the moral panic surrounding the issue, previous false reports of success, and the inherent appeal of dramatic interventions to "save" innocent victims, it is likely that a raid will be considered, if not chosen, as the preferred course of action. Choosing this course of action in the future is dangerous because it is likely to be just as ineffective and result in all the same deleterious effects. Supporters of raids choose their words carefully so that it appears that raids are the obvious and necessary solution to the problem. With few or no other alternatives, critics are likely to be silenced, and thus public discourse is stunted.

Conclusion

The FLDS culture and religious leaders have historically sanctioned behaviors that are illegal in the United States (e.g., polygamy, celestial marriages to underage girls). Occasionally authority figures acknowledge these behaviors and focus on the threat that they pose to the social order. During these occurrences the media, politicians, and law enforcement officials openly portray the FLDS in a negative light. In the past this has led to a socially constructed "panic," and the scale and severity of the threat posed by the FLDS was perceived to be much larger than it actually was. This threat then resulted in the large-scale raids on Short Creek and the YFZ Ranch.

This analysis indicates that these raids can be characterized as CCT; although they may have sounded noble and sensible at the time, they were actually ineffective in investigating, prosecuting, or curtailing the illegal behavior for which they were instigated. The only criterion that posed even a mild challenge to the CCT paradigm was "unquestioned support." Based on the previous discussion, it appears that the idea of rushing in to save women and children from illegal and immoral activities is initially appealing to both law enforcement officials and the general public. Once media sources and other outlets begin to publish sympathetic images and highlight the empirical failure of these raids, however, unquestioned public support for this form of legal action decreases. Previous CCT analyses indicate that political and public support for initiated laws in response to social issues (e.g., AMBER Alert) persevered for a long period (Griffin and Miller 2008). In contrast, our analysis indicates that political support for the raids persevered, whereas public support diminished quickly. This difference may be attributable to differences in media coverage following the legal responses that may have made the deleterious effects of the raids (e.g., children being ripped from their parents' arms) much more salient and obvious to the public than the potential deleterious effects of AMBER Alerts (e.g., a perpetrator seeing his face on an AMBER Alert and killing the child immediately to avoid being apprehended).

Thus the unquestioned support criterion may depend on the amount of information the public receives about the legal response. Perhaps if media coverage focused on the ineffectiveness and illusionary nature of other CCT laws, these laws, too, would lose public support. After all, child protection legislation and the moral panic that precedes them generally tend to ebb and flow (e.g., Zgoba 2004). The finding that both raids lost public support quickly does not indicate necessarily that they cannot be characterized as CCT. Rather, it simply means that the raids maintain a characteristic that is somewhat different from other CCT laws that had been previously analyzed and identified.

As with other CCT actions, large-scale raids on FLDS communities have resulted in deleterious effects such as psychological harm to FLDS members and the further isolation of FLDS communities. The raids have also created a sense of distrust toward government that will make it difficult to protect FLDS members from illegal behavior in the future. The combination of the ineffectiveness of the raids and the detrimental effects that they caused contribute to the need to develop more effective policies for discovering, investigating, and prosecuting illegal behaviors that take place within small religious communities such as the FLDS. Although more time-consuming and less inherently appealing, alternative methods are likely to prove more effective at protecting women and children from the crimes that drive the moral panic that precipitates the raids in the first place.

NOTE

1. The press reported 468 children initially but it was later determined that 29 of the young women were not minors but legal adults, thus making the number 439.

REFERENCES

Adams, Brooke. 2010. "Third FLDS Man in Texas Going to Prison for Sexual Assault." *Salt Lake Tribune,* January 22. Accessed online at http://www.sltrib.com/polygamy/ci_14247919.

Anderson, Joseph. M. 1992. "Fundamentalists," pp. 531–32 in Daniel H. Ludlow (ed.), *Encyclopedia of Mormonism,* Vol. 2. New York: Macmillan.

Berkowitz, Jason D. 2006–2007. "Beneath the Veil of Mormonism: Uncovering the Truth about Polygamy in the United States and Canada." *University of Miami Inter-American Law Review* 38:615–39.

Bradley, Martha Sonntag. 1993. *Kidnapped from That Land: The Government Raids on the Short Creek Polygamists.* Salt Lake City: University of Utah Press.

Castle, Carly. 2005. "Child Abuse in Arizona and Utah Polygamous Families: An Argument in Favor of Strict and Broad Enforcement of Punishments for Polygamy-Related Crimes against Children." *Hinckley Journal of Politics* 6:33–41.

Cohen, Stanley. 1972. *Folk Devils and Moral Panics*. New York: St. Martin's.

Cole, David. 1999. *No Equal Justice: Race and Class in the American Criminal Justice System*. New York: New Press.

Cragun, Ryan T., and Michael Nielsen. In press. "Social Scientific Perspectives on the FLDS Raid and the Corresponding Media Coverage," in Cardell K. Jacobson and Lara Burton (eds.), *Modern Polygamy in the United States: Historical, Cultural, and Legal Issues*. New York: Oxford University Press.

Darley, John M., and Thane S. Pittman. 2003. "The Psychology of Compensatory and Retributive Justice." *Personality and Social Psychology Review* 7:324–36.

Epstein, Seymour. 1990. "Cognitive-Experiential Self-Theory," pp. 165–92 in Lawrence Pervin (ed.), *Handbook of Personality: Theory and Research*. New York: Guilford.

———. 1994. "Integration of the Cognitive and the Psychodynamic Unconscious." *American Psychologist* 49:709–24.

Epstein, Seymour, Abigail Lipson, Carolyn Holstein, and Eileen Huh. 1992. "Irrational Reactions to Negative Outcomes: Evidence for two Conceptual Systems." *Journal of Personality and Social Psychology* 62:328–39.

Epstein, Seymour, Rosemary Pacini, Veronika Denes-Raj, and Harriet Heier. 1996. "Individual Differences in Intuitive-Experiential and Analytical-Rational Thinking Styles." *Journal of Personality and Social Psychology* 71:390–405.

Erwin, Andrew T. 2009. "Avoiding Another Eldorado: Balancing Parental Liberty and the Risk of Error with Governmental Interest in the Well-Being of Children in Complex Cases of Child Removal." *William and Mary Law Review* 51:1197–1235.

Festinger, Leon. 1957. *A Theory of Cognitive Dissonance*. Stanford, CA: Stanford University Press.

Francoeur, Robert T. 1995. *The Complete Dictionary of Sexology*. 2nd ed. New York: Continuum.

Goode, Erich, and Nachman Ben-Yehuda. 1994. *Moral Panics: The Construction of Deviance*. Cambridge, MA: Blackwell.

Griffin, Timothy, and Monica K. Miller. 2008. "Child Abduction, AMBER Alert, and Crime Control Theater." *Criminal Justice Review* 33:159–76.

Hammond, Michelle, Monica K. Miller, and Timothy Griffin. 2010. "Safe Haven Laws as Crime Control Theater." *Child Abuse and Neglect* 34:545–52.

Hylton, Hilary. 2008a. "The Echo of an Earlier Polygamist Raid." *Time*, April 13. Accessed online at http://www.time.com/time/nation/article/0,8599,1730472,00.html.

———. 2008b. "The Future of the Polygamist Kids." *Time*, April 15. Accessed online at http://www.time.com/time/nation/article/0,8599,1730471,00.html.

———. 2008c. "When the Polygamists Came to Town." *Time*, April 17. Accessed online at http://www.time.com/time/nation/article/0,8599,1731706,00.html?iid=sphere-inline-bottom.

———. 2008d. "Turning Up the Heat on Polygamists." *Time*, July 24. Accessed online at http://www.time.com/time/nation/article/0,8599,1826371, 00.html.

Johnson, Kirk. 2008. "Texas Polygamy Raid May Pose Risk." *New York Times*, April 12. Accessed online at http://www.nytimes.com/2008/04/12/us/12raid.html.

Lewan, Todd. 2008. "From 'Hunting Retreat' to a Polygamous Enclave." *Deseret News,* April 20. Accessed online at http://www.deseretnews.com/article/695272132/From-hunting-retreat-to-a-polygamous-enclave.html?pg=1.

Maloney, Wiley S. 1974. "Short Creek Story." *American West* 11:16–23.

McKinley, James C. 2009. "Polygamist Sect Leader Convicted on Sexual Assault." *New York Times,* November 6. Accessed online at http://www.nytimes.com/2009/11/06/us/06polygamy.html.

Michels, Scott. 2008. "Court: Texas Had No Right to Keep Polygamist Kids." *ABC News,* May 22. Accessed online at http://abcnews.go.com/TheLaw/story?id=4911318&page=1.

Peterson, H. Donl. 1992. "Manifesto of 1890," pp. 852–53 in Daniel H. Ludlow (ed.), *Encyclopedia of Mormonism,* Vol. 2. New York: Macmillan.

Sigman, Shayna M. 2006. "Everything Lawyers Know about Polygamy Is Wrong." *Cornell Journal of Law and Public Policy* 16:101–84.

Smith, Linda F. 2010. "Kidnapped from the Land II: A Comparison of Two Raids to Save the Children from the Polygamists." *Children's Legal Rights Journal* 30:1–68.

Sullivan, John. 2008. "Court Rules Sect Children Should Go Home." *New York Times*, May 29. Accessed online at http://www.nytimes.com/2008/05/29/us/29cnd-raid.html?hp.

"219 Children, Women Taken from Sect's Ranch." 2008. *CNN*, April 6. Accessed online at http://www.cnn.com/2008/CRIME/04/06/texas.ranch/.

Tyler, Tom R. 2006. "Restorative and Procedural Justice: Dealing with Rule Breaking." *Journal of Social Issues* 62:307–26.

Tyler, Tom R., and E. Allan Lind. 1992. "A Relational Model of Authority in Groups," pp. 115–92 in Mark Zanna (ed.), *Advances in Experimental Social Psychology,* Vol. 25. New York: Academic Press.

Weis, Rebecca. L. 2006. "Historical Progression of Problem Definition for the Practices of Polygamy and Prostitution in the United States." Unpublished master's thesis, Bowling Green State University, Bowling Green, Ohio. Accessed online at http://etd.ohiolink.edu/send-pdf.cgi/Weis%20Rebecca%20L.pdf?bgsu1151340686.

West, Brian. 2008. "Affidavit: FLDS Raid Spurred by Girl's Reports of Physical, Sexual Abuse." *Deseret News,* April 8. Accessed online at http://www.deseretnews.com/article/1,5143,695268544,00.html.

Winslow, Ben. 2008. "Utahans Change Mind on Backing FLDS Raid." *Deseret News,* June 25. Accessed online at http://deseretnews.com/article/1,5143,700237713,00.html.

White, O. Kendall, and Daryl White. 2005. "Polygamy and Mormon Identity." *Journal of American Culture* 28 165–77.

Wright, Stuart A. 1995. *Armageddon in Waco: Critical Perspectives on the Branch Davidian Conflict.* Chicago: University of Chicago Press.

Zgoba, Kristin M. 2004. "Spin Doctors and Moral Crusaders: The Moral Panic behind Child Safety Legislation." *Criminal Justice Studies* 17:385–404.

III

Legal and Political Perspectives

8

Strategic Dissolution and the Politics of Opposition

Parallels in the State Raids on the Twelve Tribes and the FLDS

JEAN SWANTKO WISEMAN

On June 22, 1984, the State of Vermont illegally seized 112 children from the Twelve Tribes Community in Island Pond, Vermont, following allegations of child abuse (Swantko 1998a; Palmer 1998). After individual hearings District Court Judge Frank Mahady ordered the children returned to their parents and issued five separate opinions based on the finding that the police raid on the small religious group was a "grossly unlawful scheme" (*In re Certain Children* 1984, p. 6). Research eventually revealed that the attorney general's staff and state child protection workers in Vermont had collaborated with anticult movement (ACM) leaders in carrying out a written plan devised by former deprogrammer Galen Kelly to discredit and destroy the religious community. Kelly's strategic plan, innocuously titled "Investigative Proposal Regarding Island Pond," was developed for Priscilla Coates, director of the Cult Awareness Network (CAN) in 1983, a year before the Island Pond Raid. The Vermont social services commissioner acknowledged that at "strategy meetings" in the fall before the Island Pond Raid he and other officials discussed options, including the state action to raid the Church and take its children. Coates and Kelly met with the attorney general's staff on August 9, 1983. Thereafter state investigators were sent around the country to talk to ex-members, hand-picked by ACM actors, to collect stories of abuse (Swantko 2009).

In the plan Kelly formulated an investigative strategy to identify allies within key government agencies, persuade them to investigate the targeted "cult," locate and interview disgruntled apostates, foment exaggerated media accounts, gather damaging evidence, and build a case for child abuse with the intent to impel state action. In the document Kelly proposed conducting a "well-structured investigation designed to develop and document facts about the activities" of the Church in Island Pond "as a vehicle to coordinate law enforcement, media and grass roots opposition to the group." The intent of the plan, as envisioned by Kelly, was "to prevent its [the Church's] growth" and "assist in the dissolution of it" (*Investigative Proposal* n.d., p. 1).

In an effort to implement the plan, Kelly organized local public meetings and met with residents to identify potential allies in this moral campaign and to spread apprehension and alarm about alleged abuse at Island Pond. One of the first such meetings occurred in Barton, Vermont, in November 1982, where he recruited citizen activist Suzanne Cloutier to coordinate the meeting as well as to cultivate press contacts. Cloutier was also encouraged to coax members to defect and write affidavits lodging claims against the group. As a result of this countermovement activism, Kelly obtained affidavits from a few defectors calling for criminal charges, and in some cases the affidavits were used in custody battles. The apostates, some of whom were deprogrammed, were put in touch with media and state authorities to press publicly for legal action. In a matter of months Kelly's strategy to build a broad-based coalition of opponents—defectors, reporters, ACM activists, and state officials—was effectively achieved.

The state raid based on charges of child abuse was a relatively successful effort to exploit public resources to carry out a partisan campaign. The putative "problem" at Island Pond was framed by public officials strictly in ACM terms and justified as a necessary action taken in the public interest. It is not an overstatement to say that the ill-conceived and ultimately illegal state incursion would not have occurred apart from the actions of Kelly and the coalition of opponents that served as the mobilizing force behind the raid. In preparation to lobby the state to act on behalf of opponents, Kelly was quite specific about the strategy: ACM actors should "work closely during an investigation with law enforcement and regulatory agencies to gain access to information that they developed themselves" with the goal of "establishing credibility with them" so as to "subtly or not so subtly force any reluctant enforcement or regulatory agency to take appropriate action" (*Investigative Proposal* n.d., p. 5; see also Richardson 2004; and Swantko 2004)

The Kelly plan, not discovered until 1999, outlines a stepwise strategy that has served as a prototype for assailing other minority religious groups, including the recent raid on the Fundamentalist Church of Jesus Christ of Latter Day Saints (FLDS) in Texas. Kelly proposed that Citizens' Freedom Foundation (CFF), a prominent ACM organization and precursor to CAN, assist in the Island Pond project for reasons that support this premise. In the document he provides the following rationales: (1) The group is "small enough and localized enough to be studied, investigated and researched as a microcosm," providing lessons *"applicable to other similar groups presently and in the future"*; (2) as a "research project to experiment in developing ways to teach communities how to cope with the incursion of a cult"; and (3) having the participation of CFF "will be a great step forward in taking aggressive action, since the only aggressive anti-cult action has been deprogramming which entails various controversial problems" (*Investigative Proposal* n.d., p. 2; emphasis added). The strategic plan makes explicit that the experiment to disrupt and dissolve the community at Island Pond would provide a model applicable to other nontraditional religious groups in the future, such as the FLDS. The importance of the model is made pointedly by Kelly in noting that it would propel the ACM past the quagmire of the movement's increasingly problematic reliance on deprogramming.

The Kelly Dissolution Plan

Galen Kelly, then a deprogrammer for CFF, sent investigators to Island Pond, Vermont, in the early 1980s to conduct a preliminary investigation into the activities of the Northeast Kingdom Community Church, or Twelve Tribes community. As a part of the investigation, one former member of the group was recruited successfully and voluntarily deprogrammed. CFF operatives interviewed various former members, read and collected unfavorable news reports about the group, and concluded that the Church was a "destructive cult," exhibiting any number of antisocial activities, including "variations of law" and practicing "mind control" for the purpose of exploiting members in the group (*Investigative Proposal* n.d., p. 1). The conclusions of the investigation became the foundation for the Kelly dissolution plan.

Kelly observed that the group in Island Pond was experiencing rapid growth and proposed that something needed to be done quickly to prevent its expansion. He suggested using information and materials from the investigation as a vehicle to convince law enforcement officials, the media, and the local public that the Church was dangerous and required immediate action. Kelly hoped to mobilize a network of opponents against the Church. He also saw the exercise at Island Pond as an experiment in developing ways to teach cities and towns how to combat an unwelcomed "cult" that moves into a community. Up to that point the key aggressive tactic employed by the ACM involved deprogramming individual members. Kelly conceded the problems associated with deprogramming in the report and proposed a new plan to target an entire group, providing a much broader and more effective strategy in fighting "cults." Kelly proposed abandoning the more vigilante method of deprogramming and making efforts to frame the solution to the "cult problem" as one in which the ACM would seek cooperation with and work alongside institutional authorities. ACM activists could coordinate counseling and rehabilitation services with state regulatory and social services agencies. Kelly suggested providing specialized support services for cult members who wanted to leave and to assist families who had traveled great distances to see children in the group, and, he hoped, have them removed. He envisioned a plan where ACM exit counseling and post-cult rehabilitation services could be presented as narrowly specialized and sellable to state agencies. This would also allow ACM framing to penetrate the state apparatus and dictate the "prognostic" tasks (i.e., devising plans of amelioration [Hunt, Benford, and Snow 1994]) most likely to be considered by officials. In other words, the ACM would provide a remedy to the state's "cult" problem, which the ACM itself had articulated as child abuse.

The substantive claims made by opponents against the Island Pond community built on existing rumors and allegations of "criminal, quasi-criminal and otherwise anti-social actions" (*Investigative Proposal* n.d., p. 3) regarding the Church. Kelly disseminated unsubstantiated allegations of child abuse, child neglect, child deaths from medical neglect, and unreported deaths of children or adults, or both, from natural or unnatural causes (Swantko 1998a, 1998b, 2000, 2004). Also included in the claims were alleged policies of the church to violate laws: not report births or deaths, not enroll children in school, violate zoning laws and housing regulations, violate tax laws, and distribute controlled medication without prescriptions. Finally, Kelly alleged questionable financial actions, violation of court orders in custody cases, and an incident of violent rape. Because the Church had faced its share of controversy, as many new religions have, allegations of mischief and criminal wrongdoing were easier to float.

The Kelly plan also proposed a breakdown of strategic approaches formulated for the pertinent institutions of influence that would be potential allies or components in the oppositional coalition; law enforcement officials, the media, and the local citizenry. Kelly's outline of strategies and designated targets in the plan are summarized as follows:

1. *Law enforcement.* Local ACM actors would endeavor to first establish a close relationship with law enforcement to gain access to police investigations while sharing their own information. They hoped this would give them ammunition against the religious group and forge a relationship of trust with

law enforcement. Ultimately this exchange of information would establish credibility with local police in order for the ACM to influence the government to take action against the targeted group.

2. *Media.* Specifically Kelly's aim was to influence the media to "bring scrutiny to bear on the Island Pond situation," to focus attention on the "cult issue," and to keep the clear issue of child abuse as a focus.

3. *Local public.* The goal was to educate local citizens with ACM material and to get local activists to assist in providing support services such as arranging deprogramming sessions and putting defectors and opponents in touch with the media. (*Investigative Proposal* n.d., pp. 5–6)

First and foremost the Kelly plan was designed to be a prototype to attack and dissolve minority religions in Vermont and elsewhere, but it had another distinct advantage. If successful, it could also become a lucrative venture for ACM exit counselors, legal advisers or consultants, privately run "rehabilitation" or treatment centers, and even self-proclaimed "cult experts," since it would generate a demand for their services. This may help to explain the emergence of a burgeoning ACM industry and international network of organizations in the last two decades (Bromley and Shupe 1993; Shupe and Darnell 2004, 2006), particularly in Europe where some are government-supported (Bromley and Shupe 1994; Introvigne 1998, 2000; Richardson 1996; Richardson and Introvigne 2001).

The 1984 raid on the Island Pond community was the culmination of coordinated activities put in play by the Kelly plan. Although ultimately the oppositional coalition did not prevail and the children were returned to their parents, the contours of the Kelly plan appear to be of continuing significance as a template for the ACM and allied opponents of nontraditional or new religious movements (NRMs). Research shows that similar raids have increased in the United States and Europe since the Vermont raid in 1984. An ongoing study by Wright and Palmer (2009) has identified fifty-eight state raids on new or nontraditional religious communities in the last sixty years. The bulk of these raids (77%), however, have occurred since 1984, the year of the Island Pond raid. These figures suggest a sharp increase in their frequency, and, perhaps more important, they also suggest a pattern of raids that correlates with the heightened organization of oppositional alliances. This pattern or template, which is also discussed by others in this volume (Palmer, Wright, and Wright and Fagen), is rooted in the Kelly plan.

Twenty-five years after the Kelly plan was devised we see the fruits of this strategy preceding the raid in Texas. Indeed, the 2008 Texas raid on the FLDS reveals notable parallels to the 1984 Island Pond case that compel examination. These parallels center on the Kelly dissolution plan. Although it evades proof that ACM actors and oppositional networks literally adopted the same Kelly plan used in the Vermont case, the substance of this strategic formula was repeated in Texas. This recurring pattern of attacking new or nontraditional religions strategically outlined in the Kelly plan appears to have become institutionalized and embedded in the ACM organizational culture (Bromley 1998; Hall 1995; Hall and Schuyler 1998; Wright 1995b, 1998, 2002).

Two Significant Trends

The importance of the 1984 Island Pond Raid cannot be overstated, because it appears to mark the beginning of two significant trends. First, the Vermont raid signals the beginning of an apparent surge of coordinated state raids on new or nontraditional religions. In these government raids state agents either act in response to claims by organized opponents or they become part of an organized alliance or coalition, targeting a religious group *collectively* rather than focusing on the individuals within the group who are the subjects of complaints, as the law requires (see Schreinert and Richardson, this volume). One unspoken but obvious effect of this type of action is to impose or reinforce boundaries of cultural legitimacy (Hall and Schuyler 1998, 142; Palmer 1998) even while ignoring culturally established legal limits. Such raids ultimately violate laws in fundamental ways with which state actors are undeniably familiar; they are applied routinely in cases every day. Some researchers suggest that this pattern—what Bromley calls a "dispute broadening process" (1998, 24)—is more readily carried out against "cults." Claims against these types of organizations "are easily marshaled and tend to proliferate rapidly"; minority religions are depicted as "subversive" and "are likely to be the targets of social control initiatives designed to contain, suppress, or destroy them" (Bromley 1998, 24).

Second, 1984 marks the beginning of a surge of strategic assaults focused primarily on *child abuse allegations* fomented by ACM affiliated organizations and actors. In important ways the Island Pond raid signaled the start of a shift in the ACM's strategy away from the failed efforts at deprogramming based on "brainwashing" and allegations to the more opportunistic and culturally sympathetic charges of child abuse (see Richardson 1999; Shreinert and Richardson, this volume). By the early eighties courts were beginning to reject legal pleas by families and friends of NRM devotees to detain and deprogram members. The ACM efforts to remedy the alleged claims of "brainwashing" and "mind control" were, notably, found to be illegal themselves. Kidnapping group members to deprogram them and attempting methods akin to brainwashing disguised as exit counseling did not withstand legal scrutiny. In fact the Cult Awareness Network was bankrupted in 1995 by a lawsuit challenging such tactics (Shupe and Darnell 2004, 2006). Consequently ACM leaders began to revise and reformulate their methods regarding their strategic assaults on NRMs.

In the 1980s many of the members of new religions born in the 1960s or early 1970s were having children, thereby resulting in a second generation in any given group. ACM activists soon recognized new opportunities to exploit, targeting NRMs for dissolution by setting out to attack their marriage, family, and child-rearing practices as unconventional and therefore suspect (Homer 1999; Richardson 1999). By alleging child abuse the ACM promoted, influenced, and exploited aggressive child protection laws (Hardin 1988) in concert with efforts to create "moral panic"; that is, the ACM fomented exaggerated fears and unfavorable public opinion regarding "cults" (Bromley and Cutchin 1999; Introvigne 2000; Richardson and Introvigne 2001). They combined these strategies in order to wage more effective campaigns against NRMs. It was in this context that the Kelly dissolution plan was introduced, centering on the strategy of fueling child abuse claims, and working to build key alliances with religious apostates and duty-bound state child protection agencies. ACM activists selectively sought out disaffected members with the worst stories or "atrocity tales" (Bromley and Shupe 1994), framing these narratives as typical or commonplace to social service agencies and the media. By portraying the experiences of disgruntled apostates as both common and pervasive, state agents wielding the full power of the state were pressed to take action in order to protect children and disrupt the alleged abusive practices of the religious group.

There are significant social and legal problems with this more recent pattern of state control of minority religions, however. Social service agents in both the Vermont and Texas cases (and in a number of others as well) allowed themselves to be persuaded by weak evidence and unsubstantiated claims. In both cases the states launched massive, joint-agency raids, employing the most extreme form of police action predicated on unreliable sources and the slimmest of evidence. Moreover, it appears that both these raids were preplanned and not a necessary response to an actual emergency to protect children. Alternative methods of investigation and enforcement could have been employed with less risk to families or possible harm to the targeted communities and with equal effectiveness in achieving the legally mandated goal of protecting children (Beaman 2008; Homer 1999).

A Comparative Analysis of the Island Pond and Eldorado Raids

The Kelly plan advised ACM actors to influence government agencies and create public pressure so strong that the state would be forced to act against the group. In both Vermont and Texas key ACM actors and apostates influenced the decision of the state to launch raids by creating the appearance of an emergency: a manufactured risk of immediate harm to children in the groups. But in neither case was there real evidence that the children were threatened by an immediate harm that would justify the state's drastic actions. State juvenile laws allow the removal of children from parents only in extreme circumstances where there is a danger to the physical health or safety of the child, where reasonable efforts have been made to prevent the removal, and where every reasonable effort has been made to enable the child to return home (see Schreinert and Richardson, this volume).[1] Vermont and most other states have virtually identical legal provisions. In Vermont and Texas, despite the fact that there was no immediate danger to any child in residence and that social workers, law enforcement, and state attorneys were well aware of the limits of the law, children were forcibly removed en masse from their homes. In Texas all the seized children were put in state custody for weeks without specific evidence of harm to all but 1 of the 439 children seized. In its review of the District Court's decision to allow the mass seizure of the FLDS children, the Texas Court of Appeals noted that,

> Even if one views the FLDS belief system as creating a danger of sexual abuse by grooming boys to be perpetrators of sexual abuse and raising girls to be victims of sexual abuse . . . there is no evidence that this danger is "immediate" or "urgent" . . . with respect to every child in the community. (*In re Sara Steed et al.* 2008, p. 3)

The claim of "urgency" by opponents and the state was predicated in part on an association theory that advanced the notion that all the children were at risk because of their membership in a community with common religious beliefs. As such, it was necessary for opponents to create the appearance of widespread child abuse based upon beliefs, not actual evidence, strategically directing state actors to disgruntled former members or others with grievances to establish evidence. In August 1983 ACM leaders Galen Kelly and Priscilla Coates provided the Vermont Attorney General's Office with a list of selected apostates to interview. Subsequently state investigators traveled to seven states to interview those on the list and others who were allegedly knowledgeable of the group to "unearth" claims of child abuse (Wiseman 2005). Among the dozen people interviewed two were children, two were visitors, one was a professional deprogrammer, and about half of those interviewed were deprogrammed. As a result of the interviews, investigators produced a thirty-two-page affidavit (known as the Moran affidavit, the name of the officer who compiled the data) of stale claims, hearsay, and information largely irrelevant to the seized children. The Moran affidavit was filed in support of the state's request for a search warrant. After the raid, some former members even contacted Vermont state authorities and Church members to complain that their statements had been distorted or exaggerated and that the investigators had come only to "look for the dirt" (Wiseman 2005). In reviewing the evidence for the search warrant and the raid, District Court Judge Frank Mahady chided prosecutors and law enforcement for conducting a mass raid with little specific evidence and overly broad claims.

> The theory is that there is some evidence of some abuse at some time in the past of some other children in the community. The same, of course, may be shown of Middlebury, Burlington, Rutland, Newport or any other community. Such generalized assumptions do not warrant mass raids by the police removing the children of Middlebury, Burlington, Rutland, Newport or any other community (even a small, unpopular one). Adlai Stevenson once noted that "guilt is personal," and I might add "not communal." Our Court has held many times that mere presence at a particular place is not sufficient to establish participation in a particular act. (*In re Certain Children* 1984, p. 3)

The State of Vermont's attempt to employ an environment theory to justify jurisdiction over the children here is quite clear. There was a simple assault case pending against one leader for spanking a child not his own. The state reasoned, however, that all the children in the community were "at risk" because they lived in the same community as the man charged with the misdemeanor of simple assault. In effect, state attorneys argued that "all the children were at risk because they lived in the same Community as the defendant." District Court Judge Mahady roundly rejected the logic of the state's legal argument:

> No person who cares the least about individual dignity would claim that such evidence would allow the State to round up all such children to be inspected for evidence of abuse. To select an unpopular neighborhood

labeled a "cult" compounds the threat. If the Court were to allow the State action here, a Pandora's Box would be opened which would prove difficult, if not impossible, ever to close again." (*In re Certain Children* 1984, p. 26 n. 1)

The State of Texas essentially advanced the same environment theory in the FLDS case. Not surprisingly, a similar finding of error was made by the Texas Court of Appeals. The Appellate Court rejected the overly broad claims by the Department of Family and Protective Services (DFPS) concerning the raid and mass custodial detention of FLDS children. The DFPS claimed that removing all the FLDS children was necessary because communal organization of the group constituted a single "household" under Texas law. The DFPS also asserted that the group's religious beliefs concerning polygamy had created a "pervasive system of abuse." Below the Texas Court of Appeals and the Texas Supreme Court, respectively, repudiate these arguments.

> The notion that the entire ranch constitutes a "household" as contemplated by section 262.201 and justifies removing all children from the ranch community if there is even one incident of suspected child sexual abuse is contrary to the evidence. The Department's witnesses acknowledged that the ranch community was divided into separate family groups and separate households. While there was evidence that the living arrangements on the ranch are more communal than most typical neighborhoods, the evidence was not legally or factually sufficient to support a theory that the entire ranch community was a "household" under section 262.201.

> The simple fact, conceded by the Department, that not all FLDS families are polygamous or allow their female children to marry as minors demonstrates the danger of removing children from their homes based on the broad-brush ascription of every aspect of a belief system to every person living among followers of the belief system or professing to follow the belief system. (*In re Texas Department of Family and Protective Services, Relator, Supreme Court of Texas* 2008, p. 6)

The Search Warrants

In both Vermont and Texas ACM actors influenced law enforcement officials to persuade judges to issue search warrants based on generalities without meeting legal standards for reliability of evidence. Before a search warrant can be issued, a judge must be satisfied that the information is reliable and credible. This is a critical step in adhering to the rule of law so that citizens are protected from unconstitutional intrusions. The failure to meet this standard leaves citizens subject to the lies of malefactors and those with bad intentions. However, when state agents lack legal grounds for entry and cannot meet the necessary standards, sometimes pressure can be applied to judges to issue a warrant anyway in the hope of finding the desired evidence once inside.

The Kelly plan specifically directs ACM actors to apply pressure once they have gained the trust of a state agency. Kelly advocates using former members and their accounts to leverage influence with state actors, even though research shows that apostate narratives are notoriously unreliable (Bromley 1998; Johnson 1998; Wright 1998). This strategy was effectively implemented in Vermont. The former social services commissioner in Vermont, John Burchard, later admitted that ACM actors provided important information upon which the agency relied: "those individuals [ACM actors] had some very compelling information which guided their actions; information which was not available to the public" (Burchard 1984). Such an approach is illegal, however; seizing people or evidence on this basis is called "investigative detention," and it is unlawful under the U.S. Constitution, as well as the state constitutions of Vermont and Texas (Swantko 2000, pp. 12, 15).[2] Judge Mahady's comments in the Island Pond case bear this out.

Indeed, it is all too clear that the State's request for protective detention permitted by the statute upon an appropriate showing was entirely pretextual. What the State really sought was investigative detention. In effect, each of the children was viewed as a piece of evidence. It was the State's admitted purpose to transport each of the 112 children to a special clinic where they were to be examined . . . Not only were the children to be treated as mere pieces of evidence; they were also to be held hostage to the ransom demand of information from the parents. (*In re Certain Children* 1984, p. 5)

The element of pressure placed on judges to sign search warrants was evident in the Vermont case. In the aftermath of the Island Pond raid, Judge Joseph Wolchik, who signed the search warrant, stated that he had been "pressured by bad information" and that he had made "a terrible mistake" ("Judge Who Ordered Raid Questions Info He Had" 1987).

Two warrants were executed in Texas. The first was not signed until after the authorities had surrounded and entered the YFZ Ranch on April 3, 2008, and seized the children. The warrant allowed officials to search for the elusive Sarah Jessop and the alleged perpetrator, Dale Barlow, based upon the complaint. In the process of the search, DFPS authorities removed more than four hundred children in what officials claimed was an "emergency" action, without obtaining a court order. DFPS subsequently petitioned the court for temporary conservatorship of the children, which was granted by District Court Judge Barbara Walther. But the ruling was challenged by FLDS mothers, and the Texas Court of Appeals determined that the state had overreached. The District Court was ordered to vacate the temporary conservatorship order. A second warrant issued on April 6 seeking records about underage children revealed that the state was not looking for at-risk children but instead wanted to justify the mass removal of FLDS children based on the religious beliefs of their parents, much in the same manner as carried out during the Island Pond raid. Having failed to find the nonexistent Sarah and perhaps realizing the calls to Flora Jessop were a hoax, it became evident that the Texas DFPS was acting on broader claims supplied by anti-FLDS activists and apostates whose narratives painted a "pervasive system of abuse." DFPS and other state officials apparently failed to see the logical and legal fallacies of this "broad-brush ascription."

According to an April 11, 2008, news report in *The Arizona Republic*, child protection officials in that state received calls "similar to the one in Texas" that led to the FLDS raid (Crawford 2008) The calls in Arizona and Texas came within a week of each other; both were made by a girl of the same age and involved similar allegations of abuse. The caller to Arizona, however, claimed to be at the FLDS community in Colorado City, Arizona. In both cases the calls were made to "outside organizations" first and were then referred to state child protection authorities. In the Texas case the "outside organization" was Flora Jessop's Child Protection Project, but no mention was made in the news report of the organization or the person receiving the call in Arizona. Another news source suggests, however, that the calls in Arizona went to Joni Holm, an anti-FLDS activist who volunteered at the Child Protection Project in Phoenix (Gallagher 2008; "New Details on Polygamist Ranch" 2008). Curiously what stands out in these two almost identical incidents is the manner in which state officials responded. Unlike the reaction by Texas authorities, Arizona officials said that they lacked sufficient information and authority to act on the calls (Crawford 2008).

In Arizona, where state officials have a long history of investigating charges made against the FLDS in Colorado City, they have learned to be more deliberate in following the law. Allegations are often found to be made without sufficient evidence. Since 2000 the Arizona Child Protective Services (CPS) has received sixty-one reports of abuse involving children at Colorado City. But CPS workers have only been able to verify the specific allegations leading to investigations in ten cases (Crawford 2008). That means that allegations or charges made against the FLDS in the preceding eight years produced sufficient grounds for investigation in only 16 percent of the complaints. These figures are striking and shed considerable light on the hurried and illegal reactions by Texas state officials. The statements by Arizona Attorney General Goddard are also revealing, telling the *Arizona Republic* weeks before the Texas court decision to overturn the state custody of the YFZ children that Arizona "officials don't have the authority to go in . . . based on an unverified phone call [and] sweep up 400 children" (Crawford 2008). As it turned out, neither did Texas officials. Ken Deibert, deputy director of Arizona's CPS parent agency, told the *Arizona Republic* that the agency had "limited information about the 16-year old girl" who made the allegations, but proceeded to investigate the charges, albeit in a much less dramatic fashion.

Arizona officials have labored to build trust and cooperation with the Mormon sect since the disastrous 1953 raid, when the state rounded up 263 FLDS children only to see a widespread public backlash (see Bradley 1991; Evans, this volume). CPS officials told the *Arizona Republic* that they "have made strides to build stronger connections with Colorado City residents, which has improved cooperation from members of the sect" (Crawford 2008). As a result of these efforts, investigations have become less complicated, and the willingness of members to report abuse has increased in recent years, indicating "evidence of growing trust with members" (Crawford 2008). Although anti-FLDS activists such as Flora Jessop and Carolyn Jessop have criticized Arizona's CPS for not being more aggressive (Jessop and Brown 2009; Jessop and Palmer 2008), the agency is apparently attempting to comply with the law and avoid the mistakes of the past. As if to drive the point home, Arizona Attorney General Goddard told the *Arizona Republic*, "In Arizona, we need to have a verifiable statement of abuse from the person who has been abused" (Crawford 2008). Notably the newspaper contacted apostate Flora Jessop for a comment on the calls in Arizona a few days after the Texas raid, and she said that she believed the calls were "legitimate" (Crawford 2008), a story she later revised when the Texas calls were determined to be a hoax.

Religious Intolerance

In both Vermont and Texas the children were seized in large part because their parents belonged to an unconventional religion or "cult." The Kelly plan of manipulating or co-opting state agencies and actors for the purpose of destroying small religious movements seems implausible without the presumption of some preexisting institutional bias and religious intolerance. Both seizures were premised on suspicions fueled by cult stereotypes and inflated perceptions of threat that officials accepted more or less uncritically. Why? Though the U.S. Constitution offers broad protections for the right of parents to raise their children in their chosen faith,[3] ACM organizations and actors have been relatively successful in persuading state officials, news media, and the public that "cults" are not "real" or authentic religions, and thus are not subject to First Amendment protections (Anthony and Robbins 1992; Richardson 2004). Indeed, the Kelly strategy is based on the presumption that institutional actors are more readily manipulated when faced with a perceived religious threat to the status quo.

Of course, ACM activists and state officials in Vermont and Texas denied attacking religious beliefs and claimed to be focused on evidence of physical harm or abuse. Marleigh Meisner, the spokesperson for the Texas DFPS, told CNN after the raid on Eldorado, "This is not about religion—this is about keeping children safe from abuse" ("ACLU Weighs In on Texas Polygamist Custody Case" 2008). But the courts rightly found that the mass removal of children could not be justified based on evidence in only a few individual cases. The unfounded extrapolation of abuse claims to the entire religious community by state officials exposes the tacit but core ACM conviction that "cults" are inherently abusive and destructive. It also exposes the ACM corollary that all followers of a "cult" conform without question to the dictates of the leader and cannot exercise independent thought. At the evidentiary hearing on April 17–18, 2008, in front of Judge Barbara Walther, DFPS officials presented no evidence of actual harm to the FLDS children, only offering testimony as to the alleged *beliefs* of the community as a whole ("pervasive belief system"). In effect, DFPS asked the court to infer from these beliefs that mere exposure to the religion amounts to a danger to the physical health and safety of the children. Judge Walther granted the state's request but the Texas Court of Appeals rejected the argument, finding that the "existence of the FLDS belief system . . . by itself, does not put children of FLDS parents in physical danger" (*In re Sara Steed et al.* 2008, p. 3). The Court recognized that not every FLDS member practiced polygamy and that not every young girl wanted to be married at a young age. When Texas CPS supervisor Angie Voss was asked by attorneys in the evidentiary hearing where her agency obtained its knowledge about the FLDS belief system, she told the court that she relied on two "experts." She identified the two experts as FLDS apostate Becky Musser and "cult expert" Dr. Bruce Perry (Perkins 2008; see also Wright and Fagen, this volume).

The state's implicit condemnation of religious beliefs as a pretext for protecting children did not escape the American Civil Liberties Union (ACLU). In a statement issued in the weeks after the FLDS raid, the ACLU said that "State officials have an important obligation to protect children against abuse. However, such actions should not be indiscriminately targeted against a group as a whole—particularly when the group is perceived as being different or unusual" ("ACLU Weighs In on Texas FLDS Raid" 2008). An amicus curiae brief filed with the Texas Supreme Court by the ACLU noted that "The State's sole evidence on harm was limited to general allegations that these parents are part of 'culture,' and subscribe to a 'belief' and a 'mindset'" that put children at risk (*In Re: Texas Department of Family and Protective Services, Relator, Supreme Court of Texas, Brief of Amici Curiae, ACLU*, 2008, p. 2). It went on to say that the state lacked constitutional grounds for separating and holding the children.

Statements by officials in Vermont revealed even less subtle anticult assumptions regarding the community at Island Pond. When Vermont Assistant Attorney General Philip H. White was asked by Judge Mahady on June 22, 1984, "Just what exactly is the harm that is endangering this child?" he responded, "It is as if the child is living amongst bacteria and the bacteria in this case that jeopardizes this child's health is the teachings and doctrines of the church" (*In re Certain Children* 1984, p. 6). Mr. White's use of the disease metaphor to describe the teachings and doctrines of the Island Pond Church, and equating them with pathology, clearly conveys a religious intolerance toward the group and reflects the sentiments characteristic of ACM ideology and framing. Here a rare moment of transparency was revealed by a state official.

Conclusions and Recommendations

Two points are apparent: (1) that the 1984 Island Pond raid plan, engineered by a coalition of opponents and state actors and strategically outlined by Galen Kelly, has been developed by ACM organizations and actors as a prototype for assailing other minority religious groups; and (2) that this prototype or strategy was implemented twenty-five years later in the Texas raid on the FLDS. The striking parallels are not random or coincidental. This recurring pattern of attacking new or nontraditional religious communities, explicitly devised by former deprogrammer Kelly, has become embedded and institutionalized in the ACM organizational culture. In the wake of increasingly problematic efforts to use deprogramming to assail "cults," this emergent alternative strategy has been more effective and continues to be a model for targeting new cases when conflict arises (see Bromley 1998; Hall 1995; Hall and Schuyler 1998; Wright 1995b; and Wright, this volume). A systematic examination of the dynamics leading to the state raid on the FLDS exposes the same tactics of "dispute broadening" (Bromley 1998) and claims-making by allied apostates and ACM actors working with state officials and media to foment fear and apprehension about the group. By focusing on the more opportunistic and culturally sympathetic charges of child abuse, opponents were able to marshal claims of subversion and mobilize state agents on their behalf to take action against the FLDS. A comparative analysis of the two raids provides compelling support for the influence and continued significance of the Kelly dissolution plan.

Some differences are also apparent in the way that these raids played out, and these are worth noting for reference in future cases. In the Island Pond case the court applied the rule of law sooner to prevent the executive and its agencies from interfering with the family integrity of Church members beyond what the Constitution allows. In Vermont the administrative judge deliberately chose a different judge to review the case than the judge who signed the warrant authorizing the seizure. This seems like wise practice, especially in a case of such magnitude. On the other hand, in Texas, Judge Walther signed the warrant and reviewed it, affirming herself at great cost to the children and parents of the FLDS and also at great cost to the citizens of Texas. The legal proceedings have cost Texas more than 14 million dollars (Moritz 2008), whereas the one-day court proceeding in Vermont cost the state a scant fraction of that amount.

Scholars who have studied these raids have called for greater protections and stricter vigilance with regard to the law in order to avoid similar actions in the future (Homer 1999; Richardson 1999, 2004; Swantko 2004; Wessinger 2006; Williams 1995; Wright 1995a, 2002). Due process must be followed at every step along the way. Due process means that every individual involved must be given notice and an opportunity to be heard. At the initial Island Pond hearing on the very day of the seizure, Judge Mahady took the time to make sure that due process was followed by conducting individual evidentiary hearings. This quickly exposed the fact that the state had no substantive evidence to justify the mass seizure of the children. Judge Mahady gave the parents time to speak with their lawyers and required that the prosecution produce convincing evidence before interfering in the parent-child relationship.

In contrast, at the April 17–18 hearing in Texas, the FLDS families were given no opportunity for meaningful participation. A fresh judge reviewing the matter in the evidentiary hearings would likely have ended the calamity and the expense much sooner. It was the Texas Court of Appeals and the Texas Supreme Court that stood at the gate to prevent the government's lawless action. Although the social service departments of both states insisted that the action was "routine" and "different in size only," this was far from the case. Due process and legal protections were violated in the execution of both raids.

In 1962 the U.S. Supreme Court, in Engel v. Vitale (1962), warned of "coercive pressure upon religious minorities to conform to the prevailing officially approved religion." It is not the duty of the state to carry out the partisan moral crusades of private interest groups in order to coerce religious conformity. Although states have a duty to protect children, the pursuit of the "best interest of the child" is not a license to ignore other legal limits or run roughshod over new or nontraditional religions. As Judge Mahady observed in the Island Pond case, "The best interest of the child is a useful maxim, but it only comes into play when there is legal justification" (*In re Certain Children* 1984, p. 3). No such legal justification was produced in the Island Pond and Eldorado raids. At least some of the concern about the FLDS seemed to be rooted tacitly in the premise that a separatist ("closed") religious community deprived children of exposure to broader cultural resources (Anthony 2005; Gallagher 2008; McLaughlin 2008). It is not incumbent upon the state, however, to dictate to parents what they may teach their children based on contested boundaries of cultural legitimacy. The choices of parents regarding religious faith and the appropriate cultural enrichment of their offspring are value judgments that are rightly protected by law and beyond the excessive reach of the state.

NOTES

1. Tex. Fam. Code 262.201 (b).

2. I cite and discuss these two errors in the paper wherein Judge Mahady's opinion is cited with corresponding explanations of the unconstitutional aspects.

3. Santosky v. Kramer, 455 U.S. 745,753 (1982); Stanley v. Ill., 405 U.S. 645 (1972); Yoder v. Wisconsin, 406 U.S. 421, 431 (1962); Engel v. Vitale, 370 U.S. 421, 431(1962); *In re Certain Children* 1984.

REFERENCES

"ACLU Weighs In on Texas FLDS Raid." 2008. *Salt Lake City Tribune*, May 7.
"ACLU Weighs In on Texas Polygamist Custody Case." 2008. CNN, April 20.
Ammerman, Nancy T. 1993. "Report to the Justice and Treasury Departments Regarding Law Enforcement Interaction with the Branch Davidians in Waco, Texas." In *Recommendations of Experts for Improvements in Federal Law Enforcement after Waco*. Washington, DC: U.S. Department of Justice.
Anthony, Dick, and Thomas Robbins. 1992. "Law, Social Science, and the 'Brainwashing' Exception to the First Amendment." *Behavioral Science and the Law* 10:5–30.
Anthony, Paul. 2005. "Shrouded in Secrecy: Former Members of Eldorado Sect Speak of Abusive, Closed Society, Fanaticism." *San Angelo Standard Times*, March 27, p. 1.
Beaman, Lori. 2008. *Defining Harm: Religious Freedom and the Limits of the Law*. Vancouver: UBC Press.
Bradley, Martha Sonntag. 1993. *Kidnapped from That Land: The Government Raids on the Short Creek Polygamists*. Salt Lake City: University of Utah Press.
Bromley, David G. 1998. *The Politics of Religious Apostasy*. Westport, CT: Praeger.
Bromley, David G., and Diana Gay Cutchin. 1999. "The Social Construction of Subversive Evil: The Contemporary Anti-Cult and Anti-Satanism Movements," pp. 195–220 in Jo Freeman (ed.), *Waves of Protest*. Lanham, MD: Rowman and Littlefield.
Bromley, David G., and Anson D. Shupe. 1993. "Organized Opposition to New Religious Movements," pp. 177–98 in David G. Bromley and Jeffrey K. Hadden (eds.), *Handbook on Cults and Sects in America*. Greenwich, CT: JAI.
——. 1994. *Anti-Cult Movements in Cross-Cultural Perspective*. New York: Garland.
Burchard, John. 1984. "*Children at Risk: Why Protective Action Was Necessary in Island Pond*," July 17. Unpublished paper available online at http://www.twelvetribes.org.
Crawford, Amanda J. 2008. "Colorado City CPS Phone Call Resembles One Made in Texas." *Arizona Republic*, April 11. Accessed online at http://www.azcentral.com.
Gaffney, Edward McGlynn. 1995. "The Waco Tragedy: Constitutional Concerns and Policy Perspectives," pp. 323–58 in Stuart A. Wright (ed.), *Armageddon in Waco*. Chicago: University of Chicago Press.
Gallagher, Eugene. 2008. "FLDS 1, Texas 0: Texas Fumbles Its Child Abuse Case against the Fundamentalist Mormons." *Religion in the News* 11 (2): 6–8.
Hall, John R. 1995. "Public Narratives and the Apocalyptic Sect: From Jonestown to Mt. Carmel, pp. 205–35 in Stuart A. Wright (ed.), *Armageddon in Waco*. Chicago: University of Chicago Press.
Hall, John R., and Phillip Schuyler. 1998. "Apostasy, Apocalypse, and Religious Violence: An Exploratory Comparison of Peoples' Temple, the Branch Davidians, and the Solar Temple," pp. 141–70 in David G. Bromley (ed.), *The Politics of Religious Apostasy*. Westport, CT: Praeger.
Hardin, Mark. 1988. "Legal Barriers in Child Abuse Investigations: State Powers and Individual Rights," *Washington Law Review* 63 (3): 493–605.
Homer, Michael. 1999. "The Precarious Balance between Freedom of Religion and the Best Interests of the Child," pp. 187–209 in Susan J. Palmer and Charlotte Hardman (eds.), *Children in New Religions*. New Brunswick, NJ: Rutgers University Press.
Introvigne, Massimo. 1998."New Religious Movements and the Law: A Comparison between Two Different Legal Systems—The United States and Italy," pp. 276–90 in Eileen Barker and Margit Warburg (eds.), *New Religions and New Religiosity*. Aarhus, Denmark: Aarhus University Press.

———. 2000. "Moral Panics and Anti-Cult Terrorism in Western Europe." *Terrorism and Political Violence* 12:47–59.

Investigative Proposal regarding Island Pond. N.d. Kingston, NY: Galen Kelly Associates. Document on file with author.

Jessop, Carolyn, with Laura Palmer. 2008. *Escape.* New York: Broadway Books.

Jessop, Flora, and Paul T. Brown. 2009. *Church of Lies.* New York: Jossey-Bass.

Johnson, Daniel Carson. 1998. "Apostates Who Never Were: The Social Construction of *Absque Facto* Narratives," pp. 115–38 in David G. Bromley (ed.), *The Politics of Religious Apostasy.* Westport, CT: Praeger.

Johnson, Lamar. 2009. Interview with YFZ church member, San Angelo, TX, April 3. On file with author.

"Judge Who Ordered Raid Questions Info He Had." 1987. *Caledonian Record*, February 11.

McLaughlin, Elliott. 2008. "Ex-Sect Members Escape Polygamy but Not Pain." CNN News, April 17. Accessed online at http://www.rickross.com/reference/polygamy/polygamy834.html.

"New Details on Polygamist Ranch." 2008. CNN News, April 9.

Moritz, John. 2008. "Texans' Tab for YFZ Roundup Tops $14 Million." *Fort Worth Star-Telegram*, June 14, A1.

Palmer, Susan J. 1998. "Apostates and Their Role in the Construction of Grievance Claims against the Northeast Kingdom/Messianic Communities," pp. 191–208 in David G. Bromley (ed.), *The Politics of Religious Apostasy.* Westport, CT: Praeger.

Palmer, Susan J., and Bozeman, John. 1997. "The Northeast Kingdom Community Church of Island Pond, Vermont: Raising Up a People for Yahshua's Return." *Journal of Contemporary Religion* 12 (2): 181–90.

Perkins, Nancy. 2008. "Texas Officials Deny ex-FLDS Members Involved in Search Warrant." *Deseret News*, April 19.

Richardson, James T. 1996. "'Brainwashing' Claims and Minority Religions outside the Untied States: Cultural Diffusion of a Questionable Legal Concept in the Legal Arena." *Brigham Young University Law Review* 873–904.

———. 1999. "Social Control of New Religions: From Brainwashing Claims to Child Sex Abuse Accusations," pp. 72–86 in Susan J. Palmer (ed.), *Children in New Religions.* New Brunswick, NJ: Rutgers University Press.

———. 2004. *Regulating Religion.* New York: Plenum.

Richardson, James T., and Massimo Introvigne. 2001. "'Brainwashing' Theories in European Parliamentary and Administrative Reports. On 'Cults' and 'Sects.'" *Journal for the Scientific Study of Religion* 40:143–68.

Shupe, Anson D., and David G. Bromley. 1994. *Anti-Cult Movements in Cross-Cultural Perspective*, New York: Garland.

Shupe, Anson D., and Susan Darnell. 2004. "The North American Anti-Cult Movement: Vicissitudes of Success and Failure," pp. 184–205 in James R. Lewis (ed.), *The Oxford Handbook of New Religious Movements.* New York: Oxford University Press.

———. 2006. *Agents of Discord: Deprogrammers, Pseudo-Science and the American Anticult Movement.* New Brunswick, NJ: Transaction.

Smith, John L. 2008. "Affidavits Paint a Disturbing Picture of Texas Child Protective Services." *Las Vegas Review Journal*, June 3. Accessed online at http://www.reviewjournal.com.

Swantko, Jean A. 1998a. "An Issue of Control: Conflict between the Church in Island Pond and State Government." Paper presented to the World Congress of Sociology, July. Available online at http://www.twelvetribes.org.

———. 1998b. "The Messianic Communities in the European Union: An Issue of Parental Authority." Paper presented at the Annual Meeting of CESNUR. Available online at http://www.twelvetribes.org.

———. 2000. "Anti-Cultists, Social Policy and the 1984 Island Pond Raid." Paper presented at the Annual Meeting of CESNUR. Available at http://www.twelvetribes.org.

———. 2004. "The Twelve Tribes Communities, the Anti-Cult Movement and Government's Response," pp. 179–200 in James T. Richardson (ed.), *Regulating Religion*. New York: Plenum.

———. 2009. "State-Sanctioned Raids and Government Violations of Religious Freedom: Revealing Similarities of Constitutional Errors in Both the 1984 Island Pond Raid and the 2008 FLDS Raid." Paper presented at the Annual Meeting of CESNUR, Salt Lake City, June. Available online at http://www.cesnur.org.

Tabor, James, and Gallagher, Eugene. 1995. *Why Waco? Cults and the Battle for Religious Freedom in America*. Berkeley: University of California Press.

Wessinger, Catherine. 2005. "Culting—From Waco to Fundamentalist Mormons." Accessed online at http://www.religiousdispatches.org/art219.php.

———. 2006. "The Branch Davidians and Religion Reporting—A Ten Year Retrospective," pp. 147-172 in Kenneth Newport and Crawford Gribbon (eds.), *Expecting the End: Millennialism in Social and Historical Context*. Waco, TX: Baylor University Press.

Wiseman, Jean Swantko. 2005. *The Children of Island Pond*. A documentary film available online at http://www.twelvetribes.org.

Williams, Rhys. 1995. "Breaching the Wall of Separation: The Balance between Religious Freedom and Social Order," pp. 299–321 in Stuart A. Wright (ed.), *Armageddon in Waco*. Chicago: University of Chicago Press.

Wright, Stuart A. 1995a. *Armageddon in Waco: Critical Perspectives on the Branch Davidian Conflict*. Chicago: University of Chicago Press.

———. 1995b. "Construction and Escalation of a 'Cult' Threat: Dissecting Moral Panic and Official Reaction to the Branch Davidians," pp. 75–94 in Stuart A. Wright (ed.), *Armageddon in Waco*. Chicago: University of Chicago Press.

———. 1998. "Exploring Factors That Shape the Apostate Role," pp. 95–114 in David G. Bromley (ed.), *The Politics of Religious Apostasy*. Westport, CT: Praeger.

———. 2002. "Public Agency Involvement in Movement-State Confrontations," pp. 102–22 in David G. Bromley and J. Gordon Melton (eds.), *Cults, Religion, and Violence*. New York: Cambridge University Press.

Wright, Stuart A., and Susan J. Palmer. 2009. "Storming Zion: An Examination of State Raids on Religious Communities." Prospectus for a book that will be published by Oxford University Press.

LEGAL DOCUMENTS CITED

Engel v. Vitale, 370 U.S. 421 (1962).

In re Certain Children, District Court of Vermont, Unit 3, Orleans Circuit (1984).

In re Sara Steed et al., Texas Court of Appeals, Third District, at Austin, No.03-08-00235-CV (2008).

In re Texas Department of Family and Protective Services, Relator, Supreme Court of Texas, Brief of Amici Curiae, ACLU (2008).

Yoder v. Wisconsin, 406 U.S. 205 (1972).

9

Political and Legislative Context of the FLDS Raid in Texas

JAMES T. RICHARDSON AND
TAMATHA L. SCHREINERT

When new religious movements (NRMs) first appeared in the United States in the 1960s and 1970s they were greeted favorably, as many in society, including some parents, were pleased to see young people choosing religion over the radical political activism of that chaotic time. The circumstances changed markedly, however, once it became obvious that some of the NRMs were quite serious about commitment and lifestyle changes that included dropping out of college, perhaps going on mission activities in exotic lands, or raising money for their new allegiances by distributing literature or selling trinkets on the streets of American cities. What evolved from the growing concern about "high demand" NRMs was a dubious but effective narrative about why young people joined such groups that focused on pseudo-scientific ideas of "brainwashing" and "mind control" (Richardson 1993; Richardson and Kilbourne 1983).

These ideological weapons of brainwashing and mind control served reasonably well for at least two decades as efforts by critics and detractors to exert social control over new and unconventional religions widened. The constitutional protections usually afforded religious groups in American society were circumvented by claims that such protections did not extend to alleged mind control techniques. Brainwashing-based social control efforts were also exported by way of a growing transnational anticult (ACM) network to other countries that began to experience the NRM phenomenon (Richardson 1996; Richardson and Introvigne 2001). Yet considerable research by scholars of NRMs and a series of court cases in the United States eventually undercut social control efforts derived from brainwashing claims (Richardson and Kilbourne 1983; Anthony 1990; Anthony and Robbins 1992; Richardson 1991, 1993). It eventually became clear that such claims could not pass muster under rules of evidence generally accepted in U.S.

courts of law (Ginsburg and Richardson 1998), as well as in other societies where reasonable rules of evidence prevailed (Richardson 1996; Anthony 1999; Anthony and Robbins 1992). Thus brainwashing-based efforts at social control became less effective and less likely to be invoked by opponents of NRMS in North America as well as in some other (but not all) Western nations.[1]

By the beginning of the 1990s the NRMs that emerged two decades earlier had produced a second generation of children born to members of these groups. NRMs varied greatly in terms of their fecundity, with Christian fundamentalist groups that resisted birth-control methods having the most children and other NRMs, such as the Bhagwan Shree Rajneesh group in Oregon, producing very few. With disturbing frequency, children born into these groups soon became subject to a gauntlet of relatively new laws regarding the protection of children. Also, as some family units within the religious groups dissolved, custody disputes developed, leading to occasional legal confrontations over control of the children of such unions (Homer 1999). Those custody battles sometimes included claims of child abuse of various kinds.

This development marked an important shift in state and countermovement efforts of social control of new or unconventional religions. Religious communities that previously had been fighting social control efforts based on brainwashing claims suddenly found themselves in a new legal arena, facing the legal manifestations of the "child saver" movement (Best 1990), with its attendant mantra of "best interest of the child." NRMs discovered quickly that child protection claims would easily trump religious freedom concerns in American society.[2] The state had, through the legislation designed to protect children, functionally assumed a posture of exerting expanded control over how children were treated and raised in American society. The welfare and benefit of children had become a paramount value in American society, overwhelming nearly all other concerns such as parental rights, familial autonomy, and freedom of religion.

This shift in state and countermovement strategy regarding minority faiths became evident in the substance and dynamics of state confrontations in the following years, both here and abroad. For example, Swantko (2004) details the troubles faced by the Twelve Tribes communities in the United States, France, and Germany as authorities have attempted to take children from the group using claims of child abuse, some made in the throes of custody battles (see also Bozeman and Palmer 1997; Malcarne and Burchard 1992; and Palmer 1999). Richardson (1999) describes state efforts to exert control over

The Family International (formerly known as the Children of God) using child protection laws in a number of different countries including Australia, Spain, the United States, Peru, Norway, Argentina, and the United Kingdom. These efforts led to Family children being taken into custodial detention by governmental agencies in several of these countries, sometimes with great fanfare and media attention (see also Oliver 1994). All these efforts eventually failed, with the children finally returned to their parents, but not before causing severe disruption of these families and the communities. Some of the parents in these targeted groups spent months in jail before being released. Siegler (1999) describes how the State of California authorities used concerns about the welfare of children as a justification for infiltrating the In Search of Truth (ISOT) community and for taking dramatic action against it. Ellison and Bartkowski (1995) and Lewis (1994) detail how the alleged abuse of children was used to convince Attorney General Janet Reno to allow the deadly federal assault to go forward against the Branch Davidians, culminating in a tragic firestorm and mass casualties.

These new religious groups were also made vulnerable to this strategy by a convergence of legal cases confronting how children should be treated within a religious minority. Richardson and DeWitt (1992) describe the legal actions involving members of the Christian Science Church whose children died as a result of illnesses not medically treated (see also Schoepflin 2003; and Peters 2008.) Most of these cases developed in the late 1980s, at about the same time that other, new minority religions were beginning to feel pressure from governmental authorities concerning how their children were being raised within the groups. Moreover, several other key cases involving children in minority faiths predated these more recent concerns, among them the lengthy battles fought by the Jehovah's Witnesses concerning their right to implement their beliefs about safeguarding children's health (Wah 2001; Louderback-Wood 2005; and Beaman 2008) and determining what children should be allowed or required to do within a religious group (Prince v. Massachusetts [1944] 321 U.S. 158).

More germane to the focus of this chapter were early efforts to exert control over children in the FLDS community, Short Creek, Arizona, in July 1953. A massive predawn raid on Short Creek involving more than 100 law enforcement agents was organized by Arizona Governor John Howard Pyle. Pyle claimed to be concerned about how children were being raised in the community, saying that they were being turned into "white slaves." This raid, described elsewhere in this volume (Evans, chap.1), was perhaps the largest mass arrest of men, women, and children in U.S. history, until the recent

Texas FLDS raid. At Short Creek more than 350 people, including 236 children, were arrested or taken into custody. About 150 of the Short Creek children were not returned to their parents for more than two years, although all were eventually returned and a rapprochement was reached between authorities and the FLDS that lasted for several decades.

This earlier raid, which occurred fifty-five years prior to the raid in Eldorado, has been analyzed as a precursor to what occurred in Texas in 2008 (Evans, this volume). The earlier raid demonstrated that state concern about children in a polygamous religious group was present in the culture of mid-twentieth-century America (see Homer 1994). This initial concern preceded the later and much broader alarm about the general welfare of children in American society that sociologists have aptly described as the "child-saver" movement (Best 1990; Ellison and Bartkowski 1995). The Arizona raid itself may have been carried out more for political reasons than authentic concern for the children in the Short Creek community, but, if so, the tactic backfired. Arizona Governor Pyle mustered nearly one hundred media representatives to accompany the large contingent of state police that raided the community that early morning in July. His efforts to manipulate public opinion failed, however, and subsequent media coverage was more sympathetic to the fundamentalist community than to the governor. Pyle lost his effort at reelection, blaming the reaction to the raid for his defeat.

It remains to be seen if repercussions surrounding the Texas raid are similar, but it is already clear that media treatment of what happened in Texas mirrors, considerably, the reactions to the Short Creek raid. Questions were raised almost immediately about what happened, how such a raid could have been mounted in such a short time (based on what turned out to be hoax phone calls), and why such drastic actions as removing 439 children were taken. What follows in this chapter is an effort to demonstrate that the raid was actually *a long time in preparation and that the State of Texas and some of its politicians had been preparing for action against the FLDS community almost since it began building a community in 2003.*

Following a description of the political and legislative efforts leading up to the FLDS raid in Texas, we briefly discuss some important developments by Texas politicians as well as issues concerning the FLDS. We then place actions taken both before and after the raid within a broader context of efforts to deal with concerns about children within communal religious groups. We then discuss how the concern over children's welfare has been used as justification for social control efforts exerted by the state against such groups.

The Raid: A Process, Not Just an Event

As just indicated, the raid on the FLDS community in Texas that occurred on April 3, 2008, was not a single act developed as a rapid one-off response to a set of hoax phone calls alleging sexual and other physical violence against someone who claimed to be an underage girl in the group. The presence of this controversial group in Texas had been flagged by government officials years before, and it seems clear now that some officials had been preparing for a confrontation for an extended period. Some of the preparatory activities began almost as soon as public awareness developed about the FLDS group's move to Texas. We offer a discussion of these preparatory activities to support the contention that state officials planned for a confrontation from the inception of the Yearning for Zion (YFZ) community.

Legislative Control Efforts

Texas Governor Rick Perry signed Senate Bill 6 of the 2005 legislative session into law on June 7, 2005, almost three years before the April 2008 raid ("Governor Perry Signs SB 6 into Law" 2005; Neil 2008). That new law, effective September 1, 2005, was designed to bolster the state's Child Protective Services (CPS) agency, and included some provisions directly aimed at the FLDS group that had moved to far west Texas and developed a large presence over the previous two years.

Several parcels of property in Schleicher County, Texas, had been purchased in 2003 and 2004 by David Allred, a son-in-law of FLDS leader Warren Jeffs, leading to a flurry of building activity that caught the attention of Texas authorities. The actions of the FLDS in west Texas led directly to efforts to pass new laws designed to thwart the development of the growing FLDS community at the YFZ Ranch.

The two major provisions amended into the omnibus bill for the Texas CPS were proposed by State Representative Harvey Hilderbran, a Republican legislator from Kerrville, Texas, whose district includes Schleicher County. One provision raised the state's age of consent for marriage from fourteen to sixteen, and the other elevated bigamy and polygamy from misdemeanors to felonies. Both new statutes were relied on in subsequent legal actions against the FLDS group and its leaders. Senate Bill (SB) 6 also contained a provision disallowing the marriage of first cousins and the marriage of stepchildren to stepparents (Harris 2005).

Representative Hilderbran had introduced a far more comprehensive bill, HR 3006, earlier in the session, and stated in a clearly transparent press release, "I want to keep Eldorado, Schleicher County, and all of Texas from becoming like Colorado City, Arizona, and Hilldale, Utah, where this cult came from" ("Governor Perry Signs SB 6 into Law" 2005). His bill survived the House committee process, passing unanimously out of the Juvenile Justice and Family Issues Committee, and was sent to the House floor for a vote. Although no vote was ever taken, Hilderbran sought to include the most important provisions from HR 3006 in SB 6, which did eventually become law.

Hilderbran's much more broad-based proposal included the following provisions (House Research Organization 2005; Richter 2009):

1. Change offense of bigamy from a misdemeanor to a second-degree felony with penalties from two to twenty years in prison and a fine of up to $10,000, if partner were over sixteen years of age; but, if the partner were less than sixteen, a first degree felony with penalties of five years to life imprisonment and a fine of up to $10,000.

2. Raise the minimum age of marriage from fourteen to sixteen but require parental consent or a court order.

3. Deny spouses the right to refuse to testify in a bigamy case.

4. Prohibit an unauthorized person from conducting a marriage ceremony. If this is done and the marriage is in violation of the law, then this would be a third-degree felony with imprisonment from two to ten years and a fine of up to $10,000.

5. Prohibit marriage between a current or former stepchild and parent.

6. Prohibit marriage between first cousins by blood or adoption.

7. Change residency requirement for holding political office from one year to two years in the state, and from six months to one year in the territory from which the office is elected.

8. Require candidates for public office to sign statement that they are not violating any constitution or laws of Texas or the United States.

Hilderbran's original bill also contained provisions to modify the state's education statutes, but they were deleted from the bill passed by the House committee. Included was a proposal to clarify the roles of state truant and attendance officers charged with ensuring that children receive an education ("Hilderbran Takes Aim at YFZ Ranch" 2005). This provision apparently was aimed at the home schooling practiced at the YFZ Ranch with the community's children.

Richter (2009) reports that Hilderbran's original bill was opposed by a broad coalition of home school advocates in Texas who did not want legislation passed that would impede their ability to educate their children themselves. Richter also says that some "east Texans" opposed the bill because it would prevent marriage of second cousins, although that does not seem to have been the intent of the proposal.

The House Research Organization report (2005, p. 4) states that HR 3006 supporters claim that,

> [The bill would] strengthen Texas' laws against polygamy and election laws to protect communities from being infiltrated by fringe religious groups. A group of Fundamentalist Church of Latter-Day Saints is building a compound south of San Angelo where local residents are concerned that members may be forcing young girls to marry, engage in polygamist activities, and possibly marry their relatives. Local residents also are concerned that members of the group will run for public office and will have moved a large enough group of voters into the area to take over local governance.

The bill would pick up on elements of similar laws in Utah and Arizona that faced similar concerns about the same group.

Opponents of the bill expressed concern that Texas was passing laws aimed at a specific religious group, and noted that no actual evidence existed that the group was engaged in any of the activities covered by HR 3006. Other opponents said that the bill was overly broad and that the requirement for an oath before running for public office was particularly problematic (House Research Organization 2005, p. 4).

The Aftermath of the Raid

Notwithstanding the criticism that has been directed at the Texas CPS for the manner in which the raid was handled, as well as its cost (estimated at $14 million [Moritz 2008]), a spokesperson for the agency said that if another call came in concerning the FLDS the agency would not hesitate to respond (Winslow 2009). Patrick Crimmins, speaking for the CPS said, "We certainly would take advantage of our vast experience in this particular case if we were to get another report. There's no way to predict exactly how we would react" (Winslow 2009). Crimmins added, "We wanted to find out if those children had been abused and neglected and do whatever we needed to do to protect them from being harmed in the future. We believe we've done that" (ibid.).

Since the raid several new proposals have been introduced by representative Hilderbran and others. Hilderbran said, "We learned we weren't equipped for the situation. Our agency had limited policy and laws that didn't envision this happening. There were mistakes made and many were made because the agency didn't have the authority or options to manage it more effectively" (Winslow 2009).

In 2009 Hilderbran introduced House Bill (HB) 4255 to address his concerns. This bill includes another change in the age of consent law, moving it to seventeen from the sixteen years of age approved in the 2005 session of the Texas legislature in SB 6 (Winslow 2009). Details of other intrusive changes being suggested in HB 4255 include the following (Hoff 2009):

1. Increase the statute of limitations for bigamy from three to seven years for adults and from five to ten years in cases involving a minor.
2. Increase the penalty for parents who do not properly report births.
3. Allow a peace officer to enter a home of a student who is part of a CPS investigation and who is not meeting compulsory school requirements.
4. Increase penalties for parents who do not require that children attend school, making it a possible third-degree felony.
5. Mandating that an alleged perpetrator is removed from the home instead of the child, the remaining parent must report any effort of the alleged perpetrator to return.
6. Prohibit a parent from accompanying a child being taken into state custody.
7. Change definition of bigamy and raise offense category to a higher felony depending on age of the spouses.
8. Allow the state to circumvent the "reasonable efforts" clause concerning efforts to keep children with their parents.

This last item is quite controversial. Current state law requires CPS to make reasonable efforts to keep children and parents together. This "reasonable effort" requirement is actually mandated by federal law (Title IV-E of the Social Security Act, 42 U.S.C. 672 (a)(1) and 671 (a) (15)), and is tied to much federal funding for the child protection system. The Texas Supreme Court faulted the agency for ignoring this provision with its actions during the 2008 raid. The new provision being proposed in HB 4255 reads as follows:

The court may find that based on the circumstances, no reasonable efforts would prevent or eliminate the need to remove a child and the department satisfied the requirements even though the department made no efforts to prevent or eliminate the need to remove the child.

If the aforementioned provision were to pass, the State of Texas could potentially lose millions of dollars that it might otherwise receive from the federal government to support and pay for foster care.

In discussing the bill, representative Hilderbran said, "The bill doesn't target this group [the FLDS]. There is another case that isn't as famous in my county but involves similar situations for children and even includes child labor." The other group, however, was not named. To date, no formal action has been taken on HB 4255, and it is not clear what, if anything, might happen concerning further legislative changes.

Other post-raid developments of note include a pledge made by the FLDS not to perform any more underage marriages and instead to abide by the new 2005 law on age of consent. Some criminal prosecutions continue that are unrelated to the custody battle over the children who were removed (see the following chapter).

The Context of Concern about Children in Communal Religious Groups

We now know that children can be at risk in religious groups that are part of the religious mainstream in America, as evidenced, for example, by the flood of cases of sex abuse that have come to light recently among mainline churches and clergy (Crisp 2007; Dokecki 2004; Fater and Mullaney 2000; Franz 2002; Gerdes et al. 1996; Haywood et al. 1996; Kennedy 2000; Markham and Mikail 2004; Plante 1996, 1999; Saradijian 2003; Shupe 1998). That new information notwithstanding, there continues to be considerable concern about children in religious groups that are newer, or whose practices and beliefs are not part of the normative culture of America. Earlier in this chapter we briefly presented a number of situations involving battles over the welfare of children in minority religious groups. Some of those conflicts occurred in noncommunal religious groups with practices thought to jeopardize the health and welfare of children within the group. Other disputes occurred over the custody of children when a marriage dissolved and one member of the couple left the religious group.

Conflicts over the welfare of children may be exacerbated if the group is relatively closed and isolated, with practices and beliefs that appear strange to the general public in the society. When a religious group lives communally, is withdrawn from society, and perhaps is even geographically isolated, the level of concern about children in the group tends to increase dramatically. This is especially the case if apostates or other detractors are attempting to convince state authorities to exert expanded control over the group. Palmer (1999), Richardson (1999), and Swantko (2004) all discuss the role that apostates have played in promoting claims of child abuse in selected minority religious groups. Palmer and Swantko focused on the Twelve Tribes community discussed above, and Richardson's analysis included The Family International. The role apostates played in giving impetus to aggressive social control efforts of the Twelve Tribes and The Family is instructive of the context within which the FLDS raid developed and was carried out, given that the "trigger" for the raid was a series of hoax phone calls forwarded to Texas authorities by a disgruntled ex-member of the FLDS.

The Family International and the Twelve Tribes are both communal religions that have, more than most other NRMs, seen the exertion of governmental power brought against them over various claims of child abuse. Both groups have had large numbers of children taken from them by governmental authorities, and both suffered great disruptions of family and organizational life as a result. That in all instances the children were eventually returned to their parents does not diminish the fact that the state was able to intrude with impunity in such a dramatic fashion as to forcibly remove children from the groups.[3]

Richardson (1999) discusses in some detail the raids in various countries where hundreds of children were taken from The Family International communal settings. He compares this to the Twelve Tribes situation, particularly the first raid that occurred in Vermont in 1984, and some of the recommendations (discussed below) that were developed by authorities in the aftermath of that abortive effort at social control. He notes that there are several major concerns about the welfare of children in communal religious groups, and that the concerns have led to a coordinated effort to introduce a new concept, "collective child abuse;" an effort that is germane to what has happened (and may still be taking place) in Texas with the FLDS.

As Richardson observes in a previous work, this new concept of "collective child abuse" was defined as follows: *"All children in certain groups are being harmed just by being in a group that adheres to certain beliefs and practices thought by some to be harmful to children"* (1999, 175–76; italics in original).

He then notes four ways in which collective child abuse is being interpreted by opponents of minority religions. First is that the religious group may be forcing children to live in relative poverty, as measured by middle-class American standards. A second aspect is the home schooling of children and the concern that they may not be receiving the type of education that would afford them adequate opportunities later in life. A third concern involves the use of corporal punishment, which some claim can easily turn into physical abuse of children. Last, but by no means least, are concerns about the possibility of children being sexually abused in the religious group.

The matter of children living in poverty has not been a major legal issue even if the lifestyle of some communal religious groups has been of concern to some. Home schooling is illegal in some countries, which has led to considerable difficulty for groups such as the Twelve Tribes in Germany and France (Swantko 2004). Major battles have been fought in America and elsewhere, however, on the latter two concerns. In the legal papers presented in court in the case of the Texas FLDS raid, CPS stated that the children were living with people who share a pervasive belief system that condones under-age marriage and pregnancy (*In re Steed* 2008, p. 11). Raids on The Family International communes where children were taken away by authorities, even if temporarily, resulted mainly from accusations dealing with possible sex abuse, and the Vermont raid resulted from claims of physical abuse. All these claims were, as noted, augmented considerably by apostates' atrocity tales of what life was supposedly like within the groups.

Policy Considerations

After the Vermont state raid on the Twelve Tribes was deemed illegal and the children were ordered to be returned to their homes, one of the government officials who was largely responsible for the raid wrote a defense of the action (Burchard 1984) and later collaborated on a more thorough analysis of what they thought ought to happen when dealing with communal religious groups if and when child abuse claims are being made (Malcarne and Burchard 1992). Although Malcarne and Burchard express concern for the sanctity of the family and for religious freedom, they state that the welfare of the children is paramount and must take priority. They chronicle difficulties Vermont authorities encountered in trying to investigate claims that were made by defectors and relatives concerning physical abuse that were allegedly occurring in the group.[4] They point out that a communal group that home schools its children and refuses to allow access to the children, or even to identify them for authorities, makes a mockery of child protection statutes. Those statutes, Malcarne and Burchard contend, were developed assuming a traditional family structure where children would be seen by nonfamily members in other contexts such as school or in a neighborhood. If abuse was occurring in such a situation, others would be aware of it and could notify authorities. But if children had little or no contact with outsiders, as is the case in some communal religious groups, then normal methods of detecting abuse and notifying authorities are not possible.

To rectify this situation, Malcarne and Burchard make a series of policy recommendations, including considerations of conditions that might call for an *ex parte* warrant in cases "where widespread abuse/neglect is suspected in the context of a religious cult" (1992, 86). They recommend a number of issues to consider in such a circumstance, including a very provocative one, derived from an earlier unpublished document developed by Burchard and Wald (1988) after the 1984 raid. When discussing the amount and type of evidence that the state must present to show that each child in a religious group is at *"personal risk"* (italics theirs), Malcarne and Burchard state:

> One solution, suggested by Burchard and Wald, is to predefine, by statute, the types of cult characteristics that would justify an inference of group-wide risk, and require the court to make specified findings in this regard. Such characteristics include the internal structure of the cult family, and whether it is organized in hierarchical fashion around a single leader or group of elders; the nature of parental autonomy within the cult, and whether there has been a delegation of child-rearing authority, either to the cult as a whole or to a designated member or members, and the cult's philosophy and practice concerning child-rearing, child-care, and discipline, if any, and whether their approach comes within the statutory definitions of abuse and neglect. (1992, 86)

All Religions Are Not Equal: A Sociology of Law Approach

The work of Donald Black, a prominent sociologist of law, provides a broader context to examine social control efforts against religious groups such as the FLDS. In applying ideas from Black, we compare and contrast accusations of child sex abuse within the Catholic Church to explain why the same allegations in two religious organizations produce very different responses from state officials.

Although it is difficult to obtain sound data on the total number of sex abuse cases involving the Catholic Church, a number of claims have been offered, along with some interesting survey data. The scandal first came to light in the mid-1980s when a few legal cases were filed, resulting in some admissions by a few individual priests. It was not until 2002, however, when the *Boston Globe* published a series of articles detailing claims of sex abuse over the years by priests in that diocese, and efforts to contain them and cover up the scandal by the Church hierarchy, that the scope of the problem became more widely known. Since that time there have been accusations of large numbers of sex abuse cases throughout the United States and in other countries. The controversy has embroiled the Vatican itself, as even the Pope has been accused of ignoring the problem and being involved in efforts to cover up the extent of sex abuse by functionaries in the Church.

In 2002 the Conference of Catholic Bishops in the United States, at a major meeting in Dallas, finally began facing the problem of sex abuse within the Church. The conference authorized a major study by John Jay College of Criminal Justice to examine the extent and effects of the sex abuse by priests in America, and directed all dioceses to cooperate and furnish data to the researchers. The results, published in 2004 (John Jay College of Criminal Justice 2004), were startling. At the time of the study around 11,000 claims had been made against 4,392 priests, which represented 4 percent of all priests in the country. Claims had affected some 95 percent of dioceses in America. By 2002 approximately $1 billion had been paid to settle claims by the time of the study, and the amount paid out has grown significantly since then.

Anson Shupe, who has made significant contributions to the understanding of "clergy malfeasance" with a series of books that discuss sex abuse within the Catholic Church as well as other religions (Shupe 1995, 1998, 2007), and W. A. Stacy (Shupe, Stacy, and Darnell 2000) have done a carefully constructed survey of households in the Dallas–Fort Worth area concerning sex abuse by a priest, pastor, rabbi, or guru. The research revealed that about 8 percent of respondents reported that a member of the household or a close friend had been sexually abused by a religious leader.

Sex abuse in the Catholic Church is not confined to the United States; major scandals have erupted in recent decades in Ireland, Canada, Germany, and other countries (Pogatchnik 2010), as people in those societies seemed to follow the lead of the revelations in the United States, and began to make public claims of massive sex abuse about Catholic authority figures. Ireland has been the most notorious case, with some fifteen thousand people now claiming to have been sexually or physically abused in Catholic institutions in past decades, leading to a Papal apology that was widely viewed as insufficient. Germany has even seen Chancellor Angela Merkel speak about the scandal to the German Bundestag (Eddy 2010), and the controversy has directly involved Pope Benedict XVII, who is from Germany and under whose watch as Archbishop of Munich some of these cases are alleged to have occurred.

Why the Different Reactions?

Donald Black's (1976) work explains why the Catholic Church in various societies was able to operate for decades (centuries?) with impunity regarding sex abuse in some of its institutions, whereas authorities moved rapidly to institute raids against some smaller communal religious groups when weakly substantiated accusations were made. Black's theoretical scheme is quite thorough and elaborate, but focusing on just a few of his major variables will suffice for our analysis.

Black uses the concepts of *status* and *intimacy* as major building blocks for his theory. Status is used in the ordinary sociological sense as a way to refer to a person's (or group's) vertical position in *social space*. If one has high status and prestige, then one is higher in social space, and can direct social control actions downward toward those entities lower in social space, and more easily deflect social-control actions directed upward in social space toward them. High-status individuals or groups can assist in constructing society, including its legal system, and even carve out a protective enclave that few can enter without permission. Intimacy refers to both personal *and* cultural intimacy, with the latter term referring to whether decision makers in a society share values and cultural understanding with one another. This variable is especially crucial if decision makers such as a judge or political authority are called on to decide matters involving another person or entity about whom they know little and with whom they share little personal or cultural intimacy. If they are familiar with that person or entity, and understand the motivations behind their actions because of their own personal experiences, then they are much less prone to be punitive in their decision making.

Another concept of import from Black's theoretical scheme is that of *third-party partisans* (Black and Baumgartner 1983) by which is meant a person or entity who is willing to get involved on behalf of one of the parties in a dispute. This concept is useful for understanding situations where lower-status entities with few intimate ties with decision makers nonetheless prevail in disputes, including legal actions. When a lower-status entity prevails in a dispute Black proposes that it is usually because some higher-status entity with intimate ties with decision makers has become a partisan on behalf of the lower-status entity. However, when third-party partisans side with authorities against a lower-status entity, then the situation can quickly deteriorate into a loss for the lower-status entity.

The Catholic Church has maintained very high status for centuries in Western societies, the early colonial history in America notwithstanding. The Church also has been able to attract many third-party partisans willing to defend it or accept the Church's explanations of things that are alleged to have occurred. Indeed, the Church has been allowed to be a law unto itself, as a form of *legal pluralism* has been allowed to prevail, with the Church handling its own internal problems as it sees fit. It has only been in recent years that the crush of thousands of cases of sex abuse made public through the mass media (a powerful third-party partisan entity that has finally started looking more objectively at the Church) that the Church has lost status and prestige, and seen potential defenders defect and even turn against the Church.

Meanwhile, just the opposite situation obtains with most minority religious groups. They are almost by definition of lower status in the eyes of decision makers in society. Such groups have little prestige, and few personal or culturally intimate ties with the powerful in society. They have few friends who will defend them and, indeed, often seem to have many who will encourage authorities to take action against such groups. Few potential third-party partisans step forward to speak on their behalf or defend them in times of controversy. They are socially isolated, and social-control efforts can be mounted against them with impunity. When social-control actions are taken by authorities against a minority religion, the matter can quickly be decided in a manner quite detrimental to the group, and to the overarching values of religious freedom and familial autonomy.

The episode described herein with the FLDS is but one example that seems explicable using these concepts from Black's work in the sociology of law. Many more come to mind, such as the tragedy at Waco with the Branch Davidians and the other episodes described in this volume where authorities, with the blessing of the mass media and general public, have exerted social control over politically weak and unpopular religious groups, sometimes with catastrophic results. Meanwhile, the Catholic Church has been allowed to continue to operate in a way that has harmed thousands of people, and it has done so with almost complete impunity until quite recently. This sharp contrast should give all pause for thought.

Discussion and Conclusion

The Texas raid on the FLDS community at the YFZ Ranch was not an isolated incident in several ways. The raid must be considered within the context of considerable concern about new religions ("cults") or minority faiths in American society and elsewhere. Scholars have pointed to the development of a "moral panic" concerning NRMs that lasted several decades and has only subsided somewhat in recent times (particularly after 9/11). That concern gave impetus to many governmental actions, much negative media attention, a number of court cases, and many "self-help" remedies (including thousands of "deprogrammings") by those who opposed the spread of the new high-demand religions (see Richardson 2004; Robbins and Anthony 1990; Bromley and Richardson 1983; Lucas and Robbins 2004; and Richardson and Introvigne 2007). Efforts at social control of NRMs in America and other societies has met with mixed success, in part because of legal protections afforded religious groups in many Western societies, particularly the United States.

The early efforts at social control gave way to other tactics with the arrival of many children in some of the more controversial NRMs. Suddenly NRMs with children began to feel the full power of the state as it exerted its authority concerning the welfare of children. NRM leaders soon discovered that the usual protections afforded religious groups fell by the wayside when children were involved, and claims were made that children were being harmed in some manner by virtue of merely being in an NRM.

Thus NRMs were made aware of the larger context involving concern about children in religious groups that had been developing in America and elsewhere for several decades. This specific concern was just one aspect of the larger "child-saver" movement that had come to the fore in modern societies in the last half-century (Best 1990). The concern about children in religious groups initially involved a number of well-known minority religious groups such as Christian Science and Jehovah's Witnesses. Both these groups had endured considerable controversy about the health of children in their groups; for example, Jehovah's Witnesses refuse to allow blood transfusions, and some Christian Science children, for whom spiritual healing had been unsuccessful, died. Other religious groups with unorthodox views about medical care and the proper discipline of children also came under scrutiny and impelled social control efforts of various kinds. In the last two decades the enormous publicity given to the thousands of cases of child sex abuse within the Catholic Church in America and in other countries added to the level of concern about the welfare of children in religious groups, even traditional mainstream religions.

One final, very important contextual element for the Texas raid was the breakdown of the détente that had existed for several decades after the abortive raid on the FLDS at Short Creek, Arizona, in 1953. The controversies surrounding Warren Jeffs's rise to power in 2002 within the FLDS have been widely publicized, particularly his legal troubles stemming from the marriage of underage girls to older men in the group, including Jeffs himself. Jeffs's legal troubles, along with other political pressures, have produced attempts to exert more control over polygamous communities in Utah and Arizona, and also within Texas, as word spread of Jeffs's plans to build the YFZ community there.

These recent pressures and concerns led directly to the preconceived and overreaching actions in Texas that are described herein. It is noteworthy that Utah's attorney general participated in the hearings in Texas that preceded the passage of SB 6, making it clear that Texas officials were working with officials in other states to develop a legal structure that would facilitate state efforts to control the FLDS wherever it is located. It will be of interest to learn more about what is being contemplated in terms of further legislative changes in Texas, following the raid and its aftermath. The possible confluence of ideas such as those that were proposed after the raid in Vermont with the planning of Texas officials will be worth watching for, as this continuing saga plays out in Texas and other areas where the FLDS is located.

NOTES

1. For important exceptions to this general rule, as well as Richardson and Introvigne's (2001) assessment on the spread of brainwashing-based ideas in Western Europe, see several chapters on France and Belgium in Richardson (2004). Such ideas, however, were accepted wholeheartedly by some non-Western nations such as Russia (Shterin and Richardson 2000) and China (Edelman and Richardson 2003).

2. A concern not unrelated to the issue of brainwashing involved how NRMs raised and spent money. Some of the methods such as street and airport solicitation for funds were offensive to many in our society, leading to efforts to limit such methods. For a discussion of these issues, see Richardson 1988.

3. This kind of action actually took place in many states since raids were conducted in several different countries over several years; see Swantko 2004 and Richardson 1999 for details.

4. Note that Swantko (2004) offers evidence that the Vermont situation was promoted by key figures in the anticult movement, working with a few apostates, some of whom had been involved in custody disputes with the group or had been expelled from the group.

Anthony, Dick. 1990. "Religious Movements and Brainwashing Litigation: Evaluating Key Testimony," pp. 295–344 in Thomas Robbins and Dick Anthony (eds.), *In Gods We Trust*. New Brunswick: NJ: Transaction.

———. 1999. "Pseudoscience and Minority Religions: An Evaluation of the Brainwashing Theories of Jean-Marie Abgrall." *Social Justice Research* 12:421–56.

Anthony, Dick, and Thomas Robbins. 1992. "Law, Social Science, and the 'Brainwashing' Exception to the First Amendment." *Behavioral Science and the Law* 10:5–30.

Beaman, Lori. 2008. *Defining Harm: Religious Freedom and the Limits of the Law*. Vancouver: University of British Columbia Press.

Best, Joel. 1990. *Threatened Children*. Chicago: University of Chicago Press.

Black, Donald. 1976. *The Behavior of Law*. New York: Academic Press.

Black, Donald, and Mary P. Baumgartner. 1983. "Toward a Theory of the Third Party," pp. 84–114 in Keith O. Boyum and Lynn Mather (eds.), *Empirical Theories about Courts*. New York: Longman.

Bozeman, John, and Susan J. Palmer. 1997. "The Northeast Kingdom Community Church of Island Pond, Vermont: Raising Up a People for Yahshua's Return." *Journal of Contemporary Religion* 12:181–90.

Bromley, David G., and James T. Richardson. 1983. *The Brainwashing/Deprogramming Controversy*. Lewiston, NY: Edwin Mellen.

Burchard, John. 1984. "Children at Risk: Why Protective Action in Island Pond was Necessary." *Burlington Free Press,* July 17, p. 6.

Crisp, Beth R. 2007. "Spirituality and Sexual Abuse." *Theology and Sexuality* 13 (3): 301–14.

Dokecki, Paul R. 2004. *The Clergy Sexual Abuse Crisis*. Washington, DC: Georgetown University Press.

Eddy, Melissa. 2010. "Merkel: Sex Abuse Scandal Major Challenge." *Deseret News*, March 17.

Edelman, Brian, and James T. Richardson, 2003. "Falun Gong and the Law: Development of Legal Social Control in China." *Nova Religio* 6:312–31.

Ellison, Christopher, and John Bartkowski. 1995. "'Babies Were Being Beaten': Exploring Child Abuse Allegations at Ranch Apocalypse," pp. 11–152 in Stuart A. Wright (ed.), *Armageddon in Waco*. Chicago: University of Chicago Press.

Fater, Kerry, and Jo Ann Mullaney. 2000. "The Lived Experience of Adult Male Survivors Who Allege Childhood Sexual Abuse by Clergy." *Issues in Mental Health Nursing* 21 (3): 281–95.

Franz, Thaeda. 2002. "Power, Patriarchy, and Sexual Abuse in Churches of Christian Denomination." *Traumatology* 8 (1): 4–17.

Gerdes, Karen E., Martha N. Beck, Sylvia Cowan-Hancock, and Tracey Wilkinson Sparks. 1996. "Adult Survivors of Childhood Sexual Abuse: The Case of Mormon Women." *Affilia* 11 (1): 39–60.

Ginsburg, Gerald, and James Richardson. 1998. "'Brainwashing' Testimony in Light of *Daubert*," pp. 265–88 in Helen Reece (ed.), *Law and Science*. Oxford: Oxford University Press.

"Governor Perry Signs SB 6 into Law." 2005. *Eldorado Success,* June 9.

Harris, Geraldine. 2005. "Texas Marriage and Marriage License Application Changes." Memorandum to all county clerks in Texas, August 22.

Haywood, Thomas W., Howard Kravitz, Linda Grossman, Orest Wasyliw, and Daniel Hardy. 1996. "Psychological Aspects of Sexual Functioning among Cleric and Noncleric Alleged Sex Offenders." *Child Abuse and Neglect* 20 (6): 527–36.

"Hilderbran Takes Aim at YFZ Ranch." 2005. *Eldorado Success,* March 24.

Hoff, Jenny. 2009. "Lawmakers Tackle FLDS Raid." Broadcast on KXAN Television, April 15. Available online at http://www.kxan.com/dpp/news/texas/Lawmakers_tackle_FLDS_raid (January 19, 2010).

Homer, Michael. 1994. "New Religions and Child Custody Cases: Comparisons between the American and European Experience," pp. 129–35 in James R. Lewis and J. Gordon Melton (eds.), *Sex, Sin, and Slander: Investigating The Family/Children of God.* Stanford, CA: Center for Academic Publication.

———. 1999. "The Precarious Balance between Freedom of Religion and the Best Interests of the Child," pp. 187–209 in Susan J. Palmer and Charlotte Hardman (eds.), *Children in New Religions.* New Brunswick, NJ: Rutgers University Press.

House Research Organization. 2005. Analysis of HR 3006, Texas Legislature.

John Jay College of Criminal Justice. 2004. "Executive Summary of "The Nature and Scope of the Problem of Sexual Abuse of Minors by Catholic Priests and Deacons in the United States." Accessed online at http://www.usccb.org/nrb/johnjaystudy/exec.pdf (August 17, 2010).

Kennedy, Margaret. 2000. "Christianity and Child Sexual Abuse: The Survivors' Voice Leading to Change. *Child Abuse Review* 9 (2): 124–41.

Kilbourne, Brock, and James Richardson, 1984. "Psychotherapy and New Religions in a Pluralistic Society." *American Psychologist* 39:237–51.

Lewis, James R. 1994. "Child Abuse in Waco," pp. 159–64 in James R. Lewis and J. Gordon Melton (eds.), *Sex, Sin, and Slander: Investigating The Family/Children of God.* Stanford, CA: Center for Academic Publication.

Louderback-Wood, Kerry. 2005. "Jehovah's Witnesses, Blood Transfusions, and the Tort of Misrepresentation." *Journal of Church and State* 47:783–822.

Lucas, Phillip, and Thomas Robbins. 2004. *New Religious Movements in the 21st Century.* New York: Routledge.

Malcarne, Venessa, and John Burchard, 1992. "Investigations of Child Abuse/Neglect Allegations in Religious Cults: A Case Study in Vermont." *Behavioral Sciences and the Law* 10:75–88.

Markham, D. J., and S. F. Mikail. 2004. "Perpetrators of Clergy Abuse: Insights from Attachment Theory." *Studies in Gender and Sexuality* 5 (2): 197–212.

Moritz, John. 2008. "Texans' Tab for YFZ Roundup Tops $14 Million." *Fort Worth Star-Telegram,* June 14, p. A1.

Neil, Martha. 2008. "Texas Changed Marriage Age to Restrict Rights of Polygamy Ranch Residents." *ABA Journal,* May 2.

Oliver, Moorman. 1994. "Today's Jackboots: The Inquisition Revisited," pp. 137–51 in James R. Lewis and J. Gordon Melton (eds.), *Sex, Sin, and Slander: Investigating the Family/Children of God.* Stanford, CA: Center for Academic Publication.

Palmer, Susan J. 1999. "Frontiers and Families: The Children of Island Pond," pp. 153–71 in Susan J. Palmer and Charlotte Palmer (eds.), *Children in New Religions.* New Brunswick, NJ: Rutgers University Press.

Peters, Shawn. 2008. *When Prayer Fails: Faith Healing, Children, and the Law.* Oxford: Oxford University Press.

Plante, Thomas G. 1996. "Catholic Priests Who Sexually Abuse Minors: Why Do We Hear So Much Yet Know So Little?" *Pastoral Psychology* 44 (5): 305–10.

———. 1999. *Bless Me Father for I Have Sinned: Perspectives on Sexual Abuse Committed by Roman Catholic Priests.* Westport, CT: Greenwood.

Pogatchnik, Shawn. 2010. "Vatican Tried to Keep Irish Child Rapist as Priest." Associated Press, December 17. Accessed online at http://www.thefreelibrary.com. (December 18, 2010).

Richardson, James T. 1991. "Cult/Brainwashing Cases and the Freedom of Religion." *Journal of Church and State* 33:55–74.

———. 1993. "A Social Psychological Critique of 'Brainwashing' Claims about Recruitment to New Religions," pp. 75–97 in Jeffrey Hadden and David Bromley (eds.), *Handbook of Cults and Sects in America.* Greenwich, CT: JAI.

———. 1996. "'Brainwashing' Claims and Minority Religions outside the Untied States: Cultural Diffusion of a Questionable Legal Concept in the Legal Arena." *Brigham Young University Law Review* 96:873–904.

———. 1999. "Social Control of New Religions: From 'Brainwashing' Claims to Child Sex Abuse Allegations," pp. 172–86 in Susan J. Palmer and Charlotte Hardman (eds.), *Children in the New Religions.* New Brunswick, NJ: Rutgers University Press.

———. 2004. *Regulating Religion: Case Studies from Around the Globe.* New York: Kluwer.

Richardson, James T., and John DeWitt. 1992. "Christian Science Spiritual Healing, the Law, and Public Opinion." *Journal of Church and State* 34:549–61.

Richardson, James T., and Massimo Introvigne, 2001. "'Brainwashing' Theories in European Parliamentary and Administrative Reports. On 'Cults' and 'Sects.'" *Journal for the Scientific Study of Religion* 40:143–68.

———. 2007. "New Religious Movements, Countermovements, Moral Panics, and the Media," pp. 91–111 in David G. Bromley (ed.), *Teaching New Religious Movements.* Oxford: Oxford University Press.

Richardson, James T., and Brock Kilbourne. 1983. "Classical and Contemporary Applications of Brainwashing Models: A Comparison and Critique," pp. 29–46 in David G. Bromley and James T. Richardson (eds.), *The Brainwashing/Deprogramming Controversy.* Lewiston, NY: Edwin Mellen.

Richter, Donald. 2009. "Rep. Hilderbran Ignores the Constitution and Targets FLDS." Available online at http://www.truthwillprevail.org.

Robbins, Thomas, and Dick Anthony. 1990. *In Gods We Trust* 2nd ed. New Brunswick, NJ: Transaction.

Saradijian, Adam. 2003. "Cognitive Distortion of Religious Professionals Who Sexually Abuse Children. *Journal of Interpersonal Violence,* 18 (8): 905–23.

Schoepflin, Rennie. 2003. *Christian Science on Trial: Religious Healing in America.* Baltimore, MD: John Hopkins University Press.

Shterin, Marat, and James T. Richardson. 2000. "Effects of the Western Anti-Cult Movement on Development of Laws concerning Religion in Post-Communist Russia." *Journal of Church and State* 42:247–72.

Shupe, Anson D. 1995. *In the Name of All That Is Holy: A Theory of Clergy Malfeasance.* Westport, CT: Praeger.

———. 1998. *Wolves Within the Fold.* New Brunswick, NJ: Rutgers University Press.

———. 2007. *Spoils of the Kingdom: Clergy Misconduct and Religious Community.* Champaign, IL: University of Illinois Press.

Shupe, Anson D., William A. Stacy, and Susan E. Darnell. 2000. *Bad Pastors: Clergy Misconduct in America*. New York: New York University Press.

Siegler, Gretchen. 1999. "The Children of ISOT," pp. 124–37 in Susan J. Palmer and Charlotte Hardman (eds.), *Children in New Religions*. New Brunswick, NJ: Rutgers University Press.

Swantko, Jean. 2004. "The Twelve Tribes Messianic Community, the Anti-Cult Movement, and Governmental Response," pp. 179–200 in James T Richardson (ed.), *Regulating Religion: Case Studies from Around the Globe*. New York: Kluwer.

Wah, Carolyn. 2001. "Religious Freedom and the Best Interests of the Child: The Case of Jehovah's Witnesses in Child Custody Litigation," pp. 193–233 in Pauline Cote (ed.), *Frontier Religions in Public Space*. Ottawa: University of Ottawa Press.

Winslow, Ben. 2009. "Raid Again? Texas CPS Defends '08 Actions." *Deseret News,* March 28.

10

Pyrrhic Victory?

*An Analysis of the Appeal Court Opinions
Concerning the FLDS Children*

TAMATHA L. SCHREINERT AND
JAMES T. RICHARDSON

The 2008 Texas raid on the Fundamentalist Church of Jesus Christ of Latter Day Saints (FLDS) at the Yearning for Zion (YFZ) Ranch that resulted in more than four hundred children being taken into custody by the state was not an anomalous event, as the chapters in this volume make clear. New religious movements (NRMs) and other minority faiths often find themselves subject to efforts of social control by authorities of the dominant society, and sometimes those efforts are couched in terms of concern about children (Homer 1999; Palmer, this volume; Palmer and Hardeman 1999; Richardson 1999; Swantko 2004). New or unconventional religious groups, with their seemingly strange practices and ideas, may offend the values and beliefs of those in power in a society. A number of new or minority religious groups have arisen indigenously or have immigrated to the United States over the past decades and sometimes they attract considerable attention, as the recent raid in Texas demonstrated. Some new religions such as the Children of God, the Hare Krishna, and the Unification Church that came to public consciousness in the 1960s and 1970s exacerbated this tendency by attempting to recruit some of the "brightest and best" young people from American society. When the mostly legal-age children of relatively high-status families in American society decided to forego typical education and career paths to join these new movements, calls for action were heard across the land (Barker 1984; Bromley and Shupe 1979; Robbins 1988).

The focus on control of strange religions is nothing new, however, as similar calls for action to limit the activities of new or minority faiths in American society have been made before. Miller (1983) describes anti-Catholic sentiments that developed in Protestant America in the early and mid-1800s. Societal leaders and others reacted quite negatively to the flood of hundreds of thousands of Catholics from southern Europe (see also Roy 1999). This nativist Anti-Catholic movement gave impetus to many efforts, both legal and extra-legal, to exert control over the newcomers to America. Violence was a part of this nativist movement, with convents being burned in Charleston, and Catholic Churches and homes being burned in Philadelphia in riots that left thirteen people dead and more than fifty wounded.

The Shakers, whose rise to prominence in the late 1700s and early 1800s, also caused alarm in some quarters (Miller 1983; Foster 1984; Stein 1994). Detractors and opponents trumpeted familiar claims of child abuse and issued demands for social control. The Shakers were accused of "stealing children" in a series of well-publicized custody cases involving children of couples who had been involved in the Shaker movement but had divorced. When one of the divorced parties left the community, child-stealing claims were used in court by the former member to effectively obtain custody of the children. The New York State Legislature even considered a bill that would automatically dissolve a marriage if one member of a couple wanted to leave the Shakers, with the departing parent essentially allowed to retain all personal possessions, as well as the children. The Shakers also were accused of harming children in other ways, and even beating at least one to death.

Miller states that comparable claims were made about other new or exotic religious groups of the time, such as the Oneida Community (1983, 27). After comparing the familiar kinds of accusations made about these earlier groups, he concludes, that "behind these attempts at discreditation is undoubtedly the perception that the way of life of the dominant culture is being threatened." This theme may underpin more recent actions taken to exert social control over minority faiths, including efforts based on concern for children.

Contemporary Concern about Children in Minority Religious Groups

Initial concern about children in the wave of NRMs that emerged in the late 1960s and early 1970s was not evident because most converts were young adults. As public awareness of the movements grew, studies of NRMs revealed that most members were college-age youth. Some controversy arose over the participation of a few who were underage, and some significant legal cases developed out of battles over adolescent members.[1] To the extent that new religious movements of this period were accused of "stealing children" in something of a "Pied Piper" effect, it was because many of those joining were offspring of relatively affluent families in the United States. Nonetheless, the major accusations against the NRMs concerned recruitment methods (Bromley and Richardson 1983; Robbins 1988) and how they raised funds to support their organization (Richardson 1988). A few groups were also accused of sexual license (Jacobs 1984, 1989; Richardson and Davis 1983; Rochford 1995), raising concerns and possible opportunities for exerting social control using NRM sexual behavior as leverage. Early on, however, the major accusation leveled against NRMs was that they "brainwashed" potential converts and used "mind control" techniques to retain them as participants. These powerful ideas became the "social weapons" of choice to use against unpopular NRMs, and even served as the major justification for the quasi-profession of "deprogramming" that developed in America (Shupe and Bromley 1980; Shupe and Darnell 2006). Thousands of young people were kidnapped and put through deprogramming in the 1970s and 1980s, and only in the 1990s did court decisions finally limit such activities to a considerable extent (Shupe and Darnell 2006).

Limitations of social control efforts based on "brainwashing" notions evolved through a series of court cases. The decisions were undergirded by considerable scientific research done by scholars in the area of NRM studies (Anthony 1990; Anthony and Robbins 1992; Kilbourne and Richardson 1984; Richardson 1991, 1992, 1993, 1999). This work by several scholars led eventually to the demise of such claims in cases involving new religions, with a key decision being made in a criminal case involving a Scientologist who unsuccessfully sought to use a defense based on "brainwashing" in a case where he was charged with tax fraud (U.S. v. Fishman, 1990).[2]

The curtailing of social control tactics using the "brainwashing" approach also coincided with the maturing of the NRMs. The reprieve afforded NRMs from the waning legal tactic based on "brainwashing" was short-lived, as many groups established families and welcomed the arrival of children. Because some NRMs did not practice birth control and grew rapidly, new threats were perceived and trumpeted by cultural opponents. What will happen to "children in cults?" opponents asked. Groups such as The Family International (formerly known as the Children of God) saw their demographic profile change dramatically in just a few years, as large numbers of children were born to families within the group (Chancellor 2000; Palmer and Hardeman 1999; Richardson 1994). Consequently anticult movement (ACM) organizations and actors shifted their social and legal challenges to the NRMs, focusing on the alleged harmful affects to children.

The changing demographics of these NRMs were also accompanied by a broader social trend of concern about children in American society and elsewhere. This confluence of generalized concern for children and the fact that a number of NRMs had high birth rates opened up new opportunities to exercise control over NRMs. A major shift in the social control paradigm occurred as the "brainwashing/mind control" narrative diminished in importance and the "child abuse" motif emerged as the principal rhetorical weapon to combat "cults" (Richardson 1999). Fueling this shift were custody battles that arose as some couples within NRMs split up. If one of the spouses left the group while the other remained, the former member could effectively lodge child abuse claims with little evidence. Courts were sensitive to such claims of abuse and deeply suspicious of the unconventional marriage and sexual practices of many groups. As a result, NRMs were placed on the defensive and found themselves besieged by this new strategy. The presumption of innocence was turned on its head, as NRMs were forced to prove their blamelessness in the public eye. ACM organizations and actors labored to make child abuse synonymous with "cults."

Problems with Child Abuse Accusations

Two general problems are associated with accusations about child abuse in NRMs and other minority religions in America. One concerns the very definition of child abuse; the other concerns the issue of "collective child abuse," which we discussed briefly in the previous chapter and which has been raised yet again in the FLDS situation. Concerning the definition of child abuse, there is no dispute that sex abuse of children is a violation of law and morality in most societies. Very few, if any, would sanction sexual behavior with young children, whether in a religious group or not. There are disputes, however, about what constitutes *other* types of child abuse in a collective religious setting, as detailed in Richardson (1999) and Ellison and Bartkowski (1995). These scholars note that some critics think that home schooling in religious groups is a form of child abuse in itself, since the schooling received is religiously based and may not prepare the children for a life in modern society. Others contend that the use of corporal punishment of children is child abuse. By definition, spanking is seen as a form of "child beating," with the expected consequences in terms of public concern. Some would claim, as well, that rearing children in an abstemious, communal environment, where material goods and possessions are lacking or discouraged, could be labeled child abuse. This claim, however, is usually not promoted since it has much broader implications for government responsibility toward children outside the realm of religious groups.

Whatever claims of child abuse are made must comport with the statutes in the given state where the claim is offered. And therein lies the other major difficulty, especially when dealing with a communal religious group. The issue of "collective child abuse," as it has evolved, entails deeply flawed assumptions and strained interpretations of the law. Richardson (1999, 182) has made the following observation regarding the misuse of child abuse laws to attack minority faiths:

> Accusations of collective child abuse "in a cultic setting" . . . were not contemplated when the laws of the United States and most other countries were designed (Carney 1999). Such laws were not written to support the assumption that child abuse occurs by virtue of a child's growing up in certain social, religious, or economic circumstances. Indeed, recent U.S. laws concerning child abuse were deliberately designed to *avoid* claims that abuse resulted from living in poverty. Such considerations notwithstanding, individually oriented laws have often been stretched to fit the new communal religions.

Richardson further notes that the laws require greater *specificity* when making child abuse accusations, with the accused being named, the alleged victim identified, and information provided specifying the date, time, and location of the abuse. These laws assume some access to the group and its children by third parties such as schoolteachers or neighbors, both of whom can be problematic when dealing with religious groups living in an isolated setting and home schooling the children. Few outsiders, including teachers in public schools or neighbors, have contact with children from groups that have chosen to isolate themselves, thus making it very difficult to apply the usual child abuse laws against such groups. These problems are lamented by some who were directly involved in the Twelve Tribes raid described below (Malcarne and Burchard 1992). Nonetheless nearly all statutes dealing with child abuse in this country require the kind of specificity mentioned above.

Similar Recent Cases

A number of cases in the United States and elsewhere demonstrate the difficulties dealing with allegations of child abuse in communal religious groups. Perhaps the most well-known case concerns the tragic episode at Waco, Texas, where a fifty-one-day standoff between government authorities and the Branch Davidians culminated in an inferno in which seventy-six Davidians, including a number of children, died (Wright 1995). The initial raid was ostensibly to look for illegal weapons but was justified in part by allegations of child abuse, including sexual abuse. Throughout the fifty-one-day siege considerable attention was paid to the welfare of children in the group, and the final assault was justified to Attorney General Reno with the claim that "babies were being beaten" (Ellison and Bartkowski 1995). Even though federal jurisdiction over children is questionable (this area of law is usually assigned to the states), the raid and subsequent siege were based partially on claims of concern about the children in the group (Ellison and Bartkowski 1995). It is a tragic irony indeed that the final outcome resulted in the deaths of all the children who remained inside Mt. Carmel on that fateful fifty-first day.

Palmer (1998, 1999) and Swantko (2004; Wiseman, this volume) discuss how concern about children was used as a justification by Vermont state police to raid the Twelve Tribes Messianic Community in Island Pond. Embroiled in controversies with authorities for years, the impetus for the raid was fueled mostly by custody disputes involving several member families that had divorced. Those disputes were used by some representatives of the anticult movement to foment concern among Vermont officials, culminating in a predawn raid on June 22, 1984, involving ninety Vermont state troopers and fifty social workers serving a warrant allowing them to take custody of children in the community. Authorities rounded up 112 children and their parents who were then transported to a nearby town where court proceedings were to take place. Later that day, however, the judge presiding over the hearings, who was not the judge who issued the original warrant, ruled that the warrant was faulty and ordered all children returned to their parents, without conditions or examination of the children.[3]

Swantko (2004) provides considerable detail about the various custody cases leading up to the 1984 raid, and also describes the extensive involvement of key ACM operatives in the episode. She also points out that officials' efforts to justify what happened were widely circulated in Europe, where Twelve Tribes communities are also present. Those documents, which did not contain information about the outcome of the Island Pond case, led to considerable difficulties for the group in some of its European communities, particularly in France.

Siegler (1999) discusses an episode of social control using concern about children that involved the In Search of Truth (ISOT) communal religious group located in northern California. This group supported itself in part by operating a group home for troubled youth, for which it was paid a per capita sum for each child housed there. The state sent in an undercover agent to surveil the group and its practices, and then proceeded to shut the home down, depriving the organization of that source of income. Apparently the main charge was that the group home was being used to "indoctrinate" the children within the ISOT belief system.

The Family International has also encountered strong challenges from state entities with regard to the welfare of its many children, both overseas and in the United States. Richardson (1999) describes raids on Family communal homes in Argentina, Spain, France, and Australia, actions that were also attempted in the United States. These state raids took custody of hundreds of Family children and charged their parents with crimes of child abuse. Uniformly the state agencies proceeded with these operations based on allegations of child sexual abuse by former members. They attempted to have the children designated wards of the state, thereby making them subject to placement in foster homes, with an attendant severing of parental rights. In all cases, the children were returned to their parents, but the litigation took considerable time in some countries. In Argentina, Family parents spent six months in Argentine jails before finally being released. Similar claims were made by opponents and former members of The Family in the United States, leading at least one Family communal group to invite authorities in to examine the children and their home situation. This effort at preemption was successful, and no raid occurred in the United States, but it did demonstrate the unusual lengths to which the group felt it had to go in an effort to avoid further raids.[4]

Finally, the Texas raid on the FLDS was not the first on this religious community, as has been made clear in this volume. State police launched a similar raid many years earlier on the original FLDS community residing in Short Creek, Arizona (Bradley 1993; Evans, this volume; Homer 1999). The raid involved 121 Arizona police officers, accompanied by 100 news reporters, who went unannounced to Short Creek on Sunday, July 26, 1953. The state took into custody 263 children, 36 men, and 86 women, based on third-party claims of child abuse, including sexual abuse. The raid ultimately became a political disaster for the governor, who had ordered the predawn enforcement action. He lost his next election after public sentiment turned against him and in favor of the FLDS community. Charges of statutory rape and contributing to the delinquency of a minor were dropped against the adults. The men who were arrested pleaded guilty to conspiracy to violate laws against bigamy and were given one-year suspended sentences. Eventually most of the children and their parents returned to their homes in Short Creek, and the community rejuvenated itself over the next few years.

Time Line of the FLDS Raid in Texas

A time line and brief description of the unfolding events regarding the FLDS raid and court actions taken in Texas is shown in Table 10.1.

TABLE 10.1

Date	Action
March 29, 2008	Hotline intake report receives call from an alleged 16 year old, "Sarah," asking for help to leave YFZ Ranch.
March 30, 2008	Another call from the same alleged teenager to a local family shelter.
April 3, 2008	Order to remove children and search warrants that include a history of "Sarah," the person who called and reported abuse. The Order is signed by District Court Judge Barbara Walther.
April 6, 2008	Over 400 children are removed from YFZ Ranch.
April 7, 2008	Original Petition For Protection of Children is filed. District Court Judge Barbara Walther signs the Order granting Temporary Conservatorship.
April 14 to 17, 2008	Adversary Hearings held in District Court Hearings regarding the removal. The presiding Judge is District Court Judge Barbara Walther.
Week of April 21, 2008	District Court Orders: Judge Walther issues temporary orders naming the Texas Department of Family and Protective Services temporary sole managing conservator of all of children.
May 22, 2008	Texas Court of Appeals, Third District, finds the district court abused its discretion by not returning the children to the parents. District court is ordered to vacate its temporary orders.
May 29, 2008	The Supreme Court of Texas affirms the appellate court ruling.
June 2, 2008	District Court Judge Barbara Walther signs "Order Vacating Temporary Managing Conservatorship and Additional Temporary Orders" sending the children home, with conditions.

TABLE 10.1 *(continued)*

Date	Action
July 24, 2008	District Court Judge Walther orders cases divided by mother creating 234 separate cases; 440 children are still being monitored (Schlegel, 2008).
August 19, 2008	A 14-year-old girl is ordered back into foster care because of "uncontroverted evidence of the underage marriage" and the mother refused to guarantee the girl's safety. (Note: Warren Jeffs, her alleged husband, was in jail at the time). Of the more than 400 cases, the Department has sought dismissal of over 70, and the rest are still being investigated (Roberts, 2008).
December 22, 2008	The Department releases the "Eldorado Investigation" report summarizing situation that leads to the raid, the detention of the children, subsequent release and dismissal of almost all of the cases. The report provides corrected numbers (439 actual children were detained). Of those, 424 were "non-suited" (dismissed). Remaining cases: 15 children from 5 mothers are still subject to the jurisdiction of the Department.

Legal Analysis

A. Overview of Court Documents

Original Order for the Investigation of Child Abuse

The court order obtained by the Department of Family and Protective Services (DFPS) to launch the investigation into child abuse allegations at the YFZ Ranch stemmed from phone calls of a girl presumably named "Sarah" who stated that she was being physically and sexually abused at the Ranch (Affidavit 2008; Campo-Flores and Skipp 2008). The order was quite specific and detailed, giving authorities the legal means to search for Sarah and her alleged abuser (Walther 2008a).

Upon entering the YFZ Ranch and interviewing children and adults, Texas authorities failed to find Sarah. What they did find was that the children and adults were not forthcoming with details about their relationships (who was whose parent, sibling, etc.), their ages, or even their names. Based upon this evasiveness, and the information obtained from "Sarah," the authorities determined that one or more of the adult males were sexually abusing the teenage girls and detained all the children (Affidavit In Support of Original Petition 2008). The children ranged in age from a few months old to eighteen years old (or older, as it was later determined that many of the young girls were indeed adults).

Original Petition for Protection of Children in an Emergency

This original petition was filed in District Court on April 7, 2008, the day after the children were removed from the YFZ Ranch. Since the children who were detained were not part of the original investigation order, the Petition had to be filed under the Texas Family Code §262.104a: "Taking possession of a child in an emergency without a court order" (Original Petition 2008). After the children were removed, Judge Walther signed the "Order for Protection of a Child in an Emergency," giving temporary custody of the children to the DFPS, pending the full adversary hearing set ten days hence (Walther 2008b).

Hearings on Removal

During the week of April 14–18, 2008, chaotic hearings on the removal of the more than four hundred children were held by District Court Judge Barbara Walther, the same judge who signed the original warrant to search the YFZ Ranch.[5] She ruled that the children were to remain in detention and the DFPS was to have temporary conservatorship. In addition to finding that it was contrary to the children's welfare to remain in the custody of their parents, the Court also found that because some of the parents' identities were unknown, "parentage testing" was necessary. Supervised visitation for the children was also ordered, meaning that the children could not see their parents without a DFPS worker present. Each parent was ordered to undergo a psychiatric evaluation and to provide all medical records of the children. Family counseling and parenting classes were also decreed for FLDS adults (Walther 2008c).

Appellate Court Reversed by District Court

The ruling was appealed by a group of FLDS parents to the Texas Court of Appeals, Third District, in Austin. The Appellate Court found that the District Court erred and that the Texas authorities did not carry its burden of proof required under the Texas Family Code §262.201. Specifically the Appellate Court ruled that authorities did *not* sufficiently show (1) that the children's physical health or safety was in danger; (2) that the need to protect the children was urgent, requiring their immediate removal; and (3) that the DFPS had made reasonable efforts to eliminate or prevent the children's removal from their parents.

The DFPS based the removal of the children on the assertion that they lived in a community with a "pervasive belief system" that condoned underage marriage and pregnancy. Of the more than 400 children removed, however, only 5 girls were identified as having become pregnant between the ages of fifteen and seventeen. There was no evidence of widespread abuse of the boys or the prepubescent girls, save the dubious assertion that they were part of a group with that belief system (*In re Steed* 2008).

Using creative legal theory, the DFPS alleged that the entire YFZ Ranch was one "household," and therefore returning any child to the Ranch meant that the child was returning to a residence that included a person who had sexually abused a child ("collective child abuse"). The Court of Appeals found this claim to be "contrary to the evidence." "While there was evidence that the living arrangements on the ranch are more communal that most typical neighborhoods," the Court noted, the DFPS itself had even acknowledged that the Ranch was "divided into separate family groups and separate households" (*In re Steed* 2008, n. 10). The Court of Appeals found that the District Court abused its discretion in failing to return the children and ordered the Lower Court to vacate its temporary orders granting sole managing conservatorship of the children to the DFPS.

The Appellate Court's Reversal Upheld by the Supreme Court of Texas

The DFPS appealed the adverse ruling to the Texas Supreme Court, which held that the removal of the children was not warranted (*In re Texas Department of Family and Protective Services* 2008). The Texas Supreme Court reiterated the Appellate Court's decision that adequate safeguards could be put in place to protect the children short of separating them from their parents. A dissent by Justice O'Neill concurred in the release of all the legal-age children but not the pubescent girls. Justice O'Neill stated that, in her view, the population of pubescent girls was demonstrably endangered, given the evidence presented about the "marriages" at the age of "physical development" (first menstruation) (*In re Texas Department of Family and Protective Services* 2008, p. 618).

Order Vacating the Temporary Managing Conservatorship and
Additional Orders

Based upon the Appellate Court rulings, the District Court applied the
reversal to all the parties and vacated the court's prior order granting the
DFPS sole temporary managing conservatorship over all the children
removed from the YFZ Ranch. The Court issued the following "Orders
Vacating Temporary Management Conservatorship and Additional Temporary Orders":

> The Department shall return each child after the parent executes an autho-
> rization (see information below), permits the child's picture to be taken and
> fingerprint given.
>
> Each parent shall attend and successfully complete "standard parenting
> classes."
>
> Each parent, child or other person involved "shall not interfere with
> the ongoing investigation into allegations of abuse and neglect . . ." The
> Department may visit the home of the children, and interview and exam-
> ine the children. This may include medical, psychological, or psychiatric
> examination.
>
> The Department shall have access to the residence of each child for unan-
> nounced home visits during the hours of 8:00 AM to 8:00 PM each day.
>
> The Department will provide the attorneys and GAL's [Guardian ad
> Litem's] current addresses and phone numbers of the parents and each
> child.
>
> The parent shall provide the Department with the specific address where
> that child will reside and a telephone contact for each parent. This includes
> the names of all adults and children who will be residing within the same
> household.
>
> If a child's residence is to be changed, the parent must provide the Depart-
> ment with 7 days notice or, in an emergency, notify the Department within
> 24 hours.
>
> Every child shall remain within the State of Texas at all times. (Walther
> 2008d)

It is critical to note here that this list of conditions is virtually unprecedented
in such cases. It represents a significant *continued* exertion of control over the
FLDS community, its families and children, even though they had ostensibly
won their case on appeal. In other cases of this nature that have been described
above, such as the ones involving the Twelve Tribes or The Family, when the

children were returned by court order to the group, it was done with few if any conditions. In this case, however, the effect of the rulings left the situation much the same as if the appeal courts had not ruled against the trial judge's original order. The group and its children were still under stringent controls by the very authorities who had initiated the raid, at least for a substantial period. These conditions had significant ramifications on the FLDS and its ability to regroup on the land where it resided prior to the raid.

"Non-suiting" of Cases

According to the DFPS report of December 22, 2008, all but 15 of the 439 cases were "non-suited." A case is defined by the DFPS as "non-suited" when "CPS staff believes the parents or family members have taken appropriate action to protect the children from future abuse or neglect" ("Eldorado Investigation" 2008). In effect, the DFPS reported the non-suiting of over 96 percent of the total number of children removed from their homes. The DFPS provided a rationale for the action, stating that owing to the families' cooperation in attending parenting classes and counseling for the children, the children were no longer at risk. YFZ spokesman Willie Jessop issued a press release in response to the report on December 26, 2008, stating that none of the children in any of these households ever needed supervision, nor were the children ever at risk (Jessop 2008).

The non-suiting of cases meant that the restrictions Judge Walther had ordered for the children upon release no longer applied. According to YFZ member Edson Jessop, however, one-third of the families, approximately two hundred women and children, had not returned to the Ranch, even after their cases were dismissed (Tresniowski et al. 2009). It is not known if those families were planning to return in the future. For the families who did return, the raid left a traumatic impact on their lives (ibid.).

B. Creative Attempts to Expand the Child Abuse Laws

Use of Generalities, Mass Removal, and Mass Hearings

By using generalities based on a widespread belief system, by employing the use of the Texas Rules of Civil Procedure permissive joinder law (Rule 40), and by grouping all the children together into mass hearings that were tantamount to chaos (Ward 2008), the DFPS effectively circumvented the Texas Family Code requirement that *each* child removed from his or her family's home must be *specifically* in danger.

Texas child welfare law requires specificity with regard to the removal of each child from his or her parents. In the Original Petition the DFPS used civil joinder laws to add later "unnamed defendants," and at least four of the children were detained under a "name unknown" classification and simply given numbers. Texas Family Code §262.104 (titled "Taking Possession of a Child in Emergency without a Court Order") is the section under which the children from the YFZ Ranch were removed. This section requires evidence of "facts" that "there is an immediate danger to the physical health and safety of the child" or that "the child has been a victim of sexual abuse" (Texas Family Code §262.104(a), 2008).

Texas Family Code §262.107, provides the standard for the court's decision on whether to return a child at an initial hearing. In considering if there is a "continuing danger to the physical health and safety of a child, the court may consider whether the household to which the child would be returned includes a person who has . . . sexually abused a child." The court must return the child unless:

- the evidence shows that the child has been the victim of sexual abuse . . . and that there is a substantial risk that the child will be the victim of sexual abuse in the future
- continuation of the child in the home would be contrary to the child's welfare; and
- reasonable efforts . . . were made to prevent or eliminate the need for removal of the child.

The Texas Family Code does not contemplate generalities when detaining children from their parents. The above statutes are not only mandated by federal law (Title IV-E of the Social Security Act, 42 U.S.C. §672(a)(1) and 42 U.S.C. §§671(a)(15)) but have been upheld by the Texas Appellate Court (*In the Interest of M.D.L.E, a child*, 2007). The Texas Family Code does not condone the "wait-and-see" approach that was allowed in this case by the DFPS effectively telling the court that, although all the children and parents had not been identified, the children still had to be detained. By detaining children whose identities were not known, and thus their parents were not known, it should not have been possible to meet the standard required by Texas and federal child welfare law that each child had been specifically abused, or had been allowed to be abused, by their parent or someone in their household.

The Appellate Court addressed the lack of specificity in the detention of so many children based simply on a "pervasive belief system." In discussing the children of the families who filed the appeal (together called the "Relators"), the Appellate Court noted that there was "simply no evidence specific to Relators' children at all except that they exist, they were taken into custody at the Yearning for Zion ranch, and they are living with people who share a 'pervasive belief system' that condones underage marriage and underage pregnancy" (*In re Steed* 2008, p. 11). Unfortunately neither the Appellate Court nor the Texas Supreme Court offered any discussion of the dangers of such lack of specificity, except to say that there was not enough evidence to have detained the children in the first place.

Residents of One "Household"

The DFPS erroneously argued that detention of all children from the YFZ Ranch was required because they were all living in the same household. The DFPS conveniently defined "household" in this manner, because the FLDS embraced an overarching belief system and because the group appeared to practice a communal style of raising children. But, more important, we do not see this interpretation of household in the original petition, suggesting that DFPS officials did not consider the problematic legal ramifications of unexamined assumptions.

The Texas Family Code §71.005, defines "household" as "a unit composed of persons living together in the same dwelling, without regard to whether they are related to each other." In addition, Texas Family Code §71.006, defines a "member of a household" to include "a person who previously lived in a household."

Nothing in the Original Petition speaks of the entire ranch as being one household. In the attached Affidavit several discussions concern the "widespread pattern and practice among the residents of the YFZ Ranch in which young minor female residents are conditioned to expect and accept sexual activity with adult men at the ranch upon being spiritually married to them" (Original Petition, p. 17.) The last paragraph of the affidavit states that "the child or other children located at YFZ Ranch" have been sexually abused, and evidence suggests that sexual abuse will occur in the future. Thus the affidavit asserts that returning children to the care of their parents endangers the physical health or safety of the children. There is no discussion or relevant details, however, about why the entire YFZ Ranch was considered one "household." The characterization of the Ranch as one "household" only surfaces later as the DFPS tried to justify taking all the children, not just the pubescent girls who either were pregnant or had been at an earlier age. This creative attempt to expand child welfare laws was further reinforced by District Court Judge Barbara Walther's ruling to detain the children and grant the Department temporary conservatorship pending the full adversarial hearings.

The Texas Supreme Court, in its affirmation of the reversal, did not specifically address the "one household" theory promulgated by Texas authorities. Instead, the Court's ruling was based on the lack of immediate risk to the children who had been detained, and the fact that there were other, less extreme safeguards that could have been put into place.

C. Other Attempts to Curtail the YFZ Ranch Using the Law

Three years before the raid on the YFZ Ranch, Texas officials began to prepare a legal arsenal to make Texas "unappealing to them," referring to the FLDS people settling near Eldorado (Kirk 2008). Texas State Representative Harvey Hilderbran introduced House Bill 3006 in 2005 that mirrored Utah laws aimed at targeting polygamous groups (see Richardson and Schreinert, this volume). The bill raised the age of consent for marriage from fourteen to sixteen years of age, defining any violation as a felony. The bill also changed bigamy and polygamy laws from misdemeanors to felonies. Although Hilderbran's bill stalled in committee, he attached the above requirements as an amendment to Senate Bill 6, which ultimately passed and was signed into law in June 2005 (Kirk 2008; Neil 2008). The FLDS men arrested after the raid on the Ranch were prosecuted under these laws.

In 2009, in response to the raid on the YFZ Ranch and the subsequent release of all but one of the children back to their families, Representative Hilderbran introduced another bill. House Bill 4255 would require the courts to consider the actions of all the adults in the home prior to deciding to remove a child from a home or, alternatively, to issue a restraining order barring the perpetrator from the home (Raffield 2009). Specifically the bill would allow the courts to consider if the "non-offending parent" complies with the terms of any restraining order, as well as cooperates with child protective services. If the non-offending parent does not cooperate, the child could be removed from the home ("Rep. Hilderbran Bill Seeks Strong Protection for Victims of Child Abuse" 2009). In addition, a second citation for failure to report child abuse would become a Class A Misdemeanor under HB 4255. This targets the doctor who had allegedly delivered more than one baby from underage girls at the YFZ Ranch (ibid.). In his press release

Hilderbran added, "Without H.B. 3006, which we passed during the 79th Legislative Session [in 2005 as an amendment to Senate Bill 6], none of the indictments that law enforcement got against these men would have been possible. This session, we are coming full circle to make sure we protect the children from anyone who might be complacent in abuse."

This type of targeted legislation bears watching, as it seems to be the latest legal weapon in curtailing the practices of the followers of the FLDS in Texas. The state government walks a thin line here between child protection and religious freedom, especially when specifically targeting the followers at the YFZ Ranch in the press releases and statements about the legislation.

Conclusion

The State of Texas carried out an unprecedented enforcement action—the mass detention of more than four hundred children—based on the rationale that they were being harmed by simply living in a community with a questionable belief system. For all the YFZ children, except the handful of pubescent girls who, between the ages of fifteen to seventeen, were found to have had children, no other evidence has been submitted of any abuse or neglect, physical or sexual. Although it has been reported in the media that the Texas DFPS was shown to have overreached and the children returned to their families, less widely reported is that, though not detained, the children and families, for months, were still subject to intense oversight by the Department. Prior to release, all the families had to sign agreements that they *would not leave the state, would be subjected to medical, physical, and psychological examinations, and must allow Department officials into their homes on unannounced visits.* In addition, although approximately two-thirds of the families returned to the YFZ Ranch (Roberts 2009), many set up homes off the Ranch at least while these cases were pending (Corbett 2008; Tresniowski et al. 2009). So although the children were still in their parents' care, the community at YFZ Ranch was effectively crippled, at least temporarily, by the intense scrutiny and physical relocation of members. The aggressive efforts by the DFPS to detain unknown children from unknown parents and to define the group as a single household—essentially avoiding the specificity requirements of Texas statutes—may not have been successful in a legal sense. But the Appellate Courts have allowed the original trial judge who accepted those unique arguments to establish conditions that seem to vitiate the impact of the Appellate Court decisions.

It would appear, therefore, that Texas authorities "lost the battle but won the war," and the apparent rulings in favor of the FLDS parents in the Texas Appellate Courts were largely a pyrrhic victory. The FLDS community won the battle to retain their children after nearly two months of their lives having been severely disrupted, but only under rigorous state oversight. In the end, all but one child has been returned to her parents. Yet every FLDS family experienced the devastating emotional impact of the raid, the forced removal of their children, the threat of extended or permanent state custody, allegations of sexual abuse, and the intrusive public scrutiny of their lives (Adams 2009).

The Appellate Courts in Texas rendered the FLDS group an apparent victory but at a very high cost in terms of basic civil liberties. In a disturbing Solomonic decision, the Appeals Courts have "cut the baby in half" in a manner that offers solace to those concerned about possible abuse in the FLDS group but also causes continued concern among advocates of religious freedom and family privacy.

NOTES

1. For a thorough discussion of the Robin George legal cases involving a fourteen-year-old girl who joined the Hare Krishna (HK), and the ramifications to the HK of her having done so with the group's cooperation, see, for example, Richardson 1991.

2. For an account of the legal battles over the use of "brainwashing" testimony, see Richardson 1996 and 1998.

3. For an extensive discussion on the Island Pond raid, see Malcarne and Burchard 1992, where, based on this raid, recommendations are made for changing child welfare laws so as to protect children in communal religious situations more effectively. Most relevant here is the recommendation for provisions for *ex parte* warrants, described as the ability to obtain a warrant on probable cause of abuse without notice to the offending party. This type of warrant was used in the raid on the YFZ Ranch.

4. The Family International is one of the more notorious NRMs, especially in terms of its past sexual practices (Richardson and Davis 1983). These past practices made the group especially vulnerable to accusations of child sex abuse. However, those practices ended decades ago, as demonstrated by scholarly studies and legal decisions (Lewis and Melton 1994; Richardson 1994; Bradney 1999). Note that the major court decision concerning The Family, a custody case from the United Kingdom in which James Richardson testified, resulted in severe conditions being placed on The Family if the child in question was allowed to remain in the group. These conditions, and the group's acquiescence to them, demonstrated yet again the state's immense power when accusations of harm to children are made.

5. Contrast this with the raid on Island Pond, in which one judge signed the warrant for the removal of the children, and a different judge, upon hearing the evidence, dismissed the case and returned the children home (Malcarne and Burchard 1992). Here not only did Judge Walther sign the original search warrant order and then order the children detained at the "fourteen-day" hearings, she was also the same judge available to hear motions filed in the grand jury polygamy investigations of some of the men from the YFZ Ranch (Adams 2008). In 2009, moreover, Judge Walther was presiding over the criminal prosecutions of the same men, including hearings on motions to suppress evidence gathered because of the very search warrant that the judge signed (Hawkins 2009).

REFERENCES

Adams, Brooke. 2008. "Texas Judge Bars Contact from FLDS Spokesman. *Salt Lake Tribune*, June 21. Accessed online at http://www.rickross.com/reference/polygamy/polygamy975.html.

———. 2009. "Texas vs. FLDS: 1 Year after the Raid." *Salt Lake Tribune*, March 26.

Anthony, Dick. 1990. "Religious Movements and Brainwashing Litigation," pp. 295–344 in Thomas Robbins and Dick Anthony (eds.), *In Gods We Trust*. New Brunswick, NJ: Transaction.

Anthony, Dick, and Thomas Robbins. 1992. "Law, Social Science, and the "Brainwashing" Exception to the First Amendment." *Behavioral Sciences and the Law* 10:5–30.

Barker, Eileen. 1984. *The Making of a Moonie: Brainwashing or Choice?* London. Blackwell.

Bradley, Martha Sonntag. 1993. *Kidnapped from That Land: The Government Raids on the Short Creek Polygamists*. Salt Lake City: University of Utah Press.

Bradney, Anthony. 1999. "Children of a Newer God: The English Courts, Custody Disputes, and NRMs," pp. 210–226 in Susan J. Palmer and Charlotte Hardman (eds.), *Children in New Religions*. New Brunswick, NJ: Rutgers University Press.

Bromley, David, and James T. Richardson. 1983. *The Brainwashing/Deprogramming Controversy*. Lewiston, NY: Edwin Mellen.

Bromley, David, and Anson D. Shupe. 1979. *Moonies in America*. Beverly Hills, CA: Sage.

Campo-Flores, Arian, and Catharine Skipp. 2008. "Rozita Swinton's Bad Call." *Newsweek*, July 26.

Carney, Terry. 1993. "Children of God: Harbingers of Another (Child Law) Reformation?" *Criminology Australian* 5:2–5.

Chancellor, James D. 2000. *Life in The Family: An Oral History of the Children of God*. Syracuse, NY: Syracuse University Press.

Corbett, Sara. 2008. "Children of God." *New York Times Magazine*, July 27.

"Eldorado Investigation: A Report by the Texas Department of Family and Protective Services." 2008. December 22. Available online at http://www.dfps.state.tx.us/documents/about/pdf/2008-12-22_Eldorado.pdf.

Ellison, Christopher G., and John P. Bartkowski. 1995. "Babies Were Being Beaten: Exploring Child Abuse Allegations at Ranch Apocalypse," pp. 111–52 in Stuart A. Wright (ed.), *Armageddon in Waco*. Chicago: University of Chicago Press.

Foster, Lawrence. 1984. *Religion and Sexuality: The Shakers, the Mormons, and the Oneida Community*. Urbana: University of Illinois Press.

Hawkins, Dave. 2009. "Motion in FLDS Case in Texas Called a Long Shot." Special to the *Standard Times*, May 20. Available online at http://www.gosanangelo.com/news/2009/may/20/motion-flds-case-texas-called-long-shot/.

Homer, Mike. 1999. "The Precarious Balance between Freedom of Religion and the Best Interests of the Child," pp. 187–209 in Susan J. Palmer and Charlotte Hardman (eds.), *Children in New Religions* (pp. 187–209). New Brunswick, NJ: Rutgers University Press.

Jacobs, Janet. 1984. "The Economy of Love in Religious Commitment: The Deconversion of Women from Nontraditional Religious Movements." *Journal for the Scientific Study of Religion* 23 (2): 155–71.

———. 1989. *Divine Disenchantment: Deconverting from New Religions*. Bloomington: Indiana University Press.

Jessop, Willie. 2008. "YFZ Raid Was Never Justified." Press release from the YFZ Ranch, December 26.

Kilbourne, Brock, and James T. Richardson. 1984. "Psychotherapy and New Religions in a Pluralistic Society. *American Psychologist* 39:237–51.

Kirk, Andrew. 2008. "Texans Had Been 'Reining in' FLDS via State Laws." *Deseret News,* June 2.

Lewis, James R., and J. Gordon Melton. 1994. *Sex, Sin, and Slander: Investigating The Family/Children of God*. Stanford, CA: Center for Academic Publication.

MacLaggan, Corrie. 2008. "Is Sect's West Texas Ranch One Household?" *Austin American-Statesman*, May 30.

Malcarne, Vanessa, and John Burchard. 1992. "Investigations of Child Abuse/Neglect Allegations in Religious Cults: A Case Study in Vermont." *Behavioral Sciences and the Law* 10:75–88.

Miller, Donald. 1983. "Deprogramming in Historical Perspective," pp. 15–28 in David G. Bromley and James T. Richardson (eds.), *The Brainwashing/Deprogramming Controversy.* Lewiston, NY: Edwin Mellen.

Neil, Martha. 2008. "Texas Changed Marriage Age to Restrict Rights of Polygamy Ranch Residents." *ABA Journal—Law News Now,* May 2.

Palmer, Susan J. 1999. "Frontiers and Families: The Children of Island Pond," pp. 153–71 in Susan J. Palmer and Charlotte Hardeman (eds.), *Children in New Religions*. New Brunswick, NJ: Rutgers University Press.

Raffield, Danielle. 2009. "Texas Legislation Watch: Rep Hilderbran's Legislative Response to the Raid at the Yearning For Zion Ranch." *Children and the Law* blog, April 27. Accessed online at http://www.childrenandthelawblog.com/2009/04/27/rep-hilderbrans-legislative-response-to-the-raid-at-yearning-for-zion-ranch/.

"Rep. Hilderbran Bill Seeks Strong Protection for Victims of Child Abuse." 2009. Press release from HB 4255, March 18. Accessed online at http://www.house.state.tx.us/news/release.php?id=2610.

Richardson, James T. 1999. "Social Control of New Religions: From "Brainwashing" Claims to Child Sex Abuse Accusations," pp. 172–86 in Susan J. Palmer and Charlotte Hardeman (eds.), *Children in New Religions*. New Brunswick, NJ: Rutgers University Press.

———. 1998. "The Accidental Expert." *Nova Religio* 2:31–43.

———. 1996. "Sociology and the New Religions: 'Brainwashing,' the Courts, and Freedom of Religion," pp. 115–34 in Pamela Jenkins and Steve Kroll-Smith (eds.), *Witnessing for Sociology: Sociologists in Court*. Westport, CT: Praeger.

———. 1994. "Update on The Family," pp. 27–40 in James R. Lewis and J. Gordon Melton (eds.), *Sex, Sin, and Slander*. Stanford, CA: Center for Academic Publications.

———. 1993. "A Social Psychological Critique of 'Brainwashing' Claims about Recruitment to New Religions," pp.75–97 in Jeffrey K. Hadden and David G. Bromley (eds.), *Handbook of Cults and Sects in America*. Greenwich, CT: JAI.

———. 1992. "Mental Health of Cult Consumers: A Legal and Scientific Controversy," pp. 233–44 in L. Brown (ed.), *Religion and Mental Health*. Oxford: Oxford University Press.

———. 1991. "Cult/Brainwashing Cases and the Freedom of Religion." *Journal of Church and State* 33:55–74.

———. 1988. *Money and Power in the New Religions*. Lewiston, NY: Edwin Mellen.

Richardson, James T., and Rex Davis. 1983. "Experiential Fundamentalism." *Journal of the American Academy of Religion* 51:397–425.

Robbins, Thomas. 1988. *Cults, Converts and Charisma*. Newbury Park, CA: Sage.

Roberts, Michelle 2008. "Judge Orders Alleged Child Bride into State Care." *Reno Gazette Journal*, August 20, p. 3C.

———. 2009. "Life at Polygamist Ranch Was Austere, Controlled." *Reno Gazette Journal*, April 5, p. 5B.

Rochford, E. Burke, Jr. 1995. "Family Structure, Commitment, and Involvement in the Hare Krishna Movement." *Sociology of Religion* 56 (2):153–76.

Roy, Jody M. 1999. *Rhetorical Campaigns of the 19th Century Anti-Catholics and Catholics*. Lewiston, NY: Edwin Mellen.

Schlegel, Erich 2008. "Child Custody Proceedings Split into 234 Separate Cases." *Reno Gazette Journal*, July 26, p. 6B.

Shupe, Anson D., and David G. Bromley. 1980. *The New Vigilantes: Anti-Cultists and the New Religions*. Beverly Hills, CA: Sage.

Shupe, Anson D., and Susan Darnell. 2006. *Agents of Discord: Deprogrammers, Pseudo-Science, and the American Anticult Movement*. New Brunswick, NJ: Transaction.

Siegler, Gretchen. 1999. "The Children of ISOT," pp. 124–37 in Susan J. Palmer and Charlotte Hardeman (eds.), *Children in New Religions*. New Brunswick, NJ: Rutgers University Press.

Stein, Stephen J. 1994. *The Shaker Experience in America*. New Haven, CT: Yale University Press.

Swantko, Jean. 2004. "The Twelve Tribes Messianic Communities, the Anti-cult Movement, and Governmental Response," pp. 179–200 in James T. Richardson (ed.), *Regulating Religion*. New York: Kluwer.

Tresniowski, Alex, Darla Atlas, Anne Lang, and Cary Cardwell. 2009. "This Is Home." *People*, vol. 71, no. 11, pp. 60–67.

Ward, Stephanie 2008. "Discovering Eldorado." *ABA Journal*, October 8–63, p. 70

Wright, Stuart A. 1995. *Armageddon in Waco*. Chicago: University of Chicago Press.

LEGAL DOCUMENTS CITED

Affidavit for Search and Arrest Warrant. 2008. April 3. Accessed online at: http://web.gosanangelo.com/pdf/FLDSaffidavit.pdf.

Affidavit in Support of Original Petition for Protection of a Child in an Emergency and for Conservatorship in Suit Affecting the Parent-Child Relationship. 2008. April 6. Accessed online at http://web.gosanangelo.com/pdf/ConservatorshipInSuit.pdf.

In re Steed. 2008. Tex. App. Lexis 3652 (Tex. App.—Austin, May 22.

In re Texas Department of Family and Protective Services. 2008. 255 S.W.3d 613 (Tex.).

In the Interest of M.D.L.E, a child. 2007. Tex. App. Lexis 1738 (Tex. App.).

"Original Petition for Protection of Children in an Emergency and for Conservatorship in Suit Affecting the Parent-Child Relationship." 2008. Cause No. 2902, April 7. District Court of Schleicher County, Texas 51st Judicial District. Accessed online at http://web. gosanangelo.com/pdf/ConservatorshipInSuit.pdf.

Texas Family Code §71.005.

Texas Family Code §71.006.

Texas Family Code §262.104(a).

Texas Family Code §262.107.

Texas Rules of Civil Procedure, Rule 40.

Title IV-E of the Social Security Act. 2008. 42 U.S.C. §672(a)(1).

Title IV-E of the Social Security Act. 2008. 42 U.S.C. §§671(a)(15).

Walther, Barbara (Judge). 2008a. Order for Investigation of Child Abuse, Cause No. 2778, April 3. District Court of Schleicher County, Texas 51st Judicial District.

———. 2008b. Order for Protection of a Child in an Emergency and Notice of Hearing, Cause No. 2902, April 7. District Court of Schleicher County, Texas 51st Judicial District.

———. 2008c. Temporary Order Following Adversary Hearing and Notice of Hearing, Cause No. 2789, April 24. District Court of Schleicher County, Texas 51st Judicial District.

———. 2008d. Orders Vacating Temporary Management Conservatorship and Additional Temporary Orders, June 2. District Court of Schleicher County, Texas 51st Judicial District. Accessed online at http://www.dfps.state.tx.us/documents/about/pdf/2008-06-02_Court%20Order.pdf.

About the Contributors

HEATHER CLINGENPEEL is a graduate student in the Department of Psychology at Georgia Southern University.

RYAN T. CRAGUN is an assistant professor of sociology at the University of Tampa. His research interests include secularism, secularization, and Mormonism.

MARTHA BRADLEY EVANS is dean of the Honors College at University of Utah. Her books include *Four Zinas: A Story of Mothers and Daughters on the Mormon Frontier* and *Kidnapped from That Land: The Government Raids on the Short Creek Polygamists.*

JENNIFER LARA FAGEN is an assistant professor of sociology at Lamar University. Her areas of specialization include gender roles, sexual violence, feminist theory and Holocaust studies.

CARLENE GONZALES is a doctoral candidate in the Interdisciplinary Social Psychology program at the University of Nevada, Reno.

MICHAEL W. HAMILTON is on the faculty of Principia College in Elsah, Illinois. He teaches American religious history, comparative religions, and religion and ethics.

CAMILLE B. LALASZ is a doctoral candidate in the Interdisciplinary Social Psychology program at the University of Nevada, Reno.

MICHAEL NIELSEN is professor and chair of psychology at Georgia Southern University. His research focuses on Mormonism and on religious conflicts and boundaries, and he is coeditor of the journal *Archive of the Psychology of Religion.*

SUSAN J. PALMER is professor of religious studies at Dawson College in Quebec, Canada, and also teaches at Concordia University. She is the author of *Moon Sisters, Krishna Mothers, Rajneesh Lovers*, of *Aliens Adored: Rael's UFO Religion*, and *The New Heretics of France*, among other books.

JAMES T. RICHARDSON is professor of sociology and judicial studies, and director of the Grant Sawyer Center for Justice Studies at the University of Nevada, Reno. He is the coauthor and editor of ten books, including *Regulating Religion: Case Studies from Around the Globe*.

TAMARA SCHREINERT is Court Master in the Family Court, Second Judicial District Court in Reno, Nevada, where she presides over protection order, custody, and divorce cases. She is a graduate of Harvard Law School and previously worked for the U.S. Department of Health and Human Services. She also practiced law in Los Angeles, focusing on child welfare and juvenile law, before returning to her hometown of Reno.

JEAN SWANTKO WISEMAN has practiced constitutional, family, and criminal defense law for thirty years. She has represented the Twelve Tribes as a trial and appellate advocate, and is a member of the same group. She is also the producer of a documentary film, *Children of the Island Pond Raid: An Emerging Culture* (2006).

STUART A. WRIGHT is professor of sociology and director of research in the Office of Research at Lamar University. He is the author or editor of five books including *Armageddon in Waco: Critical Perspectives on the Branch Davidian Conflict* and *Patriots, Politics, and the Oklahoma City Bombing*.

Index